WHAT YOUR COLLEAGUES
ARE SAYING . . .

"I will admit, when I first began reading, I was thinking, 'Here we go again, another book on differentiation.' As I read, my feelings quickly changed. I believe this book provides different information than previous books I've read on the subject. It is very easy to read, and most teachers could make substantive changes in their instruction immediately. This may be the quickest way to improve math learning and understanding I've seen. I am anxious to incorporate the strategies in this book in my planning for all students to enhance their ability to know, understand, and do math while loving it!"

—Marcia Carlson
Classroom Teacher
Crestview School of Inquiry
West Des Moines, IA

"This is an extremely important topic right now. Young students are expected to learn concepts that used to be saved for much more mature students. The big questions are how to help those young minds understand, especially when the teachers may not have a strong mathematics background. The coverage [in this book] is very complete without being overwhelming. I am impressed that just as I began to think what an insurmountable task teaching has become, [this book] breaks it down to manageable chunks."

—Lyneille Meza
Director of Data and Assessment
Denton Independent School District
Denton, TX

"Finally! A book that is written for the elementary teacher that *gets* the elementary classroom. Dr. Smith clears up the differentiation dysfunction by giving clear examples with real content. Just this would be enough to purchase and love the resource, however, this book goes the extra mile by also giving 'use-it-now' strategies that are easily understood and implemented. For anyone wishing to have a rich toolkit of strategies to provide deep understanding in key mathematical concepts, this publication is a must-have/must-read."

—Julie W. Stevenson
Consultant, University of Missouri
Kansas City and Regional Professional Development Center

"I believe Dr. Nanci Smith's *Every Math Learner: A Doable Approach to Teaching With Learning Differences in Mind* is arguably the best book now available for math teachers. In my conversations with math teachers and observations of classrooms, there is generally good-to-great expertise in math content knowledge. Problems occur, however, when there is lock-step reliance (perhaps with minor variations) on the math textbook or when there are beliefs and practices that all students predominately learn in the same way. Dr. Smith—a master teacher and trainer—flips the paradigm from teaching to learning. I've personally seen Dr. Smith's work with teachers, and know that she creates tremendous excitement within the teaching profession for practically and substantively moving from teacher-centered classrooms to learning-centered classrooms that support the needs and interests of *all* students."

—Mark Boyer,
Retired Assistant Superintendent for Learning,
Singapore American School

"While we know that the importance of differentiation is the key to student engagement and success, implementing key differentiation practices remains elusive to us as we balance competing curriculum, student, and administrative demands. Smith's book seamlessly unpacks what differentiation is and is not and provides explicit and, dare I say, beautiful examples of what this can look like in the classroom. You will be hooked from the first page and be inspired and empowered to transform your classroom, your teaching, and your students' mathematical learning experiences through and with this practical, realistic, and meaningful differentiation system."

—Beth Kobett, Ed.D.
Assistant Professor
Stevenson University

"I trained elementary teachers how to teach mathematics for 17 years. Had this book been available, it would have been part of the curriculum. I really like the Try It! sections that gives teachers strategies they can immediately put to use in their classrooms. The Watch It! videos bring the material to life, and the discussion questions tease out the important ideas presented. I highly recommend this book for anyone wanting to learn more about how to deal with differences in the classroom."

—*Betz Frederick, PhD,*
Retired Mathematics Education Professor
Grand Canyon University

EVERY MATH LEARNER

GRADES K-5

*This book is dedicated to Carol Tomlinson whom I am
fortunate to count as my teacher, my mentor and my friend.
I don't know what you saw in me to take me under your wing,
but words cannot tell you how thankful I am.*

*To Judy, Cindy, Marcia, Jessica, Sandra, and Leslie . . .
thank you for
helping to shape my journey.*

EVERY MATH LEARNER

A DOABLE APPROACH TO TEACHING
WITH LEARNING DIFFERENCES
IN MIND
GRADES K–5

NANCI N. SMITH

FOREWORD BY CAROL ANN TOMLINSON

CORWIN
MATHEMATICS

FOR INFORMATION:

Corwin

A SAGE Company

2455 Teller Road

Thousand Oaks, California 91320

www.corwin.com

SAGE Ltd.

1 Oliver's Yard

55 City Road

London EC1Y 1SP

United Kingdom

SAGE Pvt. Ltd.

B 1/I 1 Mohan Cooperative Industrial Area

Mathura Road, New Delhi 110 044

India

SAGE Publications Asia-Pacific Pte. Ltd.

3 Church Street

#10-04 Samsung Hub

Singapore 049483

Acquisitions Editor: Erin Null

Associate Editor: Julie Nemer

Editorial Assistant: Nicole Shade

Production Editor: Libby Larson

Copy Editor: Sheree Van Vreede

Typesetter: C&M Digitals (P) Ltd.

Proofreader: Ellen Brink

Indexer: Terri Morrissey

Cover Designer: Scott Van Atta

Marketing Managers: Rebecca Eaton and Margaret O'Connor

ISBN 978-1-5063-4073-9

This book is printed on acid-free paper.

SUSTAINABLE FORESTRY INITIATIVE

Certified Chain of Custody
Promoting Sustainable Forestry
www.sfiprogram.org
SFI-01268

SFI label applies to text stock

17 18 19 20 21 10 9 8 7 6 5 4 3 2 1

CONTENTS

Downloadable at resources.corwin.com/everymathlearnerK-5

Chapter 2. Tools and Templates for Find Out

Chapter 3. Tools and Templates for Teach Up

Chapter 4. Tools and Templates for Step Up

Chapter 5. Tools and Templates for Set It Up

Chapter 6. Tools and Templates for Power On

Chapter 7. Tools and Templates for Step Back

Chapter 8. Tools and Templates for Close Up

VIDEO CLIPS BY CHAPTER

With special thanks to the following teachers from Caurus Academy principal Dameon Blair and Skyline Ranch Elementary School assistant principal Deanna Potter, who allowed us to come and film their exemplary lessons and students.

Caurus Academy is a charter elementary school, grades K–8, in Anthem, AZ. Skyline Ranch Elementary is a public school in Florence School District, grades K–8.

Grade	Teacher
Kindergarten	Taylor Bandelier is a first-year kindergarten teacher with multiple years of experience in preschool and early childhood settings. She enjoys watching students figure out in their own way how to solve mathematical problems.
Grade 1	Lori Everson has taught for 13 years at every grade level from kindergarten through eighth grade. She teaches first grade at a charter school in Arizona. Lori loves seeing children struggle through a concept, then accomplish understanding, and finally watching how proud they are to explain their thinking.
Grade 2	Amy Francis is currently teaching second grade for her second year but has been teaching for 17 years in various grade levels. Amy loves the great mathematical conversations that come from problem solving and the "oh" students give when a concept clicks!

Grade 4 	Karen Garroutte is a fourth-grade teacher with a focus on mathematics curriculum. She has been teaching for 12 years. She loves watching students light up when they understand a concept; especially a concept that has been difficult for them to grasp.
Grade 5 	Lindsay Potter is an elementary teacher and has taught fifth grade in her 4-year career. She loves watching her students celebrate as they persevere in problem solving to discover a reasonable solution.
Grades 	Kimberly Farless has been teaching for 14 years and currently teaches fifth-eighth-grade mathematics. She loves seeing her students' faces light up when they finally understand the topic. She enjoys inspiring students to love mathematics.

FOREWORD

I suppose our own stories are nearly always the ones that are most powerful in our lives. They reach us at a level of meaning that is difficult to match unless you've actually lived the events that become the story. I've watched students thrive in classes where teachers have used mathematics as a way to reveal the power and satisfaction of human thinking—where the class is a journey of discovery. I've watched students fade in classes where mathematics is a litany of numbers and rules to be committed to memory, and where some students can't seem to make sense of it all while other students are months, if not years ahead of the progression of learning that's imposed alike on everyone in the class. I've seen too few of the classes in which mathematics is a way to understand the world. I've wiggled and writhed with students in too many classes where mathematics is a burden of one sort or another.

But I most deeply understand the need for a book like this one because of my own mathematics story. The actual story happened when I was in 8th grade. What came before "prepared" me for the disaster that began to unfold when I was 13. What came after was the wake of that year.

My mom was a mathematics teacher for much of her career. In my house, there was never a sense that mathematics was inaccessible. In elementary school, I just did mathematics. It never occurred to me that it should be "hard" or "easy." It was just something you did. In retrospect, I'd have been much better prepared for 8th grade and Algebra I if I'd ever had to learn to think mathematically, to grapple, to conjure multiple ways to think about problems, to explain my thinking. That wasn't the case, so when I landed in Algebra I, I was ill-prepared for the total mystery it would instantly become for me. That reality was aggravated by a teacher who spent most of each class period facing the board and working problems for those of us who sat silently in rows behind her. Every once in a while, she'd pivot her upper body toward the class (the lower half of her body seemed permanently positioned toward the board) and say, "Got that?" in a voice that, for me, was confounding, terrifying.

I was dreadfully shy and unsure of myself and would never have indicated to her that I had not the first clue what she was doing. I was afraid and chagrined—and silent. My vanishing confidence evaporated further each time she screeched her questions and I saw my friends nod to her, indicating that indeed they did "get it." I don't know whether that was the case for everyone in my visual field, but at the time, I believed it was. And I died a bit more every day.

When you get behind in mathematics in a class where it's taught as a linear progression of skills, the sink hole gets deeper by the hour unless someone is intent on pulling you to the surface. This teacher apparently did not see that as a part of her job description.

In that year, I became the embodiment of Carol Dweck's worst nightmare. I developed a classic "fixed mindset" about mathematics. Some people were good at mathematics I concluded. I clearly was not one of them. My best option was to do whatever I could to spare myself the misery that was inevitable whenever I had to enroll in a mathematics class. I avoided taking math when that was an option (and it was in college). I shopped around for the easiest math teachers when avoidance wasn't possible. And when I could not escape taking math, I set my sights on squeaking by through dedicated memorization of the unintelligible. That approach, of course, served me quite poorly on many levels and for most of my life. It shaped who I thought I was in profoundly negative ways. It took many years and the grace of several teachers who could see beyond what I showed them before I could begin to see hope in myself. Even then, I could see no hope for math in my future.

Math matters. Beyond the fact that it is a gatekeeper for many possible futures, it has unlimited capacity to teach us to reason, to think logically, even to be imaginative. Too many students never see those possibilities. That's the case when math is taught as a series of rote operations. That's the case when students fall behind in the series and there is no systematic plan to help them recover their footing or when they surge ahead and are required to "practice" what they already know.

I'm delighted, then, that Nanci Smith has written this book—addressing both how to make math instruction more thoughtful and thought provoking, and how to meet students where they are in knowledge, understanding, skill, and interest in math instruction. Nanci has developed two areas of expertise. She has a deep and rich understanding of math developed through her long career as a high school math teacher, hundreds of hours spent in classrooms across the U.S. observing and learning from observation, hundreds of hours working with math teachers at all grade levels, and more hours than she'd probably like to count as a graduate student in mathematics. While she was a high school math teacher, Nanci regularly differentiated instruction for her students. It wasn't long before teachers in other places began to seek her help in planning for the readiness differences that inevitably existed in their math classes as well. From there, she has become a well-regarded consultant on differentiation in general and differentiation in math in particular.

This book combines a helpful framework for thinking about differentiation in math with illustrations that bring the explanations to life, practical examples, and video segments from classrooms that make it possible to say "Well, I could do that, too." Kudos to Nanci and Corwin for that rare and valuable combination of print and visual support for math teachers who want to continue to grow their competence and confidence in making math as valuable as it should be to the full range of students they teach.

I hope the book will contribute to teachers generating many more positive math stories for many more students and to diminishing the kind of math story that follows me still, many decades after it was written.

Carol Ann Tomlinson, EdD

William Clay Parrish, Jr. Professor & Chair
Educational Leadership, Foundations, & Policy
Curry School of Education
University of Virginia

PREFACE

Imagine it with me. The teacher is standing at the front of the room and about to model division. She has a pile of beans in her hand that she is about to put on the overhead projector to model putting a certain number of beans into a certain number of piles. Division. Right? The students, for the most part, are watching and rolling their eyes. Some are working on other projects. Some are politely waiting. Some are *not* politely waiting. The teacher in frustration says, "Stop acting like elementary school children! There is a reason I chose to teach high school. Now we have to divide." You see that was me, and that is a true story. It was my first year of teaching, I was teaching a pre-algebra class, and the book said the lesson was on whole number division. It never dawned on me to do anything other than to teach whole number division that day. I have never wanted a "do-over" so badly as when I think of my first year of teaching, and especially that class.

I began teaching in the age of self-esteem. That is what we talked about almost more than anything else—being careful to preserve students' self-esteem. One teacher quipped to me that we sure inherited a group of students who felt good about themselves . . . they didn't know anything, but they felt good about themselves. I took this charge seriously, and as a result tried to treat all students in my class the same, and I behaved as though all students were learning equally and doing equally well. I was, after all, preserving their self-esteem. If I recognized that a student didn't understand, wouldn't that damage him or her? If I recognized that a student was more advanced or learning more quickly than others, wouldn't that make the rest of the class feel bad? The equalizing of my students only communicated to them that I did not know them well, or did not care. I quickly realized that it was not their self-esteem that I needed to guard, but their self-efficacy that I wanted to build. Today we call that a growth mindset, which we will discuss more fully in Chapter 5. These thoughts and realizations became the foundation of my most basic beliefs in education although they have been significantly defined and refined over the last 25 years as our field has grown in research and practice.

REFRESHING THE CALL FOR DIFFERENTIATION

I'm a math person. I'm not a writer. I just assume everyone already knows anything I have to share. I have been working with states, districts, schools, and teachers for over 15 years. I have even had the opportunity to work with international schools and speak at international conferences. I find the same thing—we all *know* that students are different and learn differently. We just don't really know what to do about it! Especially in mathematics.

So why write this book now? There are several recent issues that compel me to put my practice into text. In light of more rigorous mathematics standards and increasingly high-stakes testing throughout the county, differentiation seems more of a necessity now than ever. Yet at the same time, there are noted authors and speakers who malign differentiation as an impossible dream for teachers. This is understandable considering that at the height of differentiated instruction (DI) popularity, differentiation was almost seen as a magic wand: for any ill, "differentiate!" was the battle cry. This was certainly not realistic or ever the intent of differentiation. As impossible expectations and unrealistic implementations of differentiated instruction played out, it was easy to conclude that differentiation does not work and is unfair to ask of teachers. Yet we know that we are to teach mathematics through engaging, sense-making work and provide access to rich tasks for all students! How then can we downplay the need to approach learning in various ways and through differentiated tasks? Differentiation is not only about helping struggling students, to which it is most often referred today. Differentiation is for all students, at all readiness levels, with different ways to make sense of learning, and with different interests. Differentiation enables us to allow access to rich and compelling mathematics for all students. The time is more necessary than ever for a practical approach to addressing real learning differences in our students.

WHY WRITE *EVERY MATH LEARNER?*

Thank you for picking up this book and looking inside. This book is for you—the dedicated educator. You see, today we need to be more called and more dedicated than ever before. You would probably agree that it is difficult to be an educator today. We work in a time when standards are evolving and require different types of learning and reasoning (especially in mathematics) than we may be use to. With our best efforts, we still hear, and have heard for years, how poorly the United States does as a nation in international testing, especially in math, and of the disappointing results of internal testing showing the low percentage of students that reach proficient levels on the National Assessment for Educational Progress (NAEP) test as well as state and local tests. All of this amid the confusion of the teacher evaluation process and parents upset with just about everything mentioned. And yet we recognize the awe and privilege of touching young lives every day. This book is designed to help you do just that in the area of mathematics.

I now travel for a living, working with schools and districts across the country and occasionally around the world. I find myself occasionally lying (or at least hedging the truth) to the person next to me on the airplane when they ask what I do. I sometimes just don't want to get into the evils of education, and especially mathematics education. I really don't want to hear how they are not a math person or always hated math. And yet, the majority of adults and parents we know want to go back to how math was taught when they learned it. Does anyone else find this ironical?

It probably does not come as a surprise to you that many students—and if we are honest, adults and teachers—dislike math. It doesn't appear to make sense. There is a belief that either you are or are not a math person. That math is right or wrong. Most adults, who admit to disliking math or even being math-phobic, can usually name the teacher and the event that changed their attitude about math (Boaler, 2015). This is scary stuff. Mathematics instruction and classrooms cannot continue in the same ways that they have been operating for the past 50 or more years. I remember as a young teacher in the late 1980s hearing a speaker say that we teach mathematics today as if we are preparing students to be 1940s shopkeepers. I look at classrooms today, and although there is some change in some classrooms, I wonder if the speaker would notice significant differences.

With that said, there are some differences in the mathematics classroom today. Largely due to the shift in emphasis of what it means to be proficient in mathematics from one of speed and getting correct answers to one of connections, reasoning, and representation. Some teachers have begun requiring multiple representation and strategies for operations and problem solving. There are classrooms filled with discourse and collaborative learning. These are positive changes. However, too often mathematics is still being taught as steps, formulas, and memorized facts, just like in the old days. Students too often still do not really believe that mathematics is supposed to make sense and apply to their lives. They still believe that you are either good at math or you aren't. And I truly believe that the reason for a lack of change is not a lack of desire, but rather a lack of information. It is time for practical and specific examples to illuminate what mathematics learning can and should be for every student in every classroom.

MEETING *ALL* STUDENTS' MATHEMATICS NEEDS

If we are to help all students reach high expectations, given their diverse backgrounds, methods for learning and gaps and accelerations in prior knowledge, differentiation is needed now more than ever! However, it has to be realistic and practical differentiation, not the "magic wand" approach. In the pages that follow you will find how differentiation as a structure can help reach all students in mathematics (Chapter 1).

The second chapter will discuss how to determine who your students are as learners, and how to use the information to design learning opportunities that excite and motivate your students. It gives concrete lesson examples, grouping strategies, and information management ideas.

Next we will take a look at mathematical content and what it means to *understand* mathematics, not just to know and do mathematics. We will look at how to continuously "teach up" maintaining high expectations and rigor in planning units, lessons, and assessments (Chapter 3).

The fourth chapter looks at the purposefulness of differentiation—how to make proactive decisions during planning. Chapter 4 shows you how to choose tasks that will deepen mathematical understanding, offer multiple entry points, and be accessible to all students through differentiation.

Chapters 5 and 6 address the "daily-ness" of the classroom. In Chapter 5 we look at how to set up expectations in your classroom and establish a healthy learning environment with a growth mindset. This chapter describes one area of the fine-tuning of differentiation, starting with how to keep the learning community and environment operating as the year goes on. The role of routines, such as how to move in and out of groups, how to respect others who are working on different things, turning in work, what to do when you are finished, and so on, are all part of making differentiation work.

Chapter 6 addresses the management of the classroom and balancing differentiated tasks. Differentiating working conditions does not need to be difficult. This chapter gives advice on some of the subtleties of making differentiation a natural way to learn.

Following this, we address the role of assessment. What does assessment look like in a differentiated classroom? Can you differentiate tests or other assessments? How? Is that fair? What about feedback and grading? How do you get students to self-assess? This is addressed in Chapter 7.

Finally, we will look at a week in the life of a differentiated mathematics class. We will look at the initial planning and how formative assessment each day informs adjustments to the plans. We will look at the decision-making process through a description of a week in the life of a primary teacher and an intermediate teacher.

Every Math Learner provides detailed information for turning every aspect of your mathematics class into a differentiated mathematics class. With that said, there are special areas of expertise that benefit from differentiation that were not able to be fully addressed in this book, including English language learners and special education students. All of the strategies in this book are appropriate for these identified learners; however, the depth of these fields is not represented in this book. The appendixes provide further resources for reading in these areas.

THE DIFFERENCE OF *EVERY MATH LEARNER*

There have been many books on differentiation, and even several on differentiating mathematics. *Every Math Learner* will complement the existing books by extending the structures, strategies, and examples of differentiation; however, it will also be different in several ways.

GOALS

I see a greater sense of pressure, frustration, and disappointment among teachers today than ever before. I wish I could change that. This book does *not* change the testing pressure. It *does* offer concrete strategies, examples, and classroom stories that help students learn mathematics more effectively and maximize each student's learning potential, thus *leading* to improved test scores.

It is my goal that this book will provide you with specific and practical tools to design and implement rich and engaging mathematics instruction, tailored to your students' needs. Along the way I will encourage you to think deeply about the mathematics content, reaching new and exciting "aha moments" to pass on to your students. Through this two-pronged approach, rich mathematical content and engaging differentiated instruction, you and your students will experience new levels of learning and accomplishment. I sincerely hope that this book will equip you, the math teacher, to make math understandable, doable, and enjoyable for you and all of our students.

FEATURES

Throughout the chapters of *Every Math Learner* you will find features to facilitate your implementation of differentiation. Each chapter will include

- Specific content across grades K–5
- Chances to pause and think about content through "Consider It!"
- Many strategy examples, including "Try It!" strategies that are immediately usable
- Balancing the "what" and the "why" of differentiation
- Frequently Asked Questions (FAQs) and answers pertaining to the chapter
- A chance for you, the reader, to reflect, summarize, and plan your next steps
- Templates and checklists to design and refine your instruction.
- And the best part . . . video!

I am excited for you to use this book, especially because we have gone out in the field and captured real classrooms with real students for you to see differentiation in action. There is just nothing like seeing what is being explained, is there? Well, the best would be for you to try it in your own setting, but of course I couldn't capture that for you. I trust you will though.

WHO IS THIS FOR?

This book is for anyone who teaches math. It was written primarily with the elementary classroom teacher in mind; however, math coaches and curriculum developers will also benefit from the structures of thought and practical examples and tasks. Additionally, administrators will find the book helpful when determining what should be seen in mathematics classrooms.

USING *EVERY MATH LEARNER*

Corwin has a saying: Corwin books are not meant to be read—
they are meant to be used. This book was written with the idea of
"using." With that in mind, the book can be used

- for individual teachers to design their own lessons and
  activities
- for teacher teams to help guide differentiated tasks and
  assessments
- for coaches and mentors to guide teachers in their own
  growth and goal setting
- as a professional development tool to focus on specific
  strategies
- to adjust materials and program resources to better meet
  students' needs

CONCLUSION

This book will help you, the teacher, understand your students as
learners and why some things work with some kids, and others
don't. It is a practical guide to all aspects of the classroom, and
how to maintain order and sanity as you consider the students in
your care, and how to help them come to know, understand, and
(dare I say) LOVE mathematics!

ACKNOWLEDGMENTS

If you think about giving a thank you speech for where you are right now in your life, whom would you acknowledge? You now understand my overwhelming feeling that I am where I am because of the love, friendship, and support of so many people.

Over the past 25 years or more I have learned from and worked alongside many extraordinary educators. Mark Boyer taught me how to dream, and believed in me when there was little in which to believe. He encouraged me and provided opportunities and gentle direction. Your retirement from education is a loss for us all, so I am very thankful to my sister for having married you so that I won't lose you from my life.

Lori Everson and Amy Francis have been patient, kind, and generous in helping me grow and understand the day-to-day working of math at the primary level. Thank you for your eagerness to learn and try new things and for constantly modeling what it means to be an excellent teacher. Thank you, Lori, for providing examples and pictures and responding to every SOS e-mail I sent you toward the end of this book.

My learning and refined thinking on differentiation would be nothing without colleagues like Cathy Battles, Marcia Embeau, Eileen Goodspeed, Orit Guriel Jessica Hockett, Leslie Kiernan, Sandra Page, Judy Rex, and Cindy Strickland. Thank you for pushing, questioning, and sharing with me.

Early in my consulting career teachers and administrators grabbed hold of rough ideas, tried them and refined them, and helped me become better. Thank you to Regina Newman for believing in and supporting me, and to the Middle School Math team at North Shore School District for working so hard to do the best for your students. Thank you to the incredible teachers at Roslyn School District, Kristina Wood, Gabby Gizzi, Amy Fetters, Loretta Fonseca, Renee Huntley, and especially Orit Guriel. You helped me learn how to put experience and thought into words, stretched my thinking, and put ideas into action in ways that I would not have foreseen. Working with you all shaped all of my future work.

My life would not be the same without Lisa Fritz, Ellen Shields, and Betz Frederick. Everyone should have such unwavering love and support to get you through amazingly tough times.

I would not have become involved in this project if not for Erin Null. Your perseverance, generosity, and helpfulness made my qualms go away and encouraged a vision beyond anything I thought possible. Then you made the vision reality. Thank you for being constantly available and quick to respond with sound ideas and feedback. Your patience, willingness to wait, and expert advice while I figured out how to get it right is unparalleled.

Carol Tomlinson is my role model for graciousness, wisdom, encouragement, and gentleness. Your brilliant mind strikes awe in me, and I shudder to think that I am trying to write a book in your field. My words echo hollow to my ears in comparison to your voice in my head. Again I thank you for all that you have done in my life the past 16 years.

To my family that has ridden the road with me—my husband and best friend Russ and my children Josh, Abbi, and Chris and their spouses Tory, Jeff, and Jen— thank you for being there in all the ups, downs, and round-abouts. You encourage and tease equally . . . well, maybe tease more . . . and I wouldn't have it any other way. Thank you for putting up with me and loving me and being proud of me. And thank you for giving me grandchildren: Maddi, Izzi, Lexi, Sophi, Judah, Landon, Elena, and Charlotte (at this writing—but I'm not pushing). To Maddi, Izzi, Lexi and Sophi—thank you for writing math work for me.

Above all, I give my praise to my Lord and Savior, Jesus Christ. You are the perfect model of a teacher who loves, reaches individuals in individual ways, and never gives up.

PUBLISHER'S ACKNOWLEDGMENTS

Corwin would like to thank the following individuals for their editorial insight and guidance:

Emily Bonner
Associate Professor of Curriculum and Instruction
University of Texas at San Antonio
San Antonio, TX

Marcia Carlson
Classroom Teacher
Crestview School of Inquiry
West Des Moines, IA

JoAnn Hiatt
Mathematics Instructor
Belton High School
Olathe, KS

Lyneille Meza
Director of Data and Assessment
Denton Independent School District
Denton, TX

Daniel Kikuji Rubenstein
Executive Director
Brooklyn Prospect Charter School
Brooklyn, NY

ABOUT THE AUTHOR

 **Dr. Nanci Smith** is currently a full-time national and international consultant and featured conference speaker in the areas of mathematics, curriculum and assessment, differentiated, instruction and Mathematics PLCs. Her work includes professional development in forty five states and nine countries.

Nanci taught math at the high school and university levels, and differentiated instruction as a master's course.

Dr. Smith received her PhD in curriculum and instruction, mathematics education from Arizona State University. She is Nationally Board Certified in Adolescent and Young Adult Mathematics.

Nanci is also author of *Every Math Learner: A Doable Approach to Teaching With Learning Differences in Mind, 6–12,* and *A Mind for Mathematics: Meaningful Teaching and Learning in Elementary Classrooms,* and *A Handbook for Unstoppable Learning.* She was the consultant, designer, and author of the *Meaningful Math: Leading Students Toward Understanding and Application* DVD series and developed an NSF-funded CD/DVD professional development series for middle school math teachers. She has various published chapters in the areas of differentiation, effective mathematics instruction, curriculum design, and standards implementation and has given interviews for publications and NPR. She has been a featured speaker for the NCTM national conference as well as numerous other conferences in the United States and abroad.

Nanci lives in Phoenix, Arizona, with her husband Russ and three cats. Besides educating all students; her; passions are her family, especially her eight grandchildren, travel, and knitting.

CHAPTER ONE

START UP

WHY KNOWING AND ADDRESSING STUDENTS' LEARNING DIFFERENCES IS CRITICAL

I always hear from teachers that differentiation seems too hard because they don't even know where to start. This chapter will focus on the fundamentals to get you going with differentiation. In this chapter, you will find:

Introduction

What Differentiation
    Is and Is Not

A Glance at a Differentiated
    Classroom

Frequently Asked Questions

Keepsakes and Plans

INTRODUCTION

Welcome to school! There is something so very exciting about a new class of students, a new year of potential, and the fulfillment of touching the future. As teachers, we love getting to know our students. We love thinking about how much they will grow this year. We are excited to share activities that we love to do, and we hope our students will not only love to do them too but more importantly also will learn from them.

And very quickly, as we get to know our students, we recognize who each student is as an individual human being and as an individual learner. We come to understand that Maddi already knows much of what is in our grade-level content and that what she doesn't already know, she will learn in less than half the time it takes the rest of the class. There is outgoing Elena who prefers to learn with others, asks for help freely, and offers help equally as freely. Judah is a constant bundle of energy and desires to follow directions, even if he usually forgets what the directions were. There is Izzi who prefers to draw and think in color and pictures, and there is Landon who is shyly constant in his learning. There is also Alexia who reads voraciously and above grade level, but she is less inclined to enjoy mathematics. Sophia is extremely shy, bright, and capable but doesn't want to show it and does not like to do anything in front of the class. And then there is Justin, who you didn't even realize was a special education student with an Individualized Education Plan (IEP) until the IEP showed up in your mailbox. Aamino just moved to this country from Somalia and hasn't been in a formal school before, and he does not speak English. Nick is very bright but is slowly losing interest in school because he is tired from taking care of his little brother and sister after school, even though he really needs to be taken care of himself. And that is just a few of the students in your class. When we consider all of the students, and the overwhelming amount there is to learn this year, we don't lose our love for students and enthusiasm, but we begin to wonder just how to pull all of this off!

Let's face it. We didn't go into teaching for the prestige or money. We care about students. We care about the quiet and shy, the rowdy and rambunctious, the leaders and followers, the musicians, artists, athletes, cheerleaders, scholars, strugglers, and everyone in between. And in most classrooms, I have just described your student population! Our kids come to us from a wide range of backgrounds and families, experiences, and mastery levels. And we need to reach and teach them all: to have high expectations for each student and help each one fulfill his or her potential and beyond. And that is where differentiation comes in.

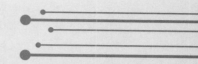

WATCH IT!

As you watch Video 1.1, *Getting Started With Differentiation*, consider the following questions:

1. How is differentiation not considered individualization, yet still about the individual?

2. What descriptions confirm your understanding of what differentiation is and is not?

3. What is new or surprises you in the descriptions?

4. Why a three-legged stool? Why balance the three "legs" of differentiation?

Video 1.1 Getting Started With Differentiation

WHAT DIFFERENTIATION IS AND IS NOT

If you ask a group of educators what is differentiation, you will undoubtedly hear it is about helping every student succeed to the best of his or her ability. That is true. Nevertheless, if you dig deeper for details, explanations can vary drastically and have changed in emphasis over the years. I have heard everything from "it's just the old individualized instruction back again with a new name." Or, "this is just about multiple intelligences," or even, "all you have to do is give choices." Today, largely because of a common description of Tier 1 of the Response to Intervention (RTI) as quality core instruction for all students that is differentiated, most educators equate differentiation with interventions for struggling learners. Just like the story of the blind men describing an elephant based on the part of the elephant they can feel, all of these explanations give a small sliver of the bigger picture of differentiation. Far too often a person's sliver of differentiation is taken as the whole and applied in ways that are neither appropriate nor purposeful, and the conclusion is that differentiation just does not work.

According to Carol Ann Tomlinson (2014, p. 4), "Teachers in differentiated classrooms begin with a clear and solid sense of what constitutes powerful curriculum and engaging instruction. Then they ask what it will take to modify that curriculum and instruction so that each learner comes away with knowledge, understanding, and skills necessary to take on the next important phase of learning." In essence, differentiation is a teacher's decisions about instructional and assessment design to best equip his or her students for learning.

Sounds simple, and in some ways, it is. In some ways, though, it absolutely is not! The decisions teachers make need to be based on the foundation of explicitly clear standards and learning goals, knowledge of their students as learners, effective pedagogical strategies and task choices, and assessment data. When thinking about students as learners, there are three areas as defined by Tomlinson (2001) that provide a structure for decision-making: Readiness, Interest, and Learning Profile. These three characteristics of learners will be the basis on which we discuss and develop how we can embrace and address the differences in our learners. What follows is a brief introduction to each characteristic that will be developed in detail with lesson examples in the following chapters.

READINESS

"This is easy." "This is too hard. I can't do this." Neither of these reactions from students is what we want to hear. If those are honest reactions from the students, then we have not addressed their readiness. In some ways, readiness differentiation is like the Three Little Bears of Education: We want "just right." The problem is that it is usually impossible to find just one "just right" for an entire class (Hattie, 2013).

Readiness differentiation begins with determining the entry point for each student on the learning trajectory for the activity, lesson, or unit. We tend to link readiness with "ability grouping." Yet there are significant differences in what we commonly think of with readiness grouping and ability grouping, no matter how flexible the ability grouping may be designed to be. Many areas impact readiness, including but not limited to life experiences, prior knowledge, ability to abstract and generalize, and home support.

We have all experienced the wide range of learners in our classrooms that can be based on a wide variety of factors. Certainly, a student's prior knowledge plays a major role in whether the student is perceived as advanced, typical, or struggling. Additionally, there are factors that have equally (or perhaps have greater) impact on a student's alacrity with learning mathematics, such as the speed at which students process and learn new information, the help and attitudes about education students experience at home, and past experiences in school. Add to this those students who are from other countries, learning English as a second language, or are identified as gifted or with a form of learning disability, and the range of learners can seem overwhelming. To teach all students with the same strategies, at the same pace, with the same expectations does not make sense. This is the essence of readiness differentiation.

Please notice that readiness does not imply ability! In fact, we now know without a doubt that ability is based on effort and is not a fixed commodity. According to Carol Dweck (n.d., 2006), "No matter what your current ability is, effort is what ignites that ability and turns it into accomplishment."

Readiness addresses that range of challenge where learning can happen for the student, being neither too easy nor too hard. One problem with considering readiness is that when looking at the student's actions, it is easy to associate readiness with what students can and can't do . . . *especially* with what they can't do.

I remember reading an article several years ago about the new superintendent my district had just hired. In it she stated that we would be committed to finding all of the holes and gaps our students had and to filling them. At first this might sound noble and like an appropriate endeavor. But think about it. The implication is that our education was to work from a deficit model—find what is wrong and fix it! Working from this negative frame of mind leaks out in our attitudes and speech too often, leaving students to feel unsuccessful, unable to learn, and at worst, dumb.

Readiness, on the other hand, works from a position of strength on the part of the student. What is it the student does know and is able to do? This provides the entry point into the learning. When we consider the "next step" in the learning progression for a student, we are addressing readiness. Readiness differentiation offers all students an appropriate challenge, a taste of success with effort, and a developing sense of efficacy and pride in learning.

Figure 1.1 illustrates readiness differentiation as determining entry points on the learning path.

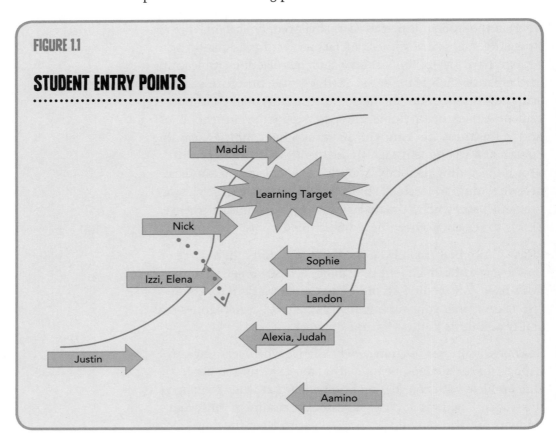

　Every Math Learner | A Doable Approach to Teaching With Learning Differences in Mind, Grades K–5

TRY IT! READINESS IMPRESSIONS

Purpose: To begin thinking about the differing readiness levels of your students

As you have gotten to know your math students, you have somewhat of an instinct as to their readiness levels. At what readiness levels would you put each of your students for mathematics, recognizing that this is a general statement and that readiness certainly changes?

1. Make a list of readiness groupings for your classroom. Next to each student's name, explain why you placed that student

in that group, for example, acquires new skills and concepts quickly or still struggles with basic facts, etc.

This initial list is based on your current knowledge of your students. Detailed information on determining readiness is provided in Chapters 2 and 7, and further examples of designing for readiness are provided in Chapter 4.

INTEREST

We all know the power of interest—when kids are really excited and hooked on what they are doing. The adage about time flying when you are having fun is never more true than when students are involved in learning and doing something they enjoy.

When I first considered differentiating by interest, I was largely stuck. For the most part, my students did not have hobbies and extracurricular activities that were mathematics related. There are only so many shopping problems you can use . . . and the boys didn't really care about shopping. Trying to print mathematical problems on their favorite color of paper wasn't exactly doing it either! What a misunderstanding I had about differentiating by interest.

It is incredibly powerful when we can link our content learning to students' hobbies and passions. It is equally important to ignite new interests through our own modeling of interest and passion for our subject. Interest differentiation is about igniting intrinsic motivation for learning. Eric Jensen (1998) gives three criteria for increasing intrinsic motivation, which fits perfectly with interest differentiation: (1) providing choices, (2) making content relevant to the learner, and (3) using engaging and energetic learning activities. Figure 1.2 models Jensen's lesson factors that contrast increasing students' motivation versus apathy.

How we figure out our students' interests is very easy—talk to them. Ask them. Our beginning of the year surveys are usually filled with interest items. We find out their hobbies, extracurricular activities, favorite movies and books, as well as hopes and dreams! We can also find out their favorite ways to learn mathematics, such as hands-on activities, and why those learning activities work for them. When we can make connections among personal interests, learning interests, and content, we have them hooked! All of these pieces of information begin to build a bank of interest differentiation possibilities.

FIGURE 1.2

MOTIVATION VERSUS APATHY LESSON FACTORS

Classroom Factors	Classroom Factors
Choices – access to content, process, product, grouping, resources, and environment	**Required** – no student voice, specific task or assignment for all
Relevance – what is being learned is meaningful in the eyes of the learner and connected to the learner's experiences. Content is developed at a conceptual and, applicable level	**Irrelevant** – content appears out of context and disconnected from student and is often learned only to pass a test
Engaging – emotional, energetic hands-on, and provides for learner's input	**Passive** – learning activities have low interaction such as seatwork and note-taking
Results In	
Increased intrinsic motivation	Increased apathy and resentment

TRY IT! THEY CARE ABOUT . . .

Purpose: To identify students' interests

1. What do you know already about your students' interests? Create an Interest List that includes general interests of students in your grade level, strategies and activities that have worked well for your class, and individual interests of your students of which you are aware.

Strategies for assessing your students' interests are given in Chapter 2.

LEARNING PROFILE

Perhaps the most debated and questioned feature of student differences is learning profile. In general, learning profile refers to the way brains best receive information, make sense of information, commit information to memory, and recall information from memory. I imagine that all of us have learning stories that exemplify when a lesson completely connected with us, and when one completely did not. Sometimes it is a connection with the teacher. Sometimes it is the type of task that really works. This could be a hint as to your preferences in learning. I know that I struggled with teachers who primarily lectured. I still do not like listening to audio books and can get bored with long phone calls. I need visuals. When sitting in a lecture, I take extensive notes to make the talk visible. How about you? What ways do you feel you learn best?

There are many different structures by which we can consider learning profile. Notice that the term is learning *profile,* which is an all-encompassing term for many different ways of learning. Often people use the term "learning style" in place of "learning profile." Nevertheless, learning style has so many different meanings that I always ask someone to clarify what he or she means when using that term.

Different authors and researchers have different opinions about learning profiles—whether we are born wired in certain ways, whether these paths change over time, and whether they vary subject to subject. For our purposes, we will have a more general conversation about learning profile and how we can use it to structure differentiated tasks.

Learning profile includes four broad categories: Group Orientation, Cognitive Style, Learning Environment, and Intelligence Preference (Tomlinson, 2001). Figure 1.3 elaborates on each of these areas.

Certainly some other factors can play into learning profile—there is plenty of research indicating learning differences between the genders as well as cultural influences. Although the learning profile structures are generalizable, none is true for every student. It is part of our job to be a student of our students—to determine what each student's combination of preferences will be as

FIGURE 1.3

CATEGORIES OF LEARNING PROFILE

Group Orientation	How do students prefer to work? Alone or with a partner? Who likes to figure things out first, and then share? Who likes to work through an activity with someone else? Which of your students work to please themselves, others, or the adults in their lives?
Cognitive Style	Which of your students need to see the big picture before they can make sense of the details, or do they need details to build to a big picture (whole-to-part or part-to-whole)? Who thinks very linearly, and who is more global and nonlinear? Which students work better with collaboration, and which work better with competition? Who are more reflective, and who are more action-oriented?
Learning Environment	Who needs a quiet and calm atmosphere to concentrate, and who can concentrate in noise and activity? How does temperature and light (bright or dim, natural or fluorescent) impact the learning of different students? How are desks arranged? What about music playing?
Intelligence Preference	Students will come with different learning intelligence preferences such as the theory of Multiple Intelligences (Gardner) and Triarchic Theory (Sternberg), which include analytical, practical, and/or creative orientations to learning.

we teach mathematics. When determining learning profiles for your students, please be aware of two very important warnings:

- It is possible that some students learn in the same ways that you do. You can also count on the fact that other students will not learn in the same way. Yet, it is completely natural for us to teach in the ways we best learn. That will always be our most natural fallback option. Thus, it is important to be aware of and plan for the wide variety of learning profiles in your classroom.

- We need to be careful not to try to determine "what kind of learners" students are and then assign them to tasks by what we assume is the student's "type." It is possible to use discussions about learning profile to help students understand differences in how people learn, and their likely strengths and weaknesses as discussed in Chapter 2. Nevertheless, in differentiating by learning profile, it is best to offer varied learning profile approaches to exploring and expressing learning, with the students making the choice of the specific task.

Consider It!

Think about your learning profile. What are your natural tendencies for preferred learning activities and instruction? How does this influence your lesson design? Who in your class learns in the same way? Who does not? Do you know how they might learn? Chapter 2 will explain how to recognize your students' learning profiles.

THREE CHARACTERISTICS OF DIFFERENCE

A friend and colleague, Cindy Strickland, uses an image of a three-legged stool to illustrate differentiation, with each leg labeled with one of the learning aspects of students. Figure 1.4 provides an illustration of the balance of the "differentiation legs."

Have you ever sat on a three-legged stool with uneven legs? I have. I can do it for a little while, but soon I am looking for a different place to sit. It wobbles and is uncomfortable. Worse would be sitting on a three-legged stool with only two legs, or what about one leg? That is a pogo stick, not a stool. This should be the picture of respectful differentiation: Decisions about differentiation need to be in balance according to students' learning needs. Just like a stool out of balance, differentiation out of balance may cause unanticipated problems.

- When we differentiate only by **readiness**, we tend to track our classrooms without meaning to. Students begin to feel that they are always working with the same other students and can classify themselves as a "bluebird" or "buzzard."

- When we differentiate only by **interest**, we can give the impression that learning for learning's sake is never necessary, and that if a student isn't really interested, the learning can be skipped.

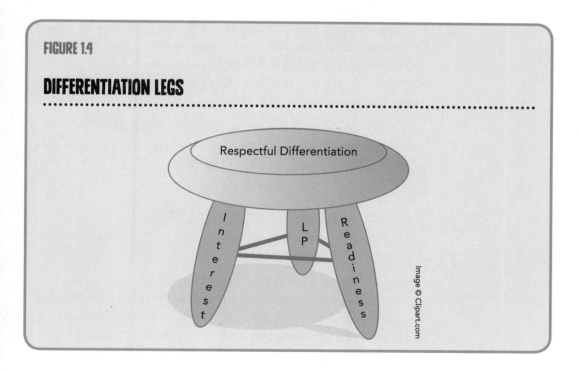

FIGURE 1.4

DIFFERENTIATION LEGS

Respectful Differentiation

Interest

LP

Readiness

Image © Clipart.com

Consider It!

As you think about your natural differentiation in class, to which of the differentiation "legs" do you most naturally lean? Is there a "leg" that you do not address often or with which you feel uncomfortable?

- When we only differentiate by **learning profile**, we can create learning cripples that are not flexible in their approaches to learning and not able to learn from a wide variety of teachers and opportunities. The three-legged stool is the perfect balance when we consider the whole of differentiation.

DIFFERENTIATION IS AND ISN'T . . .

It is interesting that of all the content areas taught in school, the way mathematics is taught is generally the most consistent of any subject across the country. It is as if there is an unspoken version of a mathematics lesson that is implemented in most classes and most grade levels, regardless of how much creative license teachers employ in other subjects. We tend to model a problem type, practice the problem type, possibly problem solve around the problem type, have homework on the problem type, and tomorrow repeat with a new problem type! And yet, we know that we are not successful overall in mathematics. There are many factors to consider when we design lessons to increase understanding in mathematics. The first factor in the process is analyzing our standards and explicitly stating the factual, skill, and conceptual expectations. This is developed in Chapter 3. We use the explication of our standards combined with the knowledge of our students, as described in Chapter 2, to develop learning goals, instruction, and design or choose tasks. Designing instruction and tasks geared to individual student's learning needs through differentiation will reach and engage students in ways that nothing else can. Chapter 4 brings all of these ideas together.

As we move forward in designing and implementing differentiation in mathematics class, let's take a final general look at what differentiation is and isn't in Figure 1.5.

A GLANCE AT A DIFFERENTIATED CLASSROOM

PRIMARY CLASSROOM

"Everyone get your math paper out. I'm going to go over the correct answers. Correct any of the answers you may have missed. Next we will use ten-frames to make tens. Now we will draw ten-frames. And then we will begin homework."

FIGURE 1.5

DIFFERENTIATION IS AND ISN'T

Differentiation Isn't	Differentiation Is
A way to make struggling students pass the test	A way to address all students and all ranges of readiness. Readiness differentiation is 1/3 of the total picture of differentiation, and it is not limited to struggling students.
Fluffy	A way for individual sense-making and connections by providing multiple methods for learning and demonstration of learning. It focuses on providing access to deep and rich content founded on standards.
The individualized instruction from the 70's	A way to address individual students and how they learn, but it does not endorse individual lessons for each student. Rather, it considers which groups of students will most benefit from which methods and tasks.
All about multiple intelligences	Inclusive of multiple intelligences, but a learning profile is 1/3 of the total picture of differentiation and multiple intelligences is one of many ways to address learning profiles. This is a small slice of the total picture of differentiation.
Just about giving choices to cover your bases	Inclusive of giving choices to increase motivation, but the design of the choices offered is significant. Again, interest differentiation is 1/3 of the total picture of differentiation.
Instinctive	Not instinctive. Our instinct is to teach the way we learn or the way we were taught. Differentiation is based on assessment data and understanding our content as well as our students.
Untenable and not worth a teacher's time	Possible. No one differentiates every lesson every day. Choosing when and what to differentiate is part of a teacher's decision-making process. Designing effective differentiation does take time and planning, especially at first. It gets easier over time and is worth it when you see students engaged and excited to learn.

It is a condensed description of most primary mathematics class sessions. Certainly differentiating in the primary classroom has certain challenges because the students are not as capably independent as older students. Yet, it is possible to differentiate and use stations or rotations with the youngest students.

"Let's all practice adding numbers by making a ten. We will use ten-frames to help us. Why would it be helpful to be able to make a ten?" The whole class lesson is using two ten-frames to add two single-digit numbers by making a ten. The students quickly realize how much easier it is to add a single digit and ten, rather than two single digits. There is now motivation to make a ten so that the addition facts become much easier.

After students practice using the ten-frames to add single-digit numbers as a whole class and individually, the teacher divides them into readiness rotation groups based on prior knowledge of students and current observation from the guided practice. Stations are set up for two different rotations based on two activities with which the students have had experience as well as their current learning. Students needing more reinforcement follow the blue rotation, and the students further along follow the orange stations as shown in Figure 1.6.

To conclude the lesson, all students come back together to discuss the strategy of "making a ten" to add numbers. Students explain why or why not it is a good strategy, and when it is easier to use or not to use. They compare the strategy with other strategies they know such as "counting on." The teacher asks students to

FIGURE 1.6

COLOR-CODED READINESS STATIONS

Blue Rotations	Orange Rotations
Roll two dice and write the corresponding addition problem and sum (students can count the pips if needed)	Play addition war
Play addition war by turning over two playing cards (with face cards removed) and adding the two cards	Use two and three ten-frames to add either two one-digit numbers or a two-digit and a one-digit number (addends are on cards that are flipped over to form the problems)
Use ten-frames to add single-digit numbers and color a ten-frame sheet to show their work	Use notation to "make a ten" for single-digit addition problems
Meet with the teacher	Meet with the teacher

complete one of two problems (blue or orange) of adding two single-digit numbers using a ten-frame picture, or a two-digit and one-digit number using a ten-frame picture.

INTERMEDIATE CLASSROOM

"There is a warm up on the board. After you complete it, please take out your homework and check your answers against the correct answers that I posted. What questions do you have?" You know how most mathematics classes run: Review homework, new notes, or learning; have some kind of practice; and start homework problems to be sure the students can finish the work at home. Often students fill in blanks in a workbook or practice with worksheets. Although there is nothing inherently wrong with any of these pieces, a steady diet of this type of learning is surely uninspiring at best and demotivating and disconnected at worst. Teachers who are responsive and creative in designing literacy lessons are sometimes at a loss as to what a differentiated mathematics class could look like.

"On the board you will find a choice of warm up problems. Please choose the one that you feel is just right for you—not too hard or too easy. Once you have completed your problem, please find a partner with whom to compare your homework answers based on the homework assignment you did last night: red, purple, or green. Do not only compare your answers, but also compare the method you used to solve it. If you have different answers, try to convince each other of your work. You can also check with someone else who did the same assignment. Only ask for help if you cannot figure it out. You have ten minutes."

Students compare their homework problems that were based on readiness. All problems were on the current topic of decimal operations; yet, problems were tiered based on applications problems, representations, and whether examples and/or reminders were provided. All assignments had three common problems, which would be the basis for whole class discussion after the independent review.

When the homework conversations are finished, the teacher asks students to meet in groups of three or four to work on an investigation relating to decimal place value, whole number place value, division, and fractions. All groups complete the same investigation; nevertheless, some groups are given base-ten blocks (with a flat representing one whole) as a concrete representation to work through the relationships, whereas other groups have a more scaffolded version of the investigation with models and hints embedded. The teacher circulates among the groups to ask questions to help students extend their thinking or help focus thinking.

As students complete the investigation, the teacher pulls the class together to discuss the findings and make the connections and understandings among place value, division, and fractions explicit. Several problems are then practiced. The class concludes with a synthesizing activity in which students can choose between working a specific problem with mathematical explanations, writing a letter to a friend explaining connections and what a problem will look like, or designing a picture or graphic to show the relationships and connections among place value, division, and fractions.

WHAT IS THE DIFFERENCE?

There are some foundational belief differences between a differentiated class and a more traditionally taught class. Figure 1.7 gives a summary list of some of these differences. All of the differentiated aspects will be developed throughout the rest of the book and through the video clips.

Consider It!

In this example, most of the mathematics lesson was differentiated. That is not always the case. Often one aspect of a lesson will be differentiated in some way, such as a choice of closure activities or a tiered practice:

- How do you respond to this lesson?

- How many types of differentiation do you feel can be done with your students?

- Of what parts are you unsure?

- Make a list of pros and cons from this lesson as a baseline for your learning as you work through this book.

FIGURE 1.7

TRADITIONAL VERSUS DIFFERENTIATED CLASSROOM

More Traditional Mathematics Classroom	Differentiated Mathematics Classroom
Student differences are ignored or avoided	Student differences form the basis of lesson design.
Texts and resources are the basis for instruction	Standards and knowledge of students as learners are the basis for instruction.
Predominantly teacher presentation	Teacher provides means for students to make connections through investigation, collaboration, and communication.
Predominantly whole class	Students are grouped to work in a variety of ways, including in pairs, in small groups, alone, and as a whole class. Pairs and groups are purposefully designed.
A single pace is expected for all students	As much as possible, flexible time and due dates are used for students who require additional time.
A single lesson or activity is used for all students	Different lesson components or activities are designed to reach all learners, varying in design among readiness, interest, and learning profile.
A single assessment is used	A variety of assessments are used to allow students to demonstrate what they know, understand, and are able to do, with options available when appropriate.
A single definition of success is expected, and it is most often speed and accuracy	Success is rooted in student growth and effort, risk taking, and perseverance.

CONCLUSION

"Educators should be champions of every student who enters the schoolhouse doors" (Tomlinson, 2014, p. 27). I don't know any educator who doesn't agree with this statement. And yet too often there are students who feel incapable, unaccepted, and unappreciated, especially in mathematics. As teachers we have incredible power to set the climate of our classrooms, as well as to inspire and transform our students. We know from brain research now that there is no such things as "math people" or "non-math people." We know effort changes everything. And we know that designing engaging lessons and activities that fit our individual students can change their and our world.

Consider It!

Think about your current classroom practice. No one is purely in one or another category. Where are your current classroom practices as you consider the two columns of "traditional" and "differentiated" classrooms?

FREQUENTLY ASKED QUESTIONS

Q: How can you differentiate when we have the same standards and give a high-stakes standardized test?

A: Differentiation is about maximizing learning for every student. The standards provide the content, or *what* we teach. Differentiation is how we craft the learning experiences for students so that they are able to reach the standards. If students can learn at deeper levels, make sense of what they are learning in ways that make most sense to their brains, and store and retrieve from memory more effectively, they will have greater success on all assessments including the high-stakes standardized tests.

Q: What about students who refuse to try?

A: I wish I had a foolproof answer. There isn't one. Nonetheless, students who are in a class where they feel accepted, have some voice in their learning, and know that the teacher believes in them will almost always start to change their behavior. Usually the behavior comes from negative past experiences, and replacing those beliefs about school and how they fit school with positive experiences and a taste of success goes a long way. There is nothing like relationships to begin to heal students who are shut down.

Q: How do you find time to do all of this?

A: First remember that no one differentiates every lesson every day. The start of differentiation can be frustrating because you don't have activities and plans ready to go. Think about what you already have, and gather ideas from colleagues and the Internet as you are able. Instead of choosing which activity you want to use, determine which students would best relate to which of the tasks. Then use them all and you have a differentiated lesson. The best advice comes from Carol Ann Tomlinson: Start slow, but start.

Keepsakes and Plans

What are the keepsake ideas from this chapter, those thoughts or ideas that resonated with you that you do not want to forget?

What Is Differentiation:

1.

2.

3.

The Learning Environment:

1.

2.

3.

A Glance at a Differentiated Classroom:

1.

2.

3.

Based on my keepsake ideas, I plan to

1.

2.

3.

Learning Profile Paper People:

Pants:
Do you like to learn math:
   on the computer - green
   with paper and pencil (worksheet) - black
   by playing math games - blue

Shirt:
Do you learn best by:
   seeing someone do math- red
   hearing them explain math - yellow
   touching/doing it yourself - purple

Shoes:
Do you like to:
   work alone - white
   in groups - black
   with a partner - brown

If you like it quiet when you work:
put stripes on your shirt

If you like it noisy/music playing while you work:
put polka dots on your shirt

If you like to be challenged to learn new things
add a hat

CHAPTER TWO

FIND OUT

STRATEGIES FOR DETERMINING WHO EACH OF YOUR STUDENTS IS AS A MATHEMATICS LEARNER

The key to differentiation is really knowing these students whose learning you are entrusted with every day. The tools and techniques in this chapter will help you understand the differences in how your students learn and what to do about it. In this chapter, you will find:

Think about yourself for a minute. How do you best learn mathematics? Do you prefer to have a detailed list of steps given followed by repeated practice? Or do you prefer to see how the mathematics applies to specific situations, and then learn how to complete the skills? Would you rather have hands-on activities or talk it out with colleagues? Do you like to work with others in tackling open-ended tasks, or would you rather think on your own? Do you take a concept and imagine how you could use it in your own life or in new situations? Our learners are as complex in how they learn mathematics as you are. You can also count on them learning differently from you as well as from each other.

Students will differ in their learning preferences, their interests, and their entry points into the learning continuum. As teachers, we need to become students of our students to design effective differentiation. Just how we "study our students" can vary by the age of the student and what we are trying to determine. The importance of studying our students does not vary. It is only when we are armed with the knowledge of our students as learners and as human beings that we are able to form strong relationships and build learning opportunities that intrigue and challenge each of them.

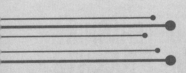

WATCH IT!

As you watch Video 2.1, *Getting to Know Students as Learners*, consider the following questions:

1. How can you get to know how your students learn differently?

2. How can you help students understand that everyone learns differently?

3. How can "Paper People" help you understand your students and help them understand each other in learning mathematics?

4. How is community built as they share their paper people?

5. How can information about how your students learn be used to design groups and tasks?

Video 2.1 Getting to Know Students as Learners

WHO OUR LEARNERS ARE

Our students come to us from varied backgrounds and life experiences, and they bring varied messages about who they believe they are as learners in school, especially in mathematics. Even within a kindergarten class you can see these differences, which escalate as the years progress. It helps to understand how our students view themselves as math learners as well as to determine strategies that can help them best learn. Before we begin with new ways to assess who your learners are, reflect on what you already do to get to know your students.

One method for finding out how your students feel about themselves as math learners is to have them write or draw their own math story. Often students have not thought about themselves as "math learners," and this activity will help them recognize their strengths and weaknesses.

Consider It!

How do you currently get to know your students? Make a list of what you currently do to get to know your students, as well as of what you are currently finding out about your students. As you look at each activity you use, identify the type of information you have gained—is it about student readiness, interest, learning profile, personal beliefs, hobbies, other? Is there any missing information about your students as learners?

TRY IT! MY MATH STORY

Purpose: Find out your students' self-perceptions on learning mathematics

Primary Version:

At the beginning of the year, and for kindergarten, conduct "My Math Story" as an interview either individually or in small groups of students. Remind students to be honest and share what they think. By the end of the year, this could be a written reflection to incorporate writing into the learning of mathematics. It is recommended to do this as a station rotation when working with the teacher, and ask only one question a day. This should be spread out over the course of several days or a week.

1. Do you enjoy learning math? Why or why not? For kindergarten, what do you like about numbers?

2. What do you like to do to learn math? Is there anything you don't like to do to learn math?

3. Show off! Tell me all you know about numbers.

Intermediate Version:

Have students write, draw, or describe their favorite mathematics classes and/or activities as they reflect on their own math stories. Use the following guidelines:

1. How do you feel about learning math? Do you enjoy learning math? Why or why not? Are you a strong math learner? Why or why not?

2. Describe your favorite math class or a specific math learning activity. It can be a specific grade or a specific activity or game. Please do not mention any teacher's name. Write about what works for you to learn math the best.

3. Why did the class or activity work well for you? What did you learn from it?

4. What does not work well for you in learning math? Why do you not like to learn that way?

5. If you could tell me one thing about how you would like to learn math this year, what would it be? Ok . . . if you want to tell me two things, that would be fine as well.

TIPS FOR ELL/SPECIAL EDUCATION STUDENTS

Students from other countries will want to share their learning experiences and backgrounds. Encourage them to draw or write about their learning experiences. Provide a word bank and sentence starters to help them. Sentence starters could include:

- I like to learn by . . .
- I do not like to . . .
- I do/do not like to learn with other students.

Word Bank Ideas with two picture support:

- Play games (picture of two students playing cards)
- Write problems (written mathematical problems)
- Talk in class (students talking to each other)
- Draw (mathematical picture)

My Math Story is a strategy to find out about your students' beliefs as math learners. In addition to finding out how your students feel, you also need to find out how your students learn. How you find this out depends on whether you are looking at students' readiness, interest, or learning profile. Interest and learning profile serve a slightly different aspect of differentiation than does readiness. Interest and learning profile are used primarily to motivate and allow students access to learning opportunities that will meet their preferences. Readiness is about appropriate challenge, prior knowledge, extensions, and the content rather than about the manner in which the content is learned. As a result, the assessment for readiness is dependent on preassessment and formative assessment. Formative assessment is fully developed in Chapter 6.

STRATEGIES TO DETERMINE READINESS

Assessments, observation data, and surveys can provide a glimpse into our students as learners, and they can be useful as tools to begin designing differentiated instruction. Perhaps the most glaring aspect of student differences in our classrooms is readiness. We often wonder what to do about Justin, Alexia, and Aamino (introduced in Chapter 1) who are behind the rest of the class in mathematics but for very different reasons, and we often worry whether we are challenging Maddi at all. The same components in class that make readiness obvious, such as homework, assessments, discussions, and activities, are also the basis on which we differentiate by readiness. All of your assessment data, whether formal or informal, form the basis of determining a student's readiness. Before beginning any unit, and in fact most lessons, it is important to preassess.

WATCH IT!

As you watch Video 2.2, *Knowing Your Learners' Readiness*, consider the following questions:

1. What information can be used to determine your students' readiness levels?

2. How often should you assess for readiness?

3. How flexible should readiness differentiation be?

Video 2.2 Knowing Your Learners' Readiness

There are many different ways by which you can preassess. Many teachers use a pretest that is an alternative version of the summative assessment that will be given. This is especially effective if you are gathering pre- and post-data to document growth. Many other options, however, are more student-friendly than giving a test on which they are not supposed to be able to do the work! No matter what form your preassessment takes, it needs to gain information about

- Key vocabulary

- Essential prerequisite skills

- Skills that will be taught in the upcoming unit

- Key concepts and big ideas undergirding the unit

- Students' individual information, not collective or collaborative

Figure 2.1 provides a list of preassessment strategies and descriptions.

FIGURE 2.1

PREASSESSMENT STRATEGIES

Strategy/Description	Example
K-W-L Check This strategy is often used in elementary classrooms. K-W-L stands for Know (what do you already know), Want to Know, and Learned (after the unit, what have you learned). This strategy is often used as a whole class activity, but when used in this manner, it is not an effective preassessment. To use a K-W-L effectively, it should be given to individual students to find out what they truly already know and want to know, and then have an individual growth reflection. Once individual K-W-L charts are completed, a class discussion would be appropriate.	Adding to 5 (as told to a teacher or independent) Know — Want to Know — I Learned 4 + 1 — More ways Words for the numbers being added and answers.

Misconception Check

A misconception check is a list of statements or work to which students will agree or disagree (or mark True or False) and explain why they believe as they do. This is especially useful to surface common errors and misconceptions. Once students have responded, you can group students according to their answers—either alike answers to have specific further tasks ready or different answers to discuss and defend their positions.

Quick Write

This is a free write for students to recall, model, draw, or calculate anything relating to the topic. This can be posed as a prompt, such as "Please write, draw, describe, plot on a number line, or anything else you know to do to show me what you know about fractions." A word bank or skill list can be provided to stimulate students' thinking.

Decimal Addition

Mark each statement as True or False. Explain your thinking:

1. To add decimal numbers, line up the numbers from the right and then add as usual.
2. You can add as many zeros (0) to the end of a decimal number and not change the value of the number.
3. You can add as many zeros (0) after the decimal point and not change the value of the number.

What Do You Know About Fractions?

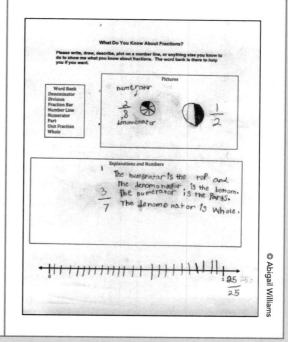

FIGURE 2.1 (Continued)

Show and Tell

Have students model and explain a concept or skill. This is especially important and useful for young learners and English-language learners (ELLs).

© Lori Everson

Another preassessment strategy that becomes formative and summative as well is a strategy I call Frayer Times Four (Smith, 2017). This is an adaptation of a Frayer model. The idea is to design a Frayer-type model for the preassessment. It does not have to be the traditional Frayer model that has sections for Definition, Information, Examples, and Non-Examples. I determine what sections I want to have, and I design my model that way. I then put the same model on a piece of paper four times: two on the front and two on the back. The first model is for the preassessment. About halfway through the unit, I give the paper back to students. I ask them to look at what they wrote on the first model and then cross out anything they now know is incorrect. On the second model, they can correct the errors from the first model and add anything else they have learned. About three fourths of the way through the unit, I repeat this process, with students crossing out anything in the first two models that they now know is incorrect and correcting and adding more information in the third model. Finally, the entire process is repeated after the summative assessment, with all corrections and additional information being added to the final model. This provides a one-page portfolio of growth through the unit, and it has students continue to reflect on their learning as well. Figure 2.2 gives a primary and intermediate example of one of the four Frayer models.

FIGURE 2.2

PRIMARY AND INTERMEDIATE MODELS FOR FRAYER TIMES FOUR

Primary Example

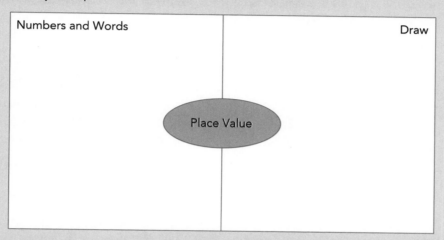

Numbers and Words	Draw

Place Value

Intermediate Version

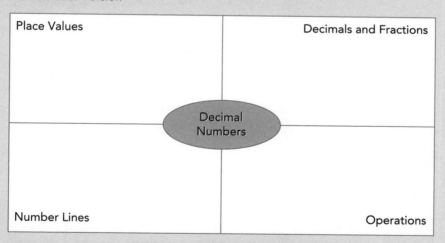

Place Values	Decimals and Fractions
Number Lines	Operations

Decimal Numbers

 Templates can be downloaded at http://resources.corwin.com/ everymathlearnerK-5

Purpose: To practice designing a preassessment other than a pretest

Design a preassessment for your next unit. Choose one of the preassessment strategies.

Sometimes a warm-up problem can serve as a preassessment in unexpected ways. Consider the following example from Tony Giorgi of Elk Grove School District, CA. Tony proposed a division problem to his students, expecting that the students would all use standard long division to solve the problem. He asked students to solve $52 \div 4$. The first student solved it the way he expected:

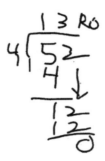

Other students raised their hands to say they had done the problem in different ways. Figure 2.3 show some of the other student's methods.

The division problem ended up being an excellent preassessment even though it was not planned to be one. This also demonstrates how powerful a task can be to provide information as to our students' readiness. Mr. Giorgi posed a problem and let his students work however they wanted. He did not suggest a specific method or ask his students to use the algorithm. Had he done so, he would not have gotten the information he did. Instead, he would only have found out who knew how to do that one procedure. He would not have found out whether his students had alternative methods or understood the meaning of division. The challenge now is how to address division for all of his students, knowing that the standard long division algorithm is not expected or standardly tested until sixth grade in most states.

FIGURE 2.3

METHODS OF DIVISION

Student A	Student A is a special education student. This student's strategy is to create the four groups and place dots one at a time into each group until counting to 52. The student then counted how many dots were in one circle. This demonstrates that the student understands the meaning of division but does not have a strategy for large numbers. The next step would be to work toward placing "groups of dots" into the four circles instead of one at a time, which will reinforce both multiplication facts as well as the relationship of multiplication and division. The next division goal will be to work toward a partial quotient strategy (See Student F), even if the partial quotient is 2 or 5 at a time.
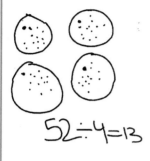 $52 \div 4 = 13$	
Student B	Student B used the inverse operation of multiplication to solve the division problem. This strategy is a good strategy, especially with manageable numbers. I would follow up with how Student B came up with 13 for a factor. Did the student look at the ones place and reason about what number times four would result in a 2 in the ones place? How does the student handle remainders with this strategy? The next step is to translate the use of multiplication into either the standard algorithm for division or partial quotients.
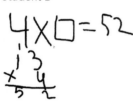	
Student C	This student uses repeated subtraction to solve. Although this does show one meaning of division, it is cumbersome to use and there are often more mistakes with this method than any other. This student presented his method on the Smart Board without showing the differences at each step. Yet, he kept track of the differences on scratch paper randomly. This student's next step is to think about subtracting "groups" of the divisor leading to multiplication practice, and using partial quotients to show groups of subtraction.
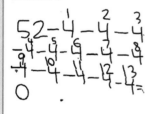	
Student D	Student D tried to use a factoring method that is a "reverse" distributive property. From the work presented, we can see strong reasoning although there are errors. The student was thinking of 44 + 8, but was not able to show the product of 4 and another factor to get to 44. This student has a strong start with reasoning about groups of 4 and may just need more practice with this strategy. The emphasis for next steps would be to continue to reinforce that groups of 4 implies multiplication.
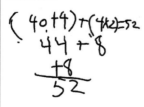	

(Continued)

FIGURE 2.3 (Continued)

Student E	Student E uses the distributive property correctly by determining two addends of 52 that are also both multiples of 4. Student E needs to show clearly the quotient to the original problem of 13 from the factors in the distributive property. For this student, it might be helpful to add another step after (4 × 10) + (4 × 3) to include 4 (10 + 3). This would benefit the student in the future when distributive property is used extensively, especially with algebra. It also more clearly shows the quotient to the orignial problem. Students with this strategy usually do not have any difficulty using the partial quotient method, or even transfering this thinking to the standard algorithm.
$$40 + 12 = 52$$ $$(4 \times 10) + (4 \times 3)$$ $$40 + 12$$ $$\underline{+12}$$ $$52$$	
Student F	Student F uses partial quotients. This strategy allows a student to use any number of "groups of 4" without having to have the exact number of tens or ones. This is a strong intermediate step toward the standard algorithm because it emphasizes the number of the groups of the divisor you are able to get in the dividend along the right side, which is one meaning of division. The number of groups are then totaled when there is not another complete group. When students easily reason in terms of place value (for example, they do not need to take two groups of 5 but see there is a group of 10 and a group of 3 for this problem, or in a larger problem, they might recognize a group of 30 rather than 10 three times), they are ready to go to the standard algorithm.
$4 \overline{\smash)52}$ -20 5 32 -20 5 12 3 -8 ⑬	

In this section, we have looked at different ways to preassess our students in terms of readiness. Because a preassessment is really about how to begin a unit in light of so many different students, it is usually most effective to preassess about a week before the start of the unit. This will give you time to reflect on what you learn about your students and decide how to begin. It is also important to realize that readiness fluctuates greatly and, as a result, must be assessed continuously. This is the role of formative assessment that will be developed in Chapter 7.

STRATEGIES TO DETERMINE INTEREST

As described in Chapter 1, interest differentiation can be about designing inquiry and tasks that relate to your students' passions and hobbies. That is incredibly powerful, and research suggests that changing the context of a problem can result in greater investment by students on the task (Walkington, Milan, & Howell, 2014). Valerie Styles quotes a letter by Howard Gardner (2015):

> Even at young ages, individuals have quite different preferences. Five year olds may be fascinated by numbers, by dinosaurs, by foods, or by certain kinds of animals. Many powerful ideas can be presented via different "vehicles," and quite possibly, strong interests and deep knowledge combine to help with learning those ideas.

How we find out about our students' interests is really quite easy—you probably do this at the beginning of the year already. Most teachers use interest surveys or inventories, creative stories, or just sharing in the morning circle what we like. Finding out about interest should be natural because students want to tell you what they like, and they want you to care about what they like. Sometimes we can get so busy, or are so focused on what we need to accomplish in class, that we forget simply to talk to our students and ask for their feedback. Let them know you are trying something different, and then ask how it worked for them. You might be surprised at the honest and usually sensitive feedback you gain.

Figure 2.4 lists other more formal strategies for finding out your students' interests.

Consider It!

- How do you currently assess your students' interests? Make a list.

- Do you assess for interests in learning as well as their families and hobbies?

- How do you use interest information in the design of learning activities?

FIGURE 2.4

ASSESSING STUDENT INTERESTS

Strategy

Mini-Me (Paper People):

Students can create a paper doll (or other symbol for older students) to represent themselves as math learners. Prompt students for what you want them to model. For example, color your pants black if you are a boy and red if you are a girl. Design your shirt to show how you like to learn mathematics—if you like games, color your shirt green; using manipulatives, blue; writing problems and steps, red. Make a hat for yourself, and color it purple if you like to work in a group and yellow if you like to work alone. If you like to challenge yourself in mathematics, put stripes on your shirt. If you like a mild challenge, put polka dots on your shirt. Once students have made their paper dolls or glyphs, have them share with partners why they designed them the way they did.

(Adapted from Tomlinson & Imbeau, 2010)

© Photo by Erin Null

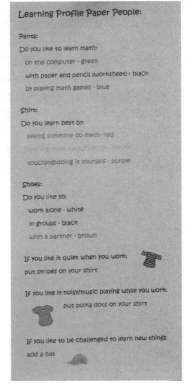

Learning Profile Paper People:

Pants:
Do you like to learn math:
on the computer - green
with paper and pencil (worksheet) - black
by playing math games - blue

Shirt:
Do you learn best by:
seeing someone do math- red
touching/doing it yourself - purple

Shoes:
Do you like to:
work alone - white
in groups - black
with a partner - brown

If you like it quiet when you work:
put stripes on your shirt

If you like it noisy/music playing while you work:
put polka dots on your shirt

If you like to be challenged to learn new things
add a hat

Surveys:

Many surveys can be found online, but it may be just as easy to design your own questions based on what you truly want to know. Don't forget to add pictures as cues for ELL students if you are using the Intermediate version.

How do you learn best?

	😀	😐	😆
Watching someone			
Using a computer			
Play a game			
Use tools like counters			

Where do you like to learn?

	😀	😐	😆
By myself			
With others in a group			
At a desk or table			
On the floor			
With music			
Quiet room			

Emojis © Clipart.com

All About Me and How I Learn!

Read each of the statements below. If it is usually true about you, circle Yes. If it is usually NOT true about you, circle No. Remember, no one is a certain way all of the time!

1.	It has to be quiet for me to learn well.	Yes	No
2.	I don't really hear noise around me when I am concentrating.	Yes	No
3.	I do math work best by myself, but then I will share with others.	Yes	No
4.	I do math work best with others so I can talk and work things out with others' help.	Yes	No
5.	When I get frustrated in math, I usually quit working.	Yes	No
6.	When I get frustrated in math, I keep trying until I get it.	Yes	No
7.	I work best at a table or desk.	Yes	No
8.	I work best on the floor.	Yes	No
9.	I like to play games to learn and practice math.	Yes	No
10.	I like to use a computer or video to learn and practice math.	Yes	No
11.	I like to follow along with my teacher to learn and practice math.	Yes	No
12.	I like to complete worksheets to learn and practice math.	Yes	No
13.	I like to follow exact instructions when doing a math project.	Yes	No
14.	I like to be able to put my own ideas into a math project.	Yes	No

Journals and Interviews:

Personal journal prompts to get to know your students work well as some students may be too shy to tell you the truth about how they feel. Writing also will help students self-assess their learning, think about their process of learning, and set goals for learning.

(Continued)

FIGURE 2.4 (Continued)

Prompts can include

- Today in math I liked how we _____ but I didn't really like _____.
- My best strategy for multiplying two-digit numbers is _____. I like this strategy because _____. An example of using this strategy is _____.
- This week in math I learned _____ really well because I learn best when _____.
- One way I learn math well is _____.
- I really struggle to learn math when _____.
- Math is most fun when _____.
- Math is most frustrating when _____.
- My favorite thing I've ever done in math class would have to be when _____.
- It helps me learn when you _____.
- It helps me learn when my friends in class _____.

Strategy

People BINGO:

People BINGO is a fun way to help students get to know one another at the beginning of the year, but if you collect the cards and notice which students signed which squares, you will learn a lot about your students' interests. Create a BINGO card (with no free space) with statements about students. There is no limit as to what can be put in the squares of the card. You can have students use the cards in various ways—have them meet each other and sign one square on each other's cards that is true about them. The goal can be a row, corners, full card, or any other pattern you choose.

Ideas include

- ➤ I have brothers (older/younger)
- ➤ I have sisters (older/younger)
- ➤ I have a pet
- ➤ I have more than one type of pet
- ➤ I play a musical instrument

> ➤ I sing in the school choir
>
> ➤ I play a sport
>
> ➤ I like math
>
> ➤ I love math
>
> ➤ Color helps me see things better
>
> ➤ I am good with numbers

Strategy

Me Box:

This is a more structured show-and-tell. Make a "Me Box" for your classroom, the size of which is up to you. Take turns sending the Me Box home with a student to fill with things that will especially explain who the student is—favorite toys, books, pictures, representations of family, food, and so on. Challenge students to fill their boxes with things that show mathematics in their lives and at home as well as their interests. Be sure that every student will have a chance to fill and show the Me Box during the first half of the year.

This can be adapted to a "Me Bag," and all students can fill their bags and bring them back to school. Several students each day can show their Me Bags if you want to use this process more quickly.

Strategy

Human Likert Scale:

Create a 1–10 (or 1–5) scale on a wall in your room. For young children, use a "frowney" face at 1 and a "smiley" face at 5 or 10. Give students a prompt, such as "How did you like working with Base 10 blocks today?" and have students put themselves along the wall in response.

 Surveys and Observation Tools can be downloaded at
http://resources.corwin.com/everymathlearnerK-5

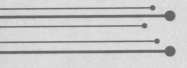

WATCH IT!

As you watch Video 2.3, *Knowing Your Learners' Interests*, consider the following questions:

1. How does interest differentiation address student motivation?

2. How does addressing students' interests engage students with learning mathematics?

3. In what ways might allowing students to choose solution methods and/or tasks promote connections and understanding in mathematics? Allow for various grouping configurations?

Video 2.3 Knowing Your Learners' Interests

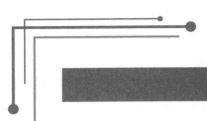

TRY IT! MY COLLAGE

Purpose: A creative way to find your students' mathematical interests

1. Provide students with pictures, magazines, and/or word phrases depending on the age of the students.

2. Have students make a collage to best represent themselves as math learners. For younger students, limit the number of items they can glue or give specific areas to show, such as family, pets, hobbies, interests, mathematical strategies, words that describe how they feel about mathematics, and so on.

STRATEGIES TO DETERMINE LEARNING PROFILE

There most likely is not a survey or test item that will reveal the complete picture of how a student learns, and even if we could figure it out, the picture is likely to change! There are, however, structures that help us define effective tasks for different learners. When working with learning profile, it is best to create purposefully designed tasks and let students choose the task that is most appealing or with which they think they can best learn or demonstrate learning rather than try to survey or determine a specific learning style for each student. When building your classroom community, and celebrating the differences in your class, it is important to develop the idea fully that not only do we enter learning at different places, but we all learn in different ways. It is great that we have different ways to make sense of mathematics, explain mathematics, and demonstrate mathematics.

In Chapter 1, broad categories of learning profiles were described. Figure 2.5 provides descriptions of two learning profile structures that are based on ways of thinking or intelligences. Gardner's Multiple Intelligences is a familiar structure and Sternberg's Triarchic Theory is another structure not quite as familiar. Both are commonly used to differentiate instruction by learning profile.

FIGURE 2.5

LEARNING PROFILE INTELLIGENCE DESCRIPTIONS AND LEARNING STRUCTURES

Name	Description	Will Learn By
Multiple Intelligences		
Verbal/ Linguistic *Word Smart*	Likes to read and write to learn and make sense of learning. Usually likes to talk. Uses words to explain concepts, relationships, and ideas	Saying, hearing, and seeing words; creative wordplay; analogies; similes; and metaphors
Logical Mathematical *Number/ Reasoning Smart*	Quick to recognize and apply patterns and relationships. Sequences naturally. Tends to be linear in thinking. Reasons using concepts, relationships, and ideas	Categorizing, working with patterns and relationships, using organizers and other structures, breaking processes into smaller steps, providing detail and explanation
Visual Spatial *Art Smart*	Appreciates and interprets pictures, charts, graphs, diagrams, and art. Uses visuals, either pictures or imagery, to depict concepts, relationships, and ideas	Visualizing; dreaming; using multiple colors; creating pictures, slideshows, or storyboards
Musical *Music Smart*	Can use various forms of music to show concepts, relationships, and ideas. Can use music or rhythm to aid memorization or practice of skills	Singing or humming, setting facts to rhythms or familiar tunes and jingles, tapping or clapping, playing music in the background while working

(Continued)

FIGURE 2.5 (Continued)

Body Kinesthetic *Body Smart*	Models concepts, relationships, and ideas through movement and objects. Often jumps into a task without reading directions. Taps, shakes a foot, paces, etc.	Engaging in hands-on tasks, physical movement, and manipulatives
Interpersonal *People Smart*	Sensitive and aware of others in the expression and learning of concepts, relationships, and ideas. Demonstrates understanding through empathy. Usually has deep friendships and may have a lot of friends	Learning through cooperative group. Thrives in a healthy learning community. Natural leaders and communicators
Intrapersonal *Self Smart*	Interprets concepts, relationships, and ideas in terms of experiences or impact on self. Aware of personal thoughts, feelings, likes, and dislikes	Opportunity to self-reflect, independent work, pursue own interest, or relate learning to prior experiences and interests
Naturalist *Nature Smart*	Recognizing concepts, relationships, and ideas in nature or the impact on nature. Enjoys relating things to their environment and making connections to nature	Observations, exploring natural phenomenon, and patterning
Sternberg's Triarchic Theory		
Analytical *School Smart*	Detail oriented about concepts, relationships, and ideas. Appreciates outlines and graphic organizers	Comparing, analyzing, critiquing, evaluating, seeing the parts and the whole, using criteria, judging, thinking logically, sequencing, ranking, and defending (Doubet & Hockett, 2015)
Practical *Street Smart*	Relates concepts, relationships, and ideas to experiences and the real world. Is concerned about when and how the learning will be used in life	Relating learning to the real world and/or prior personal experiences, putting principles into practice and action planning, demonstrating, teaching, and convincing
Creative *Imagination Smart*	Thinks "outside the box" about concepts, relationships, and ideas. Has unique and original thoughts, connects, examples, and explanations. Imagines what could be, ways to improve ideas, and what would happen if . . .	Open-ended prompts that allow for creative solutions, making new or unusual connections, predicting, transforming, analogies, representing creatively, noticing differences and changes, humor

 Surveys and Observation Tools can be downloaded at http://resources .corwin.com/everymathlearnerK-5

How do we find out which intelligences are represented in our classroom? Carefully observing your students' choices and more natural ways of reasoning can give you insight into your students' learning profiles. Additionally, there are assessment tools on the Internet that you can use, and on this book's accompanying website, there are other survey and observation examples. Figure 2.6 gives examples of the surveys and observation tools that can be downloaded at http://resources .corwin.com/everymathlearnerK-5.

It's important to pause here and note that there are some dangers in how you evaluate and establish learning profiles. One is that there has been little research evidence to support that these particular styles are accurate. Two, there is worry that teachers may consciously or unconsciously label students as a particular type of learner, which will then limit options and opportunities. Of even greater danger is that students will label and limit themselves. So, consider this category and use the inventories with caution.

There is power in teaching students some of the various ways people can think and learn, and that they will probably find ways they like to learn or mathematical strategies they like to use better than others ways. Remember to reinforce that this should never define or limit them. As students mature through the grades, they will be able to recognize learning situations in which they can apply some of their strengths, such as a visual or creative learner designing icons to accentuate notes in a lecture or a logical learner creating tables or flowcharts for a multistep process. The goal is to understand that we learn together and from each other in many different ways.

Consider It!

- Think about the students who will fit various categories based on the descriptions given in Figure 2.5. Jot their names into the space below:

- Are the tasks and activities you are using in balance to represent diverse thinkers in your class? Are there possible areas that you should consider how to address?

FIGURE 2.6

LEARNING PROFILE ASSESSMENT TOOLS

Tool

Multiple Intelligence Survey:

Students use a highlighter to mark the statements most true about them and total each box. There is not a title in the boxes so that students do not choose a title they like best and then color all the options. It is hoped that students will honestly reflect on what is *most* true of them, not just what on they like or could possibly do.

Name:_____ Date:_____

What Are Your Learning Strengths?

Use a highlighter to mark all the statements that are TRUE for you!

Verbal/Linguistic

- I like telling stories and jokes.
- I like word games like Scrabble.
- I can explain my math in writing.
- I like learning math vocabulary and use it correctly.
- If I have to memorize something, I make up a rhyme or saying to help me.
- If something breaks, I read the directions.
- Total_____

Logical/Mathematical

- I really enjoy math.
- I like logic puzzles and brainteasers.
- I like to find out how things work.
- I love playing checkers or chess.
- I like to put things in order.
- If something breaks, I look at the pieces and try to figure out how they work.
- Total_____

Interpersonal

- I get along well with others.
- I like working with others in groups to learn math.
- I like helping teach math to other students.
- Friends come to me to ask my advice in learning math.
- I have many friends.
- If something breaks, I try to find someone who can help me.
- Total_____

Intrapersonal

- I like my alone time.
- I like to work alone without anyone bothering me.
- I am willing to share my answers but prefer not to teach others.
- I like to think independently in math and often come up with my own solutions.
- I have one or two good friends.
- If something breaks, I like to fix things by myself.
- Total _____

Visual/Spatial

- My favorite problem-solving strategy is to draw a diagram.
- I daydream a lot.
- I like to imagine word problems in my head.
- In a math book, I like to look at the pictures or graphs rather than reading the words.
- If I have to remember something, I draw a picture to help me.
- If something breaks, I study a picture of it to help me.
- Total_____

Bodily/Kinesthetic

- My favorite problem-solving strategy is to use tools or manipulatives.
- When I look at things, I like to touch them.
- I move my body a lot when I'm explaining a problem.
- I like to tap my fingers or play with my pencil during a math lesson.
- If something breaks, I play with the pieces to try to fit them together.
- Total _____

Musical

- My favorite problem-solving strategy is to think about numbers in beats or rhythm.
- I like to listen to music and to sing.
- I like to have music playing when I'm doing my math homework.
- I play a musical instrument well.
- If I have to memorize something, I make up a song or rhyme to remember it.
- If something breaks, I tap my fingers to a beat while I figure it out.
- Total _____

Naturalist

- My favorite problem-solving strategy would be to apply numbers to the outdoors.
- I love to go walking in the woods and looking at trees and flowers.
- I like to do my math homework outside.
- If I have to memorize something, it might help me to relate it to something outside.
- If something breaks, I look around me to see what I can find to fix the problem.
- Total _____

Sternberg Triarchic Theory:

Students mark T or F on each statement, and then transfer their answers onto the answer key. Students count and total the number of True in each column to see their predominant learning intelligence: Analytical, Practical, Creative, or an equal combination.

Sternberg's Three Intelligences

Mark each sentence T if you like to do the activity or F if you do not like to do the activity.

1. Thinking about the characters when I'm reading or listening to a story. ___
2. Designing new things.
3. Taking things apart and fixing them. ___
4. Comparing and contrasting strategies or representations ___
5. Coming up with ideas. ___
6. Learning through hands–on activities.
7. Evaluating my own and other kids' work. ___
8. Using my imagination to solve problems or apply math. ___
9. Putting into practice things I learned. ___
10. Thinking clearly, in a step-by-step order, and figuring things out. ___
11. Thinking of other solutions. ___
12. Working with people in teams or groups. ___
13. Solving logic problems and puzzles. ___

14. Noticing things others often ignore. ___
15. Solving problems between people. ___
16. Thinking about my own and others' math strategies ___
17. Thinking about math in pictures and images. ___
18. Advising friends on their math problems. ___
19. Explaining difficult ideas or problems to others. ___
20. Supposing things were different. ___
21. Convincing someone to do something. ___
22. Using hints to draw conclusions. ___
23. Drawing in math. ___
24. Learning by interacting with others. ___
25. Sorting and classifying. ___
26. Inventing new games or approaches in math. ___
27. Applying my knowledge. ___
28. Using graphic organizers or images to organize my math thoughts. ___
29. Creating something new. ___
30. Adapting to new situations. ___

Modality:

This is a screening instrument to determine whether students are most likely to learn mathematics visually, auditorally, or kinesthetically. Students give themselves a score from 1 to 3 on the strength of each statement. They transfer their scores to the score sheet and total the columns.

Math Modality Preference Inventory

Read each statement and give yourself a score (3, 2, or 1) as to how strongly each statement applies to you. Try not to use 2 very often!

Often – 3   Sometimes – 2   Seldom/Never – 1

___ 1) I need to write math down when learning in order to remember it.
___ 2) I learn best from a lecture and not from a textbook.
___ 3) I learn best in math when I can do something with my hands, like using counters or other models.
___ 4) I need it to be quiet when I study math.
___ 5) I hate taking notes. I want to just listen to lectures and I will remember and learn that way.
___ 6) I learn and study math better when I can move—pace the floor, shift positions, tap, etc.
___ 7) It's hard for me to understand math when someone just tells about it without writing it down.
___ 8) I have difficulty following written solutions on the board unless someone also explains the steps.
___ 9) I learn math best when I can manipulate or use hands-on examples.
___10) I like to work a problem out in my mind. I usually get the right answer that way.
___11) I can remember more of what is said to me than what I see.
___12) I usually can't verbally explain how I solved a math problem, but can show it to someone.
___13) I enjoy writing in math and show my steps to stay organized.
___14) The more people explain math to me, the faster I learn it.
___15) I've always liked using my fingers to figure out math.
___16) When taking a math test, I can often see in my mind the page in my notes or in the text where the explanations or answers are located.
___17) I don't like reading explanations in my math book; I'd rather have someone explain the new material to me.
___18) It helps when I take a break and move around when I study math.
___19) I get easily distracted or have difficulty understanding in math class when there is talking or noise.
___20) I wish my math teachers would lecture more and write less on the board.
___21) If I look at my math teacher when he or she is teaching, it helps me to stay focused.
___22) I get easily distracted or have difficulty understanding in math class when there is talking or noise.
___23) It helps me when I repeat the numbers or talk to myself when working out math problems.
___24) I enjoy figuring out math games and math puzzles when I learn math.

(Continued)

FIGURE 2.6 (Continued)

Tool

Primary Observation Forms:

The instruments on the preceding pages are not appropriate for primary students. A teacher observation tool may be able to give insight into some of the natural inclinations of students.

Observation Checklist

1.Neat, clean, closes eyes to visualize, always likes to look at something, reacts to colorful stimuli, doodles and draws, chooses colorful or visual tasks, takes lots of notes								
2. Hums or talks to self often, can pay attention without looking at the front, can get information from listening without looking at pictures, elaborate explanations, tells stories even when asked not to, chooses interpersonal or listening tasks								
3. Gestures while talking, tapping, fidgeting, remembers what was done but not said or heard, touches others, rooms, chooses active hands-on tasks								
1. Details oriented, linear and sequential, likes charts and worksheets, sorts and classifies, clear explanations of what they've done, tends towards organization, frustrated with "chaos"								
2. Relates own experiences appropriately without being asked, advises others, hands-on experiences best, like to apply learning, think of ways to do things, persuasive								
3. Imaginative responses and tasks, explanations are atypical, notice things others don't, design new things, lots of idea, improves on existing ideas								
1. Learns through words, reads and writes in order to explain themselves, enjoys talking, good at memorization, finds joy in stories and poems								
2. Looks for and creates patterns, detail oriented, likes to figure things out by experimenting, asks a lot of detail questions, categorizes sorts or classifies easily								
3. Learns through pictures, charts, graphs, diagrams, and art, very colorful, likes puzzles								
4. Hums, moves rhythmically, taps in time, sings to self, learns new songs very quickly, sings what could be said, attunes to music more than others								
5. Gestures while talking, tapping, fidgeting, remembers what was done but not said or heard, touches others, roams, chooses active hands-on tasks								
6. Likes group work and working cooperatively, has an interest in their community, lots of friends, more socially adapted								
7. Enjoys the opportunity to reflect and work independently, often quiet and would rather work on his/her own than in a group, self-reflective and expressive								
8. Enjoys relating things to their environment, has a strong connection to nature								

Section 1: Modality	Section 3: Multiple Intelligences
1. Visual	1. Verbal Linguistic
2. Auditory	2. Logical Mathematical
3. Kinesthetic	3. Visual Spatial
Scciion 2: Triarchic	4. Musical
1. Analytical	5. Body Kinesthetic
2. Practical	6. Interpersonal 7. Intra Personal 8. Naturalist
3. Creative	

 Surveys and Observation tools can be downloaded at http://resources .corwin.com/everymathlearnerK-5.

WATCH IT!

As you watch Video 2.4, *Knowing Your Learners' Learning Profile*, consider the following questions:

1. In what ways can you determine your students' learning profiles?

2. What areas of learning profile are most intriguing to you?

3. How can helping students recognize their own learning strengths, as well as the learning strengths of others, help them become more independent and capable learners?

4. How does addressing students' learning profiles help them make sense of and learn mathematics more effectively?

Video 2.4 Knowing Your Learners' Learning Profile

Another way to ascertain your students' learning profile is to leverage one of our best resources—parents. Parents may be able to tell you stories and observations of their students to help you understand how they will best learn.

In the end, no matter what we do there is no absolute determination on learning profile. We can gain insights into our students and design lessons and tasks according profile structures (Multiple Intelligences, Sternberg Triarchic Theory, or Modality), and then watch to see what works with individual students.

Consider It!

What are the pros and cons of using assessment surveys in helping students identify their learning profile leanings?

How can you invoke the various aspects of learning profile in your teaching and activity designs without boxing students into a certain label?

CONCLUSION

Understanding our students in depth—who they are, what they are interested in, and how they will best learn—is something we as teachers must study if we most fully want to reach our students. Teaching is much more complex than delivering information, and our students' learning is dependent on how well we understand, and address, what each student needs in order to learn. In the end, the time we spend getting to know our students as learners also communicates care and concern for them as individuals. The relationships and lessons we build for our students through differentiation will not only best help our students reach their full potential but also develop in them a life-long love of learning.

FREQUENTLY ASKED QUESTIONS

Q: Isn't readiness differentiation just tracking in the classroom?

A: There are times when addressing readiness is necessary. Students who do not have essential perquisite understanding for a new topic need to have the missing content and skill addressed to be successful, but not all students need that. In the same way, students who are more advanced should have the opportunity to continue to grow and stretch. This is not to say that readiness differentiation is all that will happen in the classroom for students. A differentiated classroom is flexible in how tasks are designed and students are grouped, with approximately one third of the time being based on readiness. Tracking, on the other hand, groups students together based on a determined achievement criteria, and that is the course of study on which they stay. Most tracked systems say that students can move into a different level as they close gaps or accelerate, but the likelihood of that happening is very slight given that a slower and lower curriculum is usually designed for more struggling students and an enriched and accelerated curriculum is designed for more advanced learners. The gaps rarely close, and often widen.

Q: Is there a difference between learning profile and learning style?

A: Yes there is. Learning profile includes everything that encompasses ways that students take in information, make sense of the information, and get information to long-term memory. It includes gender, culture, intelligences (ways of thinking), and cognitive style. Learning style has meant many different things over the years—from the physical setup of the room to visual, auditory, and kinesthetic learning models. There are currently 71 "learning style" models! I am not sure anyone knows what the term means any longer.

Q: How do I know whether to differentiate by readiness, interest, or learning profile?

A: The choice to differentiate by readiness, interest, or learning profile is largely dependent on a teacher's decision-making process. What is the apparent need to address in the learning? Is it about what challenges students will be able to handle? Then readiness is the vehicle. If it is about motivation, then interest. If I want a way for students to make sense of learning and move the learning into memory most proficiently, then I want to choose learning profile. Often it does not have to be one clear avenue. Often these are combined in task design. For example, I can design a task based on a few of the Multiple Intelligences that best fit the learning goal and then provide extensions and supports to aid the readiness of the student. Finally, I can ask students to choose the task they are most interested in completing. I have now combined all three aspects of differentiation. How to design tasks is addressed in the next chapter.

Keepsakes and Plans

What are the keepsake ideas from this chapter, those thoughts or ideas that resonated with you that you do not want to forget?

Who Our Learners Are:

1.

2.

3.

Readiness:

1.

2.

3.

Interest:

1.

2.

3.

Learning Profile:

1.

2.

3.

Based on my keepsake ideas, I plan to:

1.

2.

3.

Learn

Pants:
Do you
on the
with
by pla

Shirt:
Do you
seeing
hearing
touch

Shoes:
Do you I
work a
in grou
with a

If you like
put stripe

If you like

If you like
add a hat

CHAPTER THREE

TEACH UP

MAKING SENSE OF
RIGOROUS MATHEMATICAL CONTENT

The second foundational key to effective differentiation is to know the mathematical content in depth. Differentiation will be purposeful and effective only when the mathematics standards are analyzed and form the basis on which instruction and activities are based. In this chapter, you will find:

Mathematics Makes
    Sense
Themes and Big Ideas in
    Mathematics
Teaching Up

What Learning Mathematics
    With Understanding Looks
    Like
Frequently Asked Questions
Keepsakes and Plans

If I were to ask you how to complete this sentence, what would you say: "The most basic idea in the learning of mathematics is . . . ?" What did you say? Patterns? Number sense? The four mathematical operations? Perhaps you went a different way and said applications. As many times as I ask teachers this question, I receive a wide variety of answers. I have never heard anyone complete the statement in accordance with the original quote, however. According to John Van de Walle (2006), "The most basic idea in the learning of mathematics is . . . mathematics makes sense." Truthfully, I didn't think of that answer the first time I saw this quote either! The more I ponder it, and the more I work with teachers in constructing powerful mathematics lessons, the more I realize that it should be every teacher's mantra. I am just wondering—are there some of you right now thinking that mathematics *doesn't* make sense? Do you have students who would not believe the statement that mathematics makes sense?

This is a chapter on mathematical content, and on trying to make sense of it, which is foundational to differentiation. If we design differentiated tasks before we have clear conceptual understanding, knowledge, and skills of the content we are teaching, we are probably dooming ourselves to a lot of extra planning and sometimes frustrating classroom experiences, with little growth or achievement to show as a result. To paraphrase something Carol Ann Tomlinson once said, "If we are somewhat foggy in what we are teaching, and then differentiate, we end up with differentiated fog." This is not our goal.

MATHEMATICS MAKES SENSE

Our brains are sense-making machines. In fact, our brains naturally seek patterns and meaning-making to store in our long-term memories (Sousa, 2015). We now know that for an idea or concept to be stored in long-term memory, it needs to make sense and be relevant to the learner. Unfortunately, we often do not teach mathematics as if it is a sense-making subject. We tend to teach skills, or problem types, and then practice, practice, practice . . . until we reach the next skill to be taught. I believe mathematics was the instigator of the phrase "drill and kill." Nevertheless, if we can begin to view mathematics as sense making, we can break this pattern, both for ourselves as teachers and for our students. Most teachers I meet have never been taught to understand mathematics, only how to do it. It makes sense then that many teachers struggle to make mathematics understandable for their students.

We have learned from cognitive science that the human brain is not well designed for memorizing data. It is most efficient and effective when it works with patterns, connections, meaning, and significance—with personal meaning being the most important (Sousa, 2015). Without the necessary time to make sense of learning, students naturally resort to memorization over sense-making. Thus, the most effective way for students to learn mathematics is to prioritize understanding rather than to perform memorization. It is our job to provide lessons that can make it happen.

How do we begin to make sense of mathematics? The first step is to clarify the big ideas that are the foundation for the topic(s) being taught in the unit. Sometimes these essential understandings are embedded in the standard we are addressing, and sometimes they can be seen in some of the exploration tasks in a resource, but they are almost always up to the teacher (or a collaborative team if you are working in one) to determine.

THEMES AND BIG IDEAS IN MATHEMATICS

Some big ideas in mathematics are true for every grade level, and in fact, they are true for every mathematics course at every level! Figure 3.1 provides a few of these concepts and understandings.

This table is just the beginning of thinking in terms of conceptual understanding in mathematics. Let's take another step. For any mathematical unit based on a group of standards to be taught, the content can be divided into what students will come to know, understand, and be able to do. In the differentiation literature, this is referred to as KUDs or KUDOs (Tomlinson & Imbeau, 2014; Tomlinson & Moon, 2013).

The Know in KUD refers to facts that can be memorized. Our mathematical content is filled with Knows: Mathematical facts, vocabulary, and formulas all fall under the Know category. If you can look it up, it is probably a Know. On the other hand, Understandings

Consider It!

- What is the difference between knowing, understanding, and doing mathematics?

- What does it look like when students exhibit understanding of mathematics? How is it different from students who know how *to do* mathematics but don't *understand* mathematics?

FIGURE 3.1

GENERAL CONCEPTS AND UNDERSTANDINGS IN MATHEMATICS

Concept	Understandings
Mathematical Operations and Properties	• Each operation in mathematics has meanings that make sense of situations, and the essential meaning of each operation remains true in every context and number system. • Every mathematical operation has specific properties that apply to it, and these properties are the basis for how these operations can and cannot be used. • The properties of operations provide the reasoning for mathematical explanations.
Number Sense and Estimation	• Developing mental mathematical strategies that reason about numbers, quantities, and the operations with numbers provides flexibility and confidence in working with numbers. • Estimation allows for establishing the reasonableness of an answer.
Units and "Unitizing"	• Determining the "base entity" in a given context or problem (e.g., apples, balloons, miles per hour, or a variable) allows you to make sense of the problem, plan a solution path, and make comparisons. • Units in measurement describe what is being measured, and what is being measured has a specific type of unit.
Equality	• An equal sign is a statement that two quantities are equivalent. That equivalency must be maintained throughout any mathematical operations.
Shape and Geometry	• Shapes and their properties describe our physical world. • Shapes are categorized and grouped according to their properties. • Relationships among shapes can be described in many ways, including algebraically.
Modeling and Representation	• There are many different representations for a given situation, and each representation can provide different aspects of the problem. • Mathematical models represent real-world contexts and provide connections, comparisons, and predictions.

Note: Several concepts presented in this figure came to light during my time working with the high-school teachers of the West Irondequoit School District, Rochester, NY.

are conceptual. They are big ideas and have many layers. Understandings connect the content unit to unit, as well as connect mathematical content to other contents. Understandings also remain true over the years, and it is powerful if the same understandings are used many times to show students clearly how topics are connected. Finally, the Do is what you expect students to be able to Do if they truly Know and Understand. Be careful not to list specific task activities (make a collage or questions 3–8) in the Do category. You are looking for the mathematics within any task that indicates knowledge and understanding. The Do will always start with a verb. To push for understanding, be sure to include high-level verbs from Blooms and Depth of Knowledge. Let's look at an example of how a KUD can be developed for both a primary and an intermediate unit.

FIRST-GRADE PLACE VALUE (BEGINNING OF THE YEAR)

Sample Common Core standards:

Count to 30, starting at any number less than 30. In this range, read and write numerals and represent several objects with a written numeral.

Understand that the two digits of a two-digit number represent amounts of tens and ones.

Understand the following as special cases:

a. 10 can be thought of as a bundle of ten ones—called a "ten."

b. The numbers from 11 to 19 are composed of a ten and one, two, three, four, five, six, seven, eight, or nine ones.

Students will Know . . .	Students will Understand that . . .	Students will demonstrate knowledge and understanding through the ability to Do . . .
K1: Definitions: more/less numeral/number object/set	**U1:** Our numbers follow a pattern that stays the same in all types of numbers.	**D1:** Count to 30 orally and count on to 30 from any number less than 30.
K2: Each number is one more than the number that comes before it.	**U2:** Our numbers are based on groups of tens. Any group of ten in one place value equals one of the next place value.	**D2:** Write numbers to 30.

D3: Represent several objects with a written numeral.

D4: Tell how many tens and how many ones are in a two-digit number, beginning with 11–19 and going up to 30. |
| **K3**: Groups of objects can be represented by a numeral that represents the number of objects. | | |
| **K4:** The last number counted in a group of objects tells how many objects there are. | **U3:** A number can be represented different ways, e.g., a numeral or group of objects. | **D5:** Count by tens (work up to 100 based on where students are at the beginning of the year).

D6: Explain why groups of 10 are important in our number system. |

FOURTH-GRADE DECIMALS

Sample Common Core standards:

Express a fraction with denominator 10 as an equivalent fraction with denominator 100, and use this technique to add two fractions with respective denominators 10 and 100. *For example, express 3/10 as 30/100, and add 3/10 + 4/100 = 34/100.*

Use decimal notation for fractions with denominators 10 or 100. *For example, rewrite 0.62 as 62/100; describe a length as 0.62 meters; locate 0.62 on a number line diagram.*

Compare two decimals to hundredths by reasoning about their size. Recognize that comparisons are valid only when the two decimals refer to the same whole. Record the results of comparisons with the symbols >, =, or < and justify the conclusions (e.g., by using a visual model).

Students will Know . . .	Students will Understand that . . .	Students will demonstrate knowledge and understanding through the ability to Do . . .
K1: Vocabulary: notation, tenths, hundredths, decimal, decimal point, fractional part, whole.	**U1:** Our numbers follow a pattern that stays the same in all types of numbers.	**D1:** Determine equivalence by converting between tenths and hundredths.
K2: Decimal numbers can represent any value in our number system, but some are not exactly equivalent values.	**U2:** Our numbers are based on groups of tens. As place values increase (to the right in a number) they are 10 times the previous place value. As they decrease (to the left in a number) they are 1/10 the previous place value.	**D2:** Compare and order decimals to hundredths.
K3: A decimal point separates the whole from the fractional value in a number. Digits after a decimal point represent a fractional part based on denominators that are powers of 10.		**D3:** Make estimates appropriate to a given situation or computation with whole numbers and decimals.
K4: Decimal notation and place value names	**U3:** A number can be represented different ways. Every fraction can be represented by an infinite number of equivalent fractions, but each fraction is represented by only one decimal (or an equivalent decimal form; for example, 0.25 0.250)	**D4:** Explain how decimals can represent fractions and how fractions can represent decimals.
K5: How to write a fraction as a decimal and a decimal as a fraction.		**D5:** Write a fraction as a decimal and a decimal as a fraction.
K6: How to compare decimals to hundredths.		**D6:** Represent decimal values in multiple representations.
K7: Adding zeros to the right of the last digit following a decimal point does not change the value of the number.	**U4:** Every decimal has a specific value, which can be compared through multiple strategies.	
K8: You can write decimals in expanded form.		

WATCH IT!

As you watch Video 3.1, *Planning a Unit Based on Rigorous Mathematical Content*, consider the following questions:

1. How do the teachers make sense of the standards in their unit?

2. What is the difference among Knowing, Understanding, and Doing mathematics?

3. In what ways could the unpacking of the standards influence what the teachers ultimately want students to be able to do, as well as the choice of specific activities in a given lesson?

4. How does writing a KUD for a unit help to align and connect mathematical content vertically (through the grades) as well as from unit to unit?

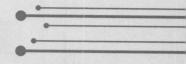

Video 3.1 Planning a Unit Based on Rigorous Mathematical Content

Did you notice that all of the understandings from the first-grade unit were also used in the fourth-grade unit, although the topics are seemingly very different? The understanding language will grow up over the years, but the meaning remains the same. This is one hallmark of an understanding. For example, "Our number system is based on groups of ten" is an understanding about a number that will *always* remain true, no matter what the topic, grade level, or skill that is being addressed. If this same idea is referred to over and over again, students make the connection with prior knowledge instead of learning the current skill or topic as a *new* thing that they now need to master. This is the power of understanding mathematics. As we learn more and more, the concepts and connections become the building blocks upon which we grow our knowledge and skills. Instead of learning decimals as a completely new topic with new procedures to be memorized, students can logically see that this is the same idea as the place value based on groups of tens that we have been learning since kindergarten! Now the connections are made, the same principles and patterns apply, and we just learn new details with a new number group.

Most mathematics resources provide the standards being addressed, and many give "essential questions" for each lesson. Some of these are helpful and others, in and of themselves, are often insufficient. For most teachers, developing KUDs for their unit is the most challenging part of differentiation. Nevertheless, it is worth the effort. The depth at which we come to know our content through this process has many benefits:

- We see connections among mathematics more readily
- We are ready to answer unexpected questions (see Chapter 4)
- We plan purposeful and targeted lessons (see Chapter 4)
- We recognize conceptual gaps and misconceptions in our students more readily (more in Chapter 7)
- We build cohesive units that ensure instruction, tasks, and all forms of assessment reach the desired learning outcomes (more in Chapters 4 and 7)
- Differentiation based on anything less may not target essential learning for all learners and, thus, not have the intended results

TEACHING UP

One misconception about differentiation that I have often heard is that differentiation "dummies down" curriculum. Nothing could be further from the truth. Research clearly shows that everyone can learn mathematics at high levels. This is the essence of teaching up. We believe that all students can learn, we can hold all students to high expectations, and we must provide the necessary support for students to accomplish the goal. This is fully developed through clarity of curriculum and expectations, instructional decisions (see Chapter 4), and our classroom culture (see Chapter 5).

The discussion of how mathematics should be taught has been going on for a long time. The National Council of Teachers of Mathematics (NCTM) first formally proposed what teaching and learning mathematics might look like in 1989 through the publication of *Curriculum and Evaluation Standards for School Mathematics*. This was followed by the *Professional Standards for Teaching Mathematics* in 1991 and the *Assessment Standards for School Mathematics* in 1995. In 2000, NCTM updated these publications with *Principles and Standards for School Mathematics*. These publications and others began a serious conversation about what it means to learn mathematics. The learning of mathematics in the mathematical community has never been about memorization and speed. In 2001, the National Research Council suggested five strands for mathematical proficiency: conceptual understanding, procedural fluency, strategic competence, adaptive reasoning, and productive disposition. All of these publications and resulting conversations and research have laid the foundation for what teaching and learning in mathematics should be ideally—balancing conceptual understandings and reasoning with procedural skills and strategies, embedded within real-world contexts.

Most recently we have NCTM's publication of *Principles to Actions* (2014) describing today's mathematics classroom. The first three principles for school mathematics according to NCTM's *Principles to Actions* are as follows:

- Teaching and Learning—Effective teaching should engage students in meaningful learning that stimulates making sense of mathematical ideas and reasoning mathematically.

- Access and Equity—All students have access to a high-quality mathematics curriculum with high expectations and the support and resources to maximize learning potential.

- Curriculum—A curriculum that develops important mathematics along coherent progressions and develops connections among areas of mathematical study and between mathematics and the real world.

So how do we do it? How do we teach and design units and lessons to accomplish all of this? How do we "teach up" to ensure a high-quality mathematics education for all students? The beginning is certainly clarifying the understandings and basing units and instruction around conceptual understandings with embedded skills. While digging into our standards, we need to make sure that we are teaching at or above our grade-level expectations. Chapter 4 will provide more specific design strategies for students who need some supportive help as well as enrichment ideas.

Teaching up also involves designing lessons, asking questions, and choosing tasks at a high level of cognitive demand. Two structures are commonly used to determine whether we are conducting class at a high level: Depth of Knowledge (DOK) and Cognitive Demand. Both structures have four levels, two levels defined as lower and two defined as upper. DOK is a structure designed by Norman Webb in the late 1990s, and it was originally designed for mathematics and science standards but has been expanded for all content areas. Cognitive Demand (Smith & Stein, 1998) is a structure specifically for mathematics. Figure 3.2 gives the level names for each framework and their characteristics.

FIGURE 3.2

STRUCTURES FOR COGNITIVE COMPLEXITY

Level	Depth of Knowledge	Cognitive Demand	Description
Lower Level 1	Recall	Memorization	• Reproducing facts, rules, formulas, procedures, or definitions from memory. • No connection to concepts.
Lower Level 2	Skill/Concept	Procedures Without Connections	• Uses information in a familiar situation. • Involves two or more steps. • Algorithmic. Use a procedure rotely. • Very little ambiguity or reasoning involved. • No student explanations required.

Level	Depth of Knowledge	Cognitive Demand	Description
Upper Level 3	Strategic Thinking	Procedures With Connections	<ul><li>Requires reasoning, developing a plan, or defining a sequence of steps.</li><li>Some complexity in the task or question.</li><li>Procedures are to develop connections and conceptual understanding.</li><li>Multiple representations.</li><li>Takes cognitive effort.</li></ul>
Upper Level 4	Extended Thinking	Doing Mathematics	<ul><li>Requires an investigation, time to think, and processing of multiple conditions.</li><li>Requires complex and nonalgorithmic thinking.</li><li>Explores and understands the nature of mathematical concepts, processes, and relationships.</li><li>Mathematics of the real world.</li></ul>

TRY IT! HOW RIGOROUS IS IT?

Purpose: To practice determining the level of rigor in a given task or problem

For each of the following tasks, determine the DOK or Cognitive Demand level. Answers are at the end of the chapter—but don't cheat!

1. Jeff had 64 action figures. He gave 12 figures to his sister. Then he divided the remaining figures equally among his FOUR friends. How many figures did each of his friends get?

2. Identify the place value of the underlined digit:

   a. 36<u>8</u>

   b. <u>2</u>52

3. Solve the following problems. Check your answers with a calculator:

   a. 24×13

   b. $832 \div 4$

4. Survey your classmates to find out how many brothers, sisters, dogs, and cats they have. Make a bar chart of one of the choices (brothers, sisters, dogs, and cats). What comparisons can you make? What questions can you ask? Find a partner who graphed a different choice. What comparisons can you make? What questions can you ask?

5. Use Base 10 blocks to model regrouping with addition and subtraction. Solve the following problems using Base 10 blocks:

   a. 42 – 17

   b. 38 + 27

Consider It!

Make a list of the tasks and questions you have used in class over the past week or two. Write the cognitive level next to each one. At what level are most of the tasks and questions with which your students engage? Do you need to make any adjustments?

Most mathematics instruction in the United States is at levels 1 and 2 only. Level one should be a supporting level to enable students to function at levels 2 and 3. Please understand that these levels are not hierarchical—that is, you do not move through the levels in order! In fact, starting with a level 4 task is often a great starting point to create the need to learn the facts, formulas, procedures, and other skills in levels 1 and 2. We need to aim for the majority of our work to be at levels 2 and 3. In Chapter 4, we will further discuss the selection and design of tasks.

There is yet another consideration to teaching up: helping students understand what it means and looks like to be an active learner of mathematics.

WHAT LEARNING MATHEMATICS WITH UNDERSTANDING LOOKS LIKE

Consider It!

What does it look like when students are involved with learning mathematics? What verbs come to mind?

How students engage with learning mathematics is equally as important as the content they are learning. In fact, if they are not invested in the process of learning, they may not learn the content to the depth we desire. As mentioned, this is not a new way of thinking, but it has rarely been made an integral part of a standards document or mathematics learning.

The realization of how important it is that students develop "mathematical habits of mind" has prompted our current focus on describing and expecting that the way students learn mathematics shifts along with the content of what students are learning. Today's standards documents describe student actions for learning in various ways. The Common Core State Standards have described them through the Standards for Mathematical Practice. Other states that have not adopted the Common Core also have Process standards that are very similar, and some states that are not using the Common Core State Standards are using the Standards for Mathematical Practice as part of their state's standards document. These behaviors are written as standards to raise the importance of students' actions and thinking in learning mathematics effectively, and they are not only expected in the classroom but also are expected to be assessed as a part of end-of-year testing. Although there are slight differences in the descriptions of each process, Figure 3.3 shows alignment among the Standards for Mathematical Practice with other states' process standards or goals.

WATCH IT!

Amy Francis taught her second-grade students the 8 Standards for Mathematical Practice at the beginning of the school year. As you watch Video 3.2, *Putting the Standards for Mathematical Practice at the Heart of Differentiation*, consider the following questions:

1. What do you believe Mrs. Francis did to establish how students participate in and engage with mathematical content in deep and meaningful ways?

2. In what ways do you see evidence that the students are aware of their own, and others', learning process?

3. What are the pros and cons in the students' actions in learning mathematics in this way?

4. Why do you believe there is such an emphasis on mathematical practices (or processes or habits of mind) in the learning of mathematics today?

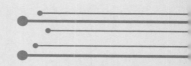

Video 3.2 Putting the Standards for Mathematical Practice at the Heart of Differentiation

Although the various documents may give different names, there is agreement on what learning mathematics should look like. Combined into a simplified list, Figure 3.3 compares the Standards for Mathematical Practice with other states' standards. Remember that these are describing student actions, not teacher actions! I believe we all do these things as mathematics teachers. In fact, if we want our students to exhibit these behaviors, we do need to model them, as well as to teach and expect them from our students.

FIGURE 3.3

STANDARDS FOR MATHEMATICAL PRACTICE (SMP) AND PROCESS STANDARDS[1]

SMP	NE	OK	SC	TX	VA
Make sense of problems and persevere in solving them	Solves mathematical Problems	Develop a deep and flexible conceptual understanding	Make sense of problems and persevere in solving them	Use a problem-solving model that incorporates analyzing given information, formulating a plan or strategy, determining a solution, justifying the solution, and evaluating the problem-solving process and the reasonableness of the solution	Mathematical Problem Solving
Reason abstractly and quantitatively		Develop mathematical reasoning	Reason both contextually and abstractly		Mathematical Reasoning
Construct viable arguments and critique the reasoning of others	Communicates mathematical ideas effectively	Develop the ability to communicate mathematically	Use critical thinking skills to justify mathematical reasoning and critique the reasoning of others	Communicate mathematical ideas, reasoning, and their implications using multiple representations, including symbols, diagrams, graphs, and language as appropriate	Mathematical communication
Model with mathematics	Models and represents mathematical problems	Develop the ability to conjecture, model and generalize	Connect mathematical ideas and real-world situations through modeling	Create and use representations to organize, record, and communicate mathematical ideas	Mathematical Representations

SMP	NE	OK	SC	TX	VA
Use appropriate tools strategically		Develop strategies for problem solving	Use a variety of mathematical tools effectively and strategically	Select tools, including real objects, manipulatives, paper and pencil, and technology as appropriate, and techniques, including mental mathematics, estimation, and number sense as appropriate, to solve problems	Mathematical Problem Solving
Attend to precision.		Develop accurate and appropriate procedural fluency	Communicate mathematically and approach mathematical situations with precision	Display, explain, and justify mathematical ideas and arguments using precise mathematical language in written or oral communication	Mathematical Problem Solving
Look for and make use of structure		Develop the ability to conjecture, model and generalize	Identify and utilize structure and patterns	Analyze mathematical relationships to connect and communicate mathematical ideas	
Look for and express regularity in repeated reasoning		Develop the ability to conjecture, model and generalize	Identify and utilize structure and patterns		
	Makes mathematical connections	Develop a productive mathematical disposition		Apply mathematics to problems arising in everyday life, society, and the workplace	Mathematical Connections

Consider It!

As you read through the combined list of mathematical learning practices, create a plan for how you will teach your students these learning actions.

Make sense of problems—reason and interpret mathematical situations. This is the obvious beginning, right? But how often do your students barely look at a problem before saying, "I don't get it." We often read the problem to the students, interpret the problem for them, and give the first step. No wonder they do not know how to make sense of problems for themselves. When students engage in learning mathematics, they wrestle with the context of a problem, what they are looking for, possible ways to start the problem, and multiple solution paths or representations. Additionally, they can begin to discuss the mathematics they see in a real-world situation, and they can describe a real-world situation that would require the mathematics being learned.

TRY IT! HOW STUDENTS MAKE SENSE OF PROBLEMS

Purpose: To shift "sense making" to students when facing a new problem

Give the students a rich problem to solve.

1. In elbow, partners have the first partner read the problem and the second partner interpret the problem in his or her own words. This should also include what the solution will look like (for example, ___ feet). Discuss as a class or check in on students' interpretations.

2. Have partner 2 suggest a way to start the problem to partner 1. Have partner 1 suggest another way to start or agree to the idea of partner 2 and explain why it will work.

3. Have partners generate strategies to represent and solve the problem.

Communicate mathematically—Students explain their thinking mathematically and ask questions of or build on other students' explanations. Students will use correct mathematical vocabulary and multiple representations to communicate their thinking. Beware of accepting an answer or retelling of steps as an explanation. Explanations need to include reasoning and the meanings and properties of operations to be considered robust.

TRY IT! STUDENT DISCOURSE

Purpose: To teach healthy mathematical discourse skills

1. Direct mathematical conversations so that they are among the students as much as possible. Do not interpret and redirect questions and answers. Teach students to restate what other students have said. To provide structures for discourse, give students sentence starters such as the following:

   - I agree with ___ because ____

   - Another way to think about this is _____

   - I did it a different way. I _____

   - I disagree with ___ because ____

   - I would like to add on to what ___ said about ____

   - Can you explain what you mean by ____

   - Can you show ____ in another way

   - I think that _____ because _____

2. Ask questions to help students clarify their thinking if they have responded incorrectly rather than calling on another student.

3. Gently correct and provide correct mathematical vocabulary.

Model with mathematics—There are two aspects to modeling mathematics: Models of mathematics and how mathematics models the real world. Models of mathematics include using manipulatives such as Base 10 blocks and two-color counters, drawings, and symbols. Whenever new material is presented in a way that students see relationships, they generate greater brain cell activity and achieve more successful long-term memory storage and retrieval (Willis, 2006, p. 15). We also use mathematics to model the real world. When we solve quantitative problems from the world around us, we are modeling the world with mathematics.

Purpose: To make mathematical processes and problems concrete and visual whenever possible.

Challenge students to represent any contextual or numerical problem as many ways as possible. Keep in mind the following tips when using models:

1. The concrete or visual model needs to come before the paper-and-pencil process. If the algorithm is taught first, students will not value or want to complete the concrete or visual activity. Also, the concrete or visual task is to develop the conceptual understanding and make sense of the process or algorithm to follow.

2. Connect the concrete or visual explicitly to the skill or process. If it cannot be explicitly connected, it is not a valid model.

3. Challenge students to represent problems in as many different ways as they can.

Choose and use tools appropriately—Tools can be anything! We usually think of physical tools such as number lines, hundreds charts, rulers, counters, and Base 10 blocks. Nevertheless, tools can also be mental strategies such as addition strategies or the distributive property (not by name) for multiplying two-digit numbers.

Knowing which tool or strategy will be appropriate and useful in a given situation is a necessary skill for solving problems and a practical life skill. Often we hand out the tools we will be using in a lesson; for example, today we need rulers. Instead, build a toolbox with all of the mathematical tools in the classroom for table groups or an area where all tools are stored.

TRY IT! THE TOOLBOX

Purpose: Have students select and defend a variety of mathematical tools

1. For a lesson, explain to the students what the task will be and ask them to choose the tools they think they will need.

2. After the task, ask students to reflect on the tools they chose. Did they get what they needed? Why or why not? Did they choose extra tools that were not needed? Why was that selected?

Recognize and use patterns and structures—The more students work with mathematics, the more they can recognize mathematical structures. For example, our whole numbers (and integers in the future) alternate between evens and odds. Place value is a key structure in the elementary grades, and that is why so many standards talk about adding and subtracting 10 or 100 to any number mentally. Structure includes understanding why the process of converting an improper fraction into a mixed number works. Patterns are more than the repeating patterns that are often taught in kindergarten: AB or ABC, and so forth. Recognizing patterns is often more related to repeated reasoning than to labeling how often a color recurs. For example, recognizing a multiplication pattern to determine equivalent fractions would be using repeated reasoning. Noticing that multiplication of whole numbers results in a product greater than the factors but multiplication of a whole number and a fraction less than one results in a product less than the whole factor is using repeated reasoning. Instead of giving students an algorithm, try modeling thinking about the structures and patterns that are inherent in operations and multiple problem examples.

Purpose: To make sense of mathematical rules or procedures, and to recognize mathematical structures that give hints to solutions

1. Give students several problems to solve that are solved using manipulatives, drawings, models, and so on, but not rules or steps.

2. Generate a list of the problems and answers.

3. Have the students find the "short cuts" or patterns they recognize. For example, multiplication facts of 5 will show all products end in either 5 or 0. Multiplication of whole numbers results in a product greater than the factors, but multiplication with a fraction less than one will result in a product less than at least one factor.

4. This will undoubtedly be the algorithm you wanted to teach, and instead it will be a student discovery.

Attend to precision—Certainly undergirding all other of these mathematical practices is the ability to attend to precision. Precision includes using correct vocabulary. It includes noticing whether an equation has a plus or minus sign and all other notation. It includes knowing mathematical facts and efficiently using various strategies for operations. It includes knowing when and how to apply the properties of operations.

Purpose: Have students catch you any time you are not mathematically precise

1. Prepare a problem presentation with which you will make precision errors.

2. Use incorrect or slang vocabulary. Make arithmetic mistakes.

3. Have students find your imprecisions.

4. You can also divide the class into two teams, and award points as students collaborate to find the errors.

Clarifying content and teaching children how to learn mathematics actively is essential for all mathematics instruction. It is certainly necessary for effective differentiation, which is based on solid curriculum.

CONCLUSION

We have developed a complete picture of clarifying content for designing differentiated instruction. We have also discussed the actions students need to employ to learn mathematics with understanding. Effective teaching is not about delivering information or creating meaning. It's melding the two to help students see the meaning in the information they are learning (Sousa & Tomlinson, 2011).

As we prepare to differentiate our mathematics instruction, consider the changes in how we teach mathematics as a whole. Figure 3.4 compares before and after of teaching mathematics, adapted from David Sousa (2015).

BEFORE AND AFTER OF MATHEMATICAL REASONING

We used to teach mathematics as . . .	But now we teach mathematics as . . .
Problems to be calculated	Situations about which we reason
Procedures to be memorized	Operations that are based on properties with multiple representations and strategies
Isolated topics	Connected concepts
A speed activity for prowess	Problem solving and reasoning for prowess
Teacher-led and valued	Student-discovered and valued
Something forgettable	Understood, so remembered

There are two keys to differentiation: Know your content, and know your students. In the last chapter, we looked at strategies to know our students as learners. In this chapter, we looked at how to know our content. In the next chapter, we will look at how knowing our content and our students come together in powerful differentiation.

FREQUENTLY ASKED QUESTIONS

Q: With the Common Core standards and other state standards so closely aligned, do we really need to go through the work of writing a KUD? Aren't they written somewhere?

A: There are many posts about big ideas online. Some are good and can be a resource. Nevertheless, some are labeled "conceptual understanding" but are actually fact or skill based. These are not understandings. Additionally, there is nothing like the struggle to make sense of the standards to help your own learning and clarify what you want students to come away with. Remember that we want our students to take a challenge and struggle with things that are challenging; therefore, we need to do the same.

Q: What if my students can't explain their thinking?

A: Chances are pretty good that your students have been asked to tell how they got an answer in mathematics, and this has always been what an "explanation" was. They need to be taught how to construct a mathematical explanation. This can be done by modeling first and foremost but also by asking questions such as "how did you know to do that" or "what allows you to do that in math (e.g., you can add in any order, etc.)."

Q: What about students who can't reach the standard?

A: It is very important to teach the grade-level standards. When we draw conclusions that certain students cannot reach the standard and, therefore, lower the expectations or, worse, lower the instruction level, we widen gaps not close them. Truthfully, most students can reach the standards given support and, if appropriate, more direct intervention. The RTI structure is designed to enable students significantly behind in learning to close gaps and reach as close to grade level as possible, if not actually reach the standard. Yet even given the RTI structure, remember that Tier 1 instruction is on grade level. Chapter 4 will more specifically address how to design for readiness.

Keepsakes and Plans

What are the keepsake ideas from this chapter, those thoughts or ideas that resonated with you that you do not want to forget?

Mathematics Makes Sense:

1.

2.

3.

Analyzing Standards and Developing Conceptual Understandings in Mathematics:

1.

2.

3.

Mathematical Learning Actions:

1.

2.

3.

Teaching Up:

1.

2.

3.

Based on my keepsake ideas, I plan to:

1.

2.

1. DOK 2/Procedures without connections. This item is an application of computational algorithms. It is a multistep problem requiring the student to make a decision on how to approach the computations.

2. DOK 1/Memorization. This is straight memorization of place value names.

3. DOK 2/Procedures without connections. This is another multistep procedure without any connections, sense-making, or application.

4. DOK 4/Doing Mathematics. This is an example of what mathematicians do in the real world.

5. DOK 3/Procedures with Connections. This task uses models to make sense of the algorithms that will be used with regrouping, and reinforcing groups of tens and place value.

NOTE

1. The full descriptions of each of these mathematical behaviors can be accessed at the following websites:

- Common Core Standards for Mathematical Practices: http://www.corestandards.org/Math/Practice/

- Nebraska Mathematical Processes: https://www.education.ne.gov/math/Math_Standards/Adopted_2015_Math_Standards/2015_Nebraska_College_and_Career_Standards_for_Mathematics_Vertical.pdf

- Oklahoma Mathematical Actions and Processes: http://sde.ok.gov/sde/sites/ok.gov.sde/files/documents/files/OAS-Math-Final%20Version_2.pdf

- South Carolina Process Standards: https://ed.sc.gov/scdoe/assets/file/agency/scde-grant-opportunities/documents/SCCCRStandardsForMathematicsFinal-PrintOneSide.pdf

- Texas Process Standards: http://www.abileneisd.org/cms/lib2/TX01001461/Centricity/Domain/1943/Texas%20Mathematical%20Process%20Standards%20Aug%202014.pdf

- Virginia Standards of Learning Mathematics Goals: http://www.pen.k12.va.us/testing/sol/standards_docs/mathematics/index.shtml

CHAPTER FOUR

STEP UP

HOW TO MAKE PROACTIVE PLANNING
DECISIONS THAT DEEPEN THINKING

For many educators, when they think of differentiation, it is the task or activity they are usually picturing, rather than the intentional design behind the task. This chapter will provide you with a variety of strategies for differentiation to match your learners' needs with deep content. In this chapter, you will find:

The Decisions Behind Differentiation	Classroom Structures
Differentiation and KUDs	Frequently Asked Questions
Strategies for Differentiation	Keepsakes and Plans

"I have this great activity. . . ." That is how most teachers begin thinking about differentiation. It is very hard not to think that way. Yet effective and purposeful differentiation is dependent on the integration of knowing both your students' learning needs and the depth of content as described in the preceding chapters. And so the foundations are in place and it is time to design. Purposeful differentiation is about making a series of decisions.

THE DECISIONS BEHIND DIFFERENTIATION

At its simplest, differentiation is a series of decisions about the most impactful learning opportunities for each student. Nevertheless, a lot of decisions need to be made: What classroom structures will work best and for which segments? What should be differentiated? How should it be differentiated? What strategies will be effective?

Before you start feeling overwhelmed, remember that in a differentiated classroom, not everything is differentiated. That often causes a great sigh of relief among teachers. It is not even desirable to differentiate everything if you could. In a differentiated classroom, very purposeful decisions are made as to what should and should not be differentiated.

There is an ebb and flow in a differentiated classroom—times when the whole class is together to establish a common language and set the groundwork for the topic or exploration; times for group work, sense making, exploration, and various tasks; times for individual work to practice; and times for the teacher and students to check for their understanding and assess their progress. Within any lesson, students move in and out of these various structures depending on the components and design of the lesson.

DIFFERENTIATION AND KUD

The starting point of effective differentiation is clear and explicit content (Chapter 3). So what do we do with that? From Chapter 1, we remember that the three areas that can be differentiated are content, process, and product, and we can differentiate any of these by readiness, interest, or learning profile. As you look at planning differentiated tasks, the Know, Understand, and Do should be the driving force. Nevertheless, not everything should be differentiated. As you think about your content, consider the following:

- *Know*—Can be differentiated. To make the determination of which "Knows" can be differentiated, determine what is essential information and what is not. Essential knowledge (such as mathematical facts, key grade-level vocabulary, formulas in the standards) is non-negotiable and the specific content is not differentiated, although the methods by which students learn the facts may be differentiated. If the "Know" is good-to-know, it may be differentiated. For example, a specific application of a skill may be differentiated. Not every application of addition needs to be taught to every student, nor could they possibly be. Different specific contexts may be given to different groups of students based on readiness or interest.

- *Understand*—The Understandings for a unit are not differentiated. All students need to develop the same connections, concepts, and big ideas that give purpose to the mathematics being learned, although they may be reached at different levels.

- *Do*—The Do in the KUD is written, activity free, to show what students should be able to do as a result of the learning in the unit. The Do is massively differentiable. How students show what they know and understand is wide open. The number of aspects and complexity level at which they demonstrate skills may be negotiable based on readiness.

Figures 4.1 and 4.2 give examples of how the KUD can guide differentiation. The figure uses specific Ks, Us, and Ds from the first- and fourth-grade-unit KUDs found in Chapter 3. Notice that not all of the KUDs for a unit could possibly be used in a single lesson. Specific K, U, and D were chosen from the unit plan to use in a single lesson. These KUDs are used to design the differentiated tasks for the lesson. The examples provide tasks for readiness, interest, and learning profile, but this is only to provide multiple examples for you, the reader. In an actual lesson, the teacher would make the decision as to the manner of differentiation. Although not all of the tasks would be used in a single lesson, they could be used over the course of the unit, or the teacher could decide to choose one aspect that is most appropriate for the lesson.

The examples in Figures 4.1 and 4.2 clearly show the different types of tasks based on readiness, interest, and learning profile. Nevertheless, it is possible that these can be combined in different ways, such as giving choices within a specific readiness level or designing tasks by learning profile and allowing students to choose the task that is most interesting to them.

Consider It!

As you look over the differentiation suggestions in Figures 4.1 and 4.2, what conditions would prompt a teacher to choose readiness or interest or learning profile for the specific lesson?

FIGURE 4.1

FIRST-GRADE DIFFERENTIATION IDEAS BASED ON KUD

KUD From Unit Plan Being Addressed:

K1: Vocabulary:

more/less

numeral/number

object

set

K3: Groups of objects can be represented by a numeral that represents the number of objects.

U2: Our numbers are based on groups of tens. Any group of ten in one place value equals one of the next place value.

U3: A number can be represented different ways, e.g., a numeral or group of objects.

D3: Represent several objects with a written numeral.

D4: Tell how many tens and how many ones are in a two-digit number, beginning with 11–19 and going up to 30.

Example for Readiness Differentiation	Michelle buys Shopkins. (Moose Toys, Melbourne, Australia) She has two bags that come with 10 Shopkins each. She also has six more Shopkins. How many Shopkins does she have? Group Tasks: 1) Use base 10 blocks and draw a picture to show the Shopkins. How many Shopkins does Michelle have? 2) Draw a picture to show Michelle's Shopkins. How many Shopkins does she have? How many tens are there in the number? How many ones? Draw an arrow from the tens to the bags, and from the ones to the extras. 3) How many Shopkins does Michelle have? How does the number you wrote show the bags of tens and the extra Shopkins?
Example for Interest Differentiation	We are going to model two-digit numbers today. Choose the way you want to practice modeling numbers. 1) Grab two handfuls of counters to build a collection. Organize the counters into groups and determine how many are there. Find at least two different ways to count your collection.

	2) Roll two different-colored dice to show the number of tens and ones (one color for ten and one for ones) in a number. Write your number. Show two different ways to represent your number (tally charts in tens and ones; drawing base 10 blocks; subitized dots, etc.)
	3) Draw a two-digit number (written on slips of paper) from the number bag. Write your number at the top of your number box. Underneath, write how many tens and how many ones in your number. Find another way to show tens and ones for your number. For example, 27 can be 2 tens and 7 ones or 1 ten and 17 ones or 27 ones. Use base 10 blocks to make exchanges of tens and ones as needed.
Example for Learning Profile Differentiation **(Differentiated by Sternberg's Triarchic Theory)**	(Analytical) Use base 10 blocks to model 2-digit numbers. Draw your blocks, and write the number under the picture. Draw arrows to show the tens and the ones. Be ready to explain your drawings and numbers to your partner. (Practical) Think of something you have a lot of or would like to have a lot of. What is it? How many would you like to have? Write your number (30 or less) and draw a picture of your collection. How many groups of ten and how many extra ones do you have? (Creative) Choose a two-digit number between 15 and 30. Show your number as many different ways as you can, but you need to show at least three different ways. It can be tally marks, tens and ones table, base 10 block drawing, subitized dots, scattered drawings grouped into tens, or any other way.

FOURTH-GRADE DIFFERENTIATION IDEAS BASED ON KUD

KUD From Unit Plan Being Addressed:

K1. Vocabulary: notation, tenths, hundredths, decimal, decimal point, fractional part, whole.

K4: Decimal notation and place value names.

K5: How to write a fraction as a decimal and a decimal as a fraction.

U4: Every fraction can be represented by an infinite number of equivalent fractions, but each fraction is represented by only one decimal (or an equivalent decimal form; example 0.25 0.250)

D4: Explain how decimals can represent fractions and fractions can represent decimals.

D5: Write a fraction as a decimal and a decimal as a fraction.

(Continued)

Chapter 4 | Step Up   81

FIGURE 4.2 (Continued)

Example for Readiness Differentiation	Finding and Modeling Fractions and Decimals You will convert fractions to decimals using models and division. Explain how the model, division, and notation all show the same thing in different ways. 1) (Craftsman) Use more complex fractions including thirds and fractions beyond unit fractions. No additional supports or examples are given. 2) (Apprentice) Provide one completed model using 1/2 as an example. Use primarily unit fractions on which students work, with one or two fractions with numerators other than one. Have fraction and decimal manipulatives available if needed. 3) (Novice) Provide scaffolded directions. Give one completed example, a second problem with steps provided, and blanks to be filled in. Show how manipulatives can be used if there is a question about relationships. Encourage drawing as well as algorithms. Use only unit fractions unless the group shows mastery and is ready to move on. Give scaffolded text with blanks for the relationship explanations.
Example for Interest Differentiation	Choose one of the following ways to relate fractions and decimals: 1) Since a fraction represents division, you can divide the numerator by the denominator and get an equivalent form. Use division to convert fractions to decimals. 2) Relate coins to decimals. Determine the number of a specific coin that is needed to equal \$1.00. Write the fraction of \$1.00 that coin represents. Then write the decimal value of the coin. Show how the decimal and the fraction are equivalent. Extend this to multiple coins and money values. Ex. A Nickel It takes 20 nickels to make \$1.00. One nickel is 1/20 of a dollar. One nickel is written as \$0.05. 0.05 = 5/100 = 1/20 3) Use Fraction/Decimal strips to equate fractions and decimals. Generate a list of equivalent fractions and decimals. Write other equivalent fractions as well, not just the simplified fraction. 4) Make a stacked number line model for equivalent fractions and decimals. Stack at least five number lines: 1st for decimals, 2nd for halves, 3rd for fourths, 4th for fifths, and the 5th for tenths. (The number of lines can be adjusted based on the fractions and decimals you are working with.)

Example for Learning Profile Differentiation (Differentiated by Modality – Visual, Auditory or Kinesthetic)	(Visual) Draw a fraction from the fraction bag (choose appropriate fractions, and write each fraction on a slip of paper and place in a bag). Divide the blank square and shade it to show your fraction. Next, overlay the hundreds grid on the rectangle. Write the decimal equivalent for your fraction based on the grid. Explain how you know the fractions and decimals are actually equivalent. 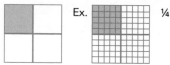 ¼ = 25/100 = 0.25 (Kinesthetic) Use base 10 blocks or other fraction/decimal manipulatives to find equivalent fractions and decimals. Draw your equivalent models next to each other, and write the fraction and decimals underneath. Find multiple equivalent fractions. Explain how you know the fractions and decimals are actually equivalent. (Auditory) Discuss with a partner or small group two different ways to change a fraction to a decimal. How will you know that they are actually equivalent? Make a "PSA" (public service announcement) infomercial on how to convert fractions to decimals. You may make a video to show your process or present your skit to another small group or the class.

It is also important to keep in mind the Depth of Knowledge/ Cognitive Demand level (see Chapter 3) of the tasks. Low-level differentiated tasks will not have the desired learning outcomes for which we are hoping. Differentiated tasks have to be the same high level as whole class tasks for the Standards for Mathematical Practice, conceptual understanding, and problem-solving skills to become a natural part of learning mathematics.

STRATEGIES FOR DIFFERENTIATION

Choosing whether to differentiate by readiness, interest, or learning profile should be based on recognizing student need coupled with decisions about keeping learning fresh and engaging. Each area of differentiation has its specific strengths. Figure 4.3 provides the rationale for choosing a specific mode of differentiation.

FIGURE 4.3

DIFFERENTIATION FOCUS

Differentiation Aspect	Purpose
Readiness	Provides an appropriate and realistic challenge and has the best potential for growth and understanding.
Interest	Addresses intrinsic motivation and creates connections and a sense of fun in learning.
Learning Profile	Eases the learning process so that our brains can get learning into and out of memory. It is "more likely to evoke positive emotional responses, engaging affective filters to open access to the brain's processing centers" (Willis, 2006).

TRY IT! WRITE A KUD FOR ONE LESSON

Choose an upcoming lesson, and write a brief KUD for the specific lesson (not the entire unit if the unit's KUD is not already developed). If you have used the unit template (see http://resources .corwin.com/everymathlearnerK-5, Chapter 2) to write your KUD, select the specific K, U, and D for one lesson. Determine how you will differentiate to best meet your students' learning needs for the lesson (readiness, interest, or learning profile) and why.

Once you have decided on the particular manner of differentiation, consider the following recommendations and strategy ideas.

READINESS DIFFERENTIATION

Readiness differentiation is probably the most visible of all student learning differences and usually the area of most concern given our high-stakes testing environment. It can also seem the most daunting to address for a teacher.

Readiness differentiation begins with determining where each student is at this moment in his or her understanding and knowledge of the content. This is based on current pre- or formative assessment (for details, see Chapter 7). A teacher once told me that she did not preassess her students, or use much formative assessment, because she knew that her students didn't know anything. Be careful with assuming what your students know or don't know without supporting evidence. It is this clarifying evidence that allows me to address readiness concerns appropriately, as well as to discover the specific misconception or skill gap that needs to be addressed. According to Judy Willis, "Challenging students at reasonable, appropriate levels is one of the most powerful strategies for success, but teachers must carefully monitor the level of challenge. If goals do not provide sufficient challenge to engage students, or if the challenge exceeds students' levels of capability, frustration replaces motivation" (2006, p. 25).

With readiness differentiation, our goal is not to create 30 lesson plans or tasks to address each student in the moment but to look for common patterns in prior knowledge, errors or misconceptions to address. In this way, groups of students can receive the same task at the appropriate level of challenge without constructing an abundance of variations.

We often think of "high–middle–low" tasks when addressing readiness. This doesn't necessarily have to be the case. Only two different tasks might be needed or perhaps more levels of tasks depending on the makeup of the class. Sometimes readiness differentiation is not based as much on the content mastery but

TIP FOR ELL/SPECIAL EDUCATION STUDENTS

It is important to assess what students truly know and understand about the mathematical content, not to be hampered by language constraints. Use multiple methods for assessing your students including drawings, gestures, and practicing repeating key vocabulary with diagrams and steps to assess the mathematical readiness apart from language readiness.

on other aspects of readiness such as independence. For example, some students may be able to self-start on a task, whereas others need more modeling and help getting started. One structure for differentiation then could be to have a group with the teacher to get started, while the other students are starting independently on the same task. At a certain point, flip the groups so the original group with the teacher is now working independently, and the students who had begun now have a time to check in and extend their thinking with the teacher.

Another way to differentiate by readiness is to have different points within whole class direct instruction when students who are ready to begin independent (or paired) work move out of the whole class instruction. Students not quite ready will continue with the teacher to see more examples and hear further explanation. At another stopping point, students are given another opportunity to work independently. Continue in this way until all students are working without guidance. It may be that some reluctant learners will not choose to work apart from the teacher if given the option—do not give that option.

WATCH IT!

As you watch Video 4.1, *Planning for Readiness Differentiation*, consider the following questions:

1. How can readiness groups be determined?

2. How were differences in readiness addressed through the specific tasks and/or stations?

3. How did the teachers plan the tiered (readiness) tasks for the various levels?

4. How did the teachers manage the tasks, making sure that students had the correct level?

5. How were students engaging with, or reacting to, their specific tasks?

Video 4.1 Planning for Readiness Differentiation

STRATEGIES

Tiered Activities The primary strategy used for differentiating by readiness is called a *tiered activity*. One reason a tiered activity is the building block for readiness differentiation is that just about anything can be tiered. The idea of designing tiers is that whatever is happening in the mathematics class—questioning, practice problems, a specific task—can be tiered by adjusting for various readiness levels. The essential key is to not weaken or change the learning objective when designing different tiers, although the same essential understandings and skills may be addressed at different levels of complexity, abstractness, and open-endedness (Tomlinson, 2014, p. 133).

To create a tiered activity:

1. Explicitly establish the essential understanding and skills to be addressed.

2. Brainstorm possible structures or activities that will elicit the essential learning—this is wide open. The activity should be interesting, high level, and cause students to use and reflect on the essential understandings and skills. Consider the activities you have already used first and check for the complexity level of the task and for whom the task as written is most appropriate.

3. If you are designing from scratch, write your first task for the highest group of students in the class. If you are using a preexisting activity that is not for the highest group of students, hold on to it for the appropriate tier, and jump to designing the top tier. Once you have designed your top task, go through your class roster and record the students who will be able to engage with this task.

4. Design your next task. It could be the same task as the original task with additional supports, models, or smaller steps embedded. It could also be a different task. Once this task is designed, review your roster and make a list of the students for whom this task is most appropriate.

5. Continue this process until you have the number of tasks designed to challenge all of the students in your class appropriately.

Figures 4.4 and 4.5 give examples of how specific KUDs from the unit's standards lead to developing a tiered activity.

FIGURE 4.4

FIRST-GRADE ADDITION

Standard:
• Add within 100, including adding a two-digit number and a one-digit number, and add a two-digit number and a multiple of 10, using concrete models or drawings and strategies based on place value, properties of operations, and/or the relationship between addition and subtraction.
• Understand that in adding two-digit numbers, one adds tens and tens, ones and ones; also, sometimes it is necessary to compose a ten. (From Common Core State Standards, 1.NBT.4)

Know:
- Place value names of tens and ones; strategies for addition including base 10 blocks, hundreds board, counting on, number-line jumps, tally method, and place value (expanded notation) method.

Understand:
- Only things that are alike can be added (tens and tens and ones and ones).
- Different methods of addition will model and explain the role of place value in different ways, but all methods lead to the same answer and understandings.

Do:
- Add numbers using multiple methods. Compare and contrast methods for addition.
- Explain the importance of adding "like things" when adding mixed numbers.

Tier	Task
1	a) Add 2 two-digit numbers using a minimum of three strategies. Explain how each strategy uses place value to add to a correct sum.
	b) Use words or pictures to show things that can be added (such as 2 apples and 3 oranges = 5 pieces of fruit or 2 balloons and 3 balloons = 5 balloons) and things that cannot be added (such as trees and people). Explain the difference.
2	a) Add a two-digit number and a single-digit number using two different strategies. Compare and contrast the strategies. How are they alike, and how are they different? How do both show the importance of place value when you add?
	b) Use words or pictures to show things that can be added (such as 2 balloons and 3 balloons = 5 balloons) and things that cannot be added (such as trees and people). Explain the difference.
3	a) Add two single-digit numbers that require regrouping. Use 2 different strategies. Explain which strategy you prefer and why. Explain why you have to regroup with your sum.
	b) Use pictures to show things that can be added (such as two balloons and 3 balloons = 5 balloons) and things that cannot be added (such as trees and people). Explain the difference.
4	Add two single-digit numbers that do not require regrouping. Use 2 different strategies. Explain which strategy you prefer and why.
	b) Use pictures to show things that can be added (such as two balloons and 3 balloons = 5 balloons) and things that cannot be added (such as trees and people). Explain the difference.

 A template to create a tiered activity can be downloaded from
http://resources.corwin.com/everymathlearnerK-5.

FIGURE 4.5

FIFTH-GRADE MIXED NUMBER ADDITION

Standard:

- Add and subtract fractions with unlike denominators (including mixed numbers) by replacing given fractions with equivalent fractions in such a way as to produce an equivalent sum or difference of fractions with like denominators. For example, $2/3 + 5/4 = 8/12 + 15/12 = 23/12$. (In general, $a/b + c/d = (ad + bc) / bd$). (Common Core State Standards, 5.NF.1)

Know:

- Numerator, denominator, equivalency, lowest common denominator, least common multiple, mixed number, how to find equivalent fractions, how to find common denominators (multiple lists, factor trees, etc.), how to convert mixed numbers to improper fractions, and vice versa.
- When adding or subtracting fractions, add or subtract numerators given common denominators.

Understand:

- Only things that are alike can be added or subtracted, and denominators determine whether fractions are alike.
- Equivalency allows us to rename quantities without changing their value to combine or compare.

Do:

- Add mixed numbers with unlike denominators. Compare and contrast methods for addition.
- Explain the importance of adding "like things" when adding mixed numbers.

Tier	Task
1	Add mixed numbers with unlike denominators in two different ways: first keeping mixed numbers and next converting to improper fractions. Compare and contrast the two methods. Explain how you are adding "like things" in the two methods. Explain the role of equivalency in adding mixed numbers.
2	Add mixed numbers with common denominators in two different ways: first keeping mixed numbers and next converting to improper fractions. Compare and contrast the two methods. What are the pros and cons of each method? How are you adding "like things" in both methods?
3	Add mixed numbers with common denominators. Provide scaffolded instructions for each step. Maintaining Mixed Numbers: 1. What are the whole numbers, and what are the fractional parts? 2. Add the fractions together. 3. Is the sum of the fractions greater than one? If so, convert the improper fraction to a mixed number. Record the fractional part of the mixed number, and carry the whole number to the whole number addition. 4. Add the whole numbers. 5. Explain whether your sum makes sense comparing your final answer to an estimation of the answer.

(Continued)

FIGURE 4.5 (Continued)

Using Improper Fractions:

1. Convert the mixed number to an improper fraction. Check your notes for the correct steps if you need them.

2. Add the improper fractions. Remember how to add fractions. Check your notes if you need them.

3. Convert the sum of your fractions back to a mixed number.

4. Explain whether your sum makes sense comparing your final answer to an estimation of the answer.

 A template to create a tiered activity can be downloaded from http://resources.corwin.com/everymathlearnerK-5.

As mentioned, most strategies and tasks can be "tiered" simply by creating additional versions to challenge students most appropriately. The next example shows how a specific strategy can be tiered to address students' readiness.

Think Dots Think Dots is a strategy conceived by Kay Brimijoin that places six different questions or tasks onto separate cards with pips (die spots) on the opposite side. Figure 4.6 shows a picture of

FIGURE 4.6

THINK DOTS

© Nanci Smith

Think Dots. Think Dots can be used in a variety of ways. Students can roll a die and complete the task they roll, or a group of students can work together with one student rolling a die and facilitating the group's work on the task. The lead and the roll then pass to the next student.

To create a set of Think Dots:

1. Design six questions or tasks that ask for information or are an application of the lesson content. Design this first set at a high level for the highest students in your class. There are a variety of methods by which you can design the six cards:

   a. Use the six levels of Blooms, one for each card.

   b. Choose six of the eight Standards for Mathematical Practice to design specific questions or tasks for the lesson content.

   c. Consider multiple representations for a task or process.

   d. Use the following prompts to design targeted tasks:

      i. Describe

      ii. Analyze

      iii. Compare and contrast

      iv. Demonstrate or model

      v. Change an element of the problem, and describe how it will affect the results

      vi. Diagram or illustrate

2. Design additional sets to address the various readiness levels in your class. Consider the following ways to design multiple levels:

   a. Manipulatives or models for more concrete examples

   b. Shortened directions or step-by-step directions

   c. Fewer facets per problem

   d. More basic applications

   e. Greater check-in points with the teacher

The Think Dots strategy is best used to develop and assess understandings embedded in skills, so typical numeric problems are not recommended as prompts. The prompts should include high-level verbs such as *explain, model, generalize, describe,* and so on.

Figure 4.7 gives a primary example for place value, and Figure 4.8 gives a multiplication example.

FIGURE 4.7

PLACE VALUE THINK DOTS

	High to Mid-High Students	
○	Arrange the digits 0, 1, 2, 3, and 4 to make at least four different numbers. Explain the differences in their values. Order them from least to greatest.	
○ ○	Roll five 0–9 dice. Make the greatest and least numbers possible. How do you know they are the greatest and least?	
○ ○ ○	Explain the role place value has in addition and subtraction.	
○ ○ ○ ○	Explain how strategically to make the least number possible if you were given certain digits to arrange.	
○ ○ ○ ○ ○	Determine a strategy to make the greatest number possible if you were given digits to arrange.	
○ ○ ○ ○ ○ ○	Explain how the expanded form of a number relates to place value. How does this help in number operations?	
	Mid-High to Mid-Low Students	
○	Rearrange the digits in the number 4,213 to make the greatest and least numbers possible. How do you know they are greatest and least?	
○ ○	Roll three dice. Make the greatest and least numbers possible. How do you know they are the greatest and least?	
○ ○ ○	Describe how you would add two- (or three-) digit numbers. What role does place value have in addition?	
○ ○ ○ ○	Explain how strategically to make the least number possible if you were given certain digits to arrange.	
○ ○ ○ ○ ○	Determine a strategy to make the greatest number possible if you were given digits to arrange.	
○ ○ ○ ○ ○ ○	Write the number 467 in expanded form. How does this form relate to place value?	

	Struggling Students
○	Explain the difference among the numbers 1, 10, and 100. Draw pictures or use models to show the difference.
○ ○	How many hundreds, tens, and ones are in the number 104? Use ten frames or base 10 blocks to show the number.
○ ○ ○	How many tens and how many ones are in the number 74? Use a model to show the number. As a challenge, use your model to determine how many more are needed to reach 100.
○ ○ ○ ○	Rearrange the digits in the number 674 to make the greatest numbers possible. How do you know it is the largest?
○ ○ ○ ○ ○	Rearrange the digits in the number 674 to make the least numbers possible. How do you know it is the least?
○ ○ ○ ○ ○ ○	Use a hundreds chart to show the pattern of ones and tens as numbers go up by one or by tens.

FIGURE 4.8

MULTIPLICATION THINK DOTS

	High to Middle Students
○	There are many ways to remember multiplication facts. Start with 0 and go through 10. Tell how to remember how to multiply by each number. For example, how do you remember how to multiply by 0? By 1? By 2? Etc.?
○ ○	There are many patterns in the multiplication chart. One pattern deals with pairs of numbers, for example, multiplying by 3 and multiplying by 6 or multiplying by 5 and multiplying by 10. What other pairs of numbers have this same pattern? What is the pattern?
○ ○ ○	Russell says that 7 × 6 is 42. Kadi says that he can't know that because we didn't study the 7 multiplication facts. Russell says he didn't need to, and he is right. How might Russell know his answer is correct?

(Continued)

FIGURE 4.8 (Continued)

○ ○ ○ ○	Max says that he can find the answer to a number times 16 simply by knowing how to multiply by 2. Explain how Max can figure it out, and give at least two examples.
○ ○ ○ ○	Alicia and her ____ friends each have _____ necklaces. How many necklaces do they have all together? Show the answer to your problem by drawing an array or another picture. Roll a number cube to determine the numbers for each blank.
○ ○ ○ ○ ○ ○	What is _____ × _____? Find as many ways to show your answer as possible. Roll the provided dice to determine the factors.
Middle to Struggling Students	
○	It's easy to remember how to multiply by 0, 1, 2, and 5! Tell how to remember.
○ ○	Jamie says that multiplying by 10 just adds a 0 to the number. Bryan doesn't understand this because any number plus 0 is the same number. Explain what Jamie means, and why her trick can work.
○ ○ ○	Explain how multiplying by 2 can help with multiplying by 4 and 8. Give at least 3 examples.
○ ○ ○ ○	We never studied the 7 multiplication facts. Explain two different ways to figure out the 7 facts. Try to find a pattern in multiplying by 7.
○ ○ ○ ○	Jorge and his ____ friends each have _____ trading cards. How many trading cards do they have all together? Show the answer to your problem by drawing an array or another picture. Roll a number cube to determine the numbers for each blank.
○ ○ ○ ○ ○ ○	What is _____ × _____? Find as many ways to show your answer as possible. Roll the provided dice to determine the factors.

TRY IT! CREATING READINESS TIERS

Take an activity you currently use in class. Think about the appropriate readiness level of the task. For which students in class is the task most appropriate? How can you create other tiers of the same task for the remaining students in class? Design the various tiers and try them out.

A final way by which you can think of differentiating with readiness is through scaffolding and compacting. Compacting addresses advanced students, whereas scaffolding provides additional supports for those students who will need it.

Compacting has three basic steps:

1. Identify and document the skills and understandings that the students have mastered based on assessments and the unit's KUD.

2. Identify and document the skills and understandings that the students have *not* mastered based on assessments and the unit's KUD.

3. When the class is working with and learning content that the students have already mastered, they will work on a related study or area of application. Students will rejoin the class to learn content that has not previously been mastered.

4. All students will remain accountable for the learning of all content within the unit on the summative assessment.

Too often we expect students to complete work they already know how to do, no matter the repetition or boredom, while the rest of the class catches up to "what they already know." We also expect them to not be a discipline problem while this is happening. Compacting allows bright students to work independently on related studies, dig deeper into content and application, and continue to learn and grow instead of holding stagnant. It provides the opportunity to use some of the wonderful tasks we could do "if only there was time" because now there is time for certain students. Additionally, compacting provides the time for these bright and gifted students to dig deeply into the concepts and understandings in the unit through tasks and explorations that replace other class assignments. Notice that compacting *replaces* certain assignments within the unit—it does not *add on to* the existing assignments for "students who finish early."

Scaffolding on the other hand is a general term for providing the support that will enable students to be successful with any given tasks. Possible supports include

- Hint Envelopes—provide a list of hints for specific sections or steps to a problem. Think of what you would ask students if they were struggling at any given point in the task, and record these in order. Put the hints (either as a list or separately on slips of paper) into an envelope for students to access as needed.

- Models—provide models or partial models of what is expected in the task. This is especially effective with procedures for solving numerical operations. When providing a model, be careful not to give away too much of the information with which you want students to wrestle and make sense.

- Reciprocal Teaching—use mixed readiness pairings to have the first student "teach" the process to the second student as the second student writes and solves the problem as the teacher teaches. Roles then reverse. Begin with the student who has the stronger readiness level as the first teacher. Be ready for pairs of students who may need help from the beginning.

- Mini-teach—pull a small group of students who need an additional example or coaching through a problem.

A final reflection on addressing student readiness: Whatever structure or task you are designing for students, remember that students with less developed readiness will benefit from:

- Someone to help them find and make up missing information and skills to close gaps and move ahead

- More direct instruction and practice

- Higher degree of structure and concrete materials to make sense of activities

- Fewer steps, less reading, a slower pace, and tasks closer to personal experiences

TIP FOR ELL/SPECIAL EDUCATION STUDENTS

When considering English-language learners (ELLs), scaffolding may need to be more about language than about mathematics. Provide a word box with illustrated definitions to help students master language and concepts in the units. Additionally, illustrated steps to a particular process will help students struggling with language to connect steps and the process to prior knowledge and reasoning.

Students with greater developed readiness will benefit from

- Skipping practice of previously documented mastered skills and understanding

- Complex, open-ended, abstract, and multifaceted problem-solving tasks

- A quick pace for mathematical skill mastery and a slower pace for building depth of conceptual understanding and problem solving (Tomlinson, 2014, pp. 18–19)

INTEREST DIFFERENTIATION

It is possible that we get stumped trying to relate the specific content to students' interests. This is usually because we approach the connection through a skill or fact rather than through a concept. For example, we can hook students' interests when studying addition by looking at addition through the lens of collections. We can study geometry through the lens of art or shapes in our community. We can even introduce algebra concepts through the lens of mystery unknowns such as "I'm thinking of a number . . ." Finding concepts that intrigue our students, and relating our studies to them, is a way to differentiate by interest.

Research also suggests that changing the context of a problem can result in greater investment by students on the task. One study that was conducted with students changed the context of word problems from a typical textbook problem to something the students were interested in, such as shopping, computers, music, and use of cell phones, without changing any of the numbers or mathematics required. Half of the 141 students in the study were given the original problems in the unit, and the remaining students were given problems with the context tailored to their interests. The group that received problems with its interests represented performed better and learned faster during the unit, and it was still performing better on more complex problems that were not adjusted four units later (Walkington et al., 2014).

We know from cognitive science that we can also intrigue and hook our students through connections (as described earlier), appropriate challenge or a puzzle-like quality, and novelty (Sousa, 2015). These qualities can be integrated at the beginning of a lesson as a hook or through the tasks we choose. Perhaps the most important way to create interest in our students is through modeling our own enthusiasm and choosing intriguing tasks.

The most common way that we differentiate by interest is by offering choice. This can be done in a wide variety of ways from using choice boards to designing activities into which choices are built.

WATCH IT!

As you watch Video 4.2, *Planning for Interest Differentiation,* consider the following questions:

1. What tips can you take from how Mrs. Potter plans for interest differentiation? What would you say was the most important tip about the design of multiple activities?

2. How does Mrs. Potter use interest to assign groups? How did she react to her students' choices?

3. How do the students respond to the choices they made?

4. What are the advantages of allowing students to choose their task? Can you think of any disadvantages?

5. What can you take from the video clip to apply to your classroom when providing choices?

Video 4.2 Planning for Interest Differentiation

STRATEGIES

Choice Boards Choice boards are a structural way to organize choice-based activities. Choice boards usually have clear pockets in which the teacher places descriptions or pictures of the tasks from which students can choose. Students post their names next to the task on which they have chosen to work. This can be accomplished through attaching a clothespin with the student's name on it, a sticky note with the student's name, or a white board signup. Students can move from task to task as they finish and check in with the teacher to have their work checked for completeness. Figure 4.9 gives an example of a choice board.

Contracts Contracts are a general term for any strategy that provides students with an opportunity for students to work somewhat independently on material that is balanced between teacher-assigned and student-choice tasks. Contracts can be used as formative or summative assessments or as a learning progression through the unit. No matter what the structure, a quality design will include

FIGURE 4.9

CHOICE BOARD

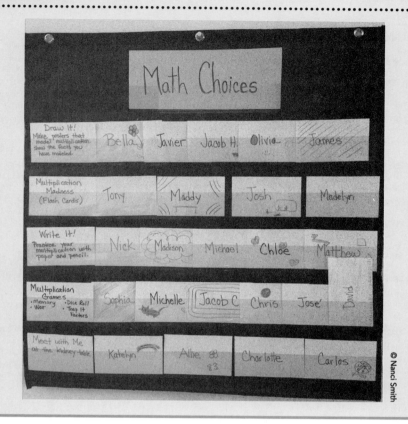

- Specific content goals from the KUD including demonstration of conceptual understandings as well as knowledge and skills that need to be practiced and mastered
- Application of skills and knowledge into context and problem-solving situations
- Allowance working conditions students follow to assume Establishment of for learning
- Allows for some student choice
- Establishes criteria for success

There are many structures by which a contract can be designed. The first example is based on a strategy by Carol Cummings (2000) called a *menu*. The menu provides three sections: Main Dish (must-do), Side Dish (choice), and Desserts (above and beyond). Figure 4.10 gives an example of a fifth-grade menu on Volume.

FIGURE 4.10

VOLUME MENU

Menu: Geometry

Final Due Date: April 17

Check-In Dates: Meet with Teacher to determine

Main Dish (Most Complete All)

1. Complete the outline sheet on Volume including definition and formulas.

2. Create a Venn diagram comparing Volume and Area

3. Explain the use of multiplication in finding volume. How is addition used in finding compound volumes? What is the role of units in volume—both with multiplication and addition?

4. Complete worksheet on volume problems—shapes and applications.

Side Dish (Choose 2)

1. Find solids (a minimum of 5) in your world—school, home, neighborhood, or anywhere else. Sketch each right rectangular prism with measurements and calculate the volume for each. Suggest what could be stored in each.

2. Compare the two volume formulas with which we have worked. Explain how the two formulas are really different versions of the same thing. Use diagrams to explain the comparison.

3. Build a composite shape from blocks or boxes. Bring in your model or sketch the model. Find the volume of your shape.

4. Find a creative way to show the difference between 2-D and 3-D shapes including what "D" means, how it affects related measurements and units, and include models.

Dessert (Optional to Go Above and Beyond)

1. Create a Volume Book with the following pages:

   a) Cover page

   b) Definitions, diagrams and formulas

   c) A minimum of six original volume problems—three simple prisms and three compound shapes with answers

   d) A minimum of two original application problems with answers

2. Design a storage chest for your room that will hold at least twelve of your toys and games. Measure the toys and games individually, and then design your storage chest. Draw your toys with their measurements, and the design for your storage chest.

 The full menu can be downloaded at http://resources.corwin.com/ everymathlearnerK-5.

Another example of a type of contract is called a Think-Tac-Toe. This is a 3×3 (or larger if desired) table of tasks from which students will choose. Most often students are to choose one task from each row, but they do not have to make a tic-tac-toe. In designing a Think-Tac-Toe, each row of options should relate to the same concept, skill, or topic. With careful design, it will not matter which tasks the students choose since the tasks in the same row all relate to the same outcome. Figure 4.11 gives an example of a third-grade think-tac-toe on multiplication and division.

FIGURE 4.11

MULTIPLICATION AND DIVISION THINK-TAC-TOE

Directions: Chose one task from each row to complete. You do not have to choose tasks to get three in a row. Choose tasks you feel you will best be able to complete.		
Practice multiplication and division facts using flash cards with a partner.	Complete a multiplication and division practice sheet.	Review your mathematical facts using a multiplication table. Identify 6 facts on which you want to continue to concentrate.
Create a page of fact families for 7, 8, and 9 (or three other numbers you want to practice).	Make a poster of how multiplication and division are related.	Make a set of multiplication and division triangle manipulatives.
Make a poster of the different meanings of multiplication and division.	Write 3 different application problems for multiplication or division that show the meanings of multiplication and division.	Model multiplication and division facts showing the meanings of multiplication and division. For example, an area model for 3×7 or a partition for 18 ÷ 9.

A final way to address interest is to use novel and fun approaches, such as games. Many commercial and computer-based games can practice mathematical skills. Also, many games can be easily made for your students.

Matching Games Matching games can be made out of any set of problems. Consider bumping up the readiness level by creating three cards to match instead of two, with the third category being a model or a representation. For example, for multiplication, use one card for the problem, one card for the product, and a third card for one of the representations such as a picture of groups, an array, an area model, or repeated addition. Another example of adding a third category would be a word problem, the expression to set up the problem, and the answer. To make the game easier to play as a memory-style game, consider running the card types in different colors, such as the multiplication problem in blue, products in green, and representations in pink. If you don't want to take the time and trouble to make copies in color, mark the backs of the cards with a P (problem), A (answer), and R (representation). This allows students to turn over one of each kind of card to see whether they match, rather than turning over three problem cards that don't have a chance to match.

Triplets Triplets is a card game played similar to a rummy game with students taking turns drawing and discarding cards and trying to get three cards to match. The playing instructions are as follows.

Instructions:

1. One student will deal each player three (or six for more advanced version) cards face down.

2. Place the remaining cards in a pile in the center, and flip up the top card.

3. The player to the right of the dealer has the first move. He or she may either draw a card from the top of the pile or pick up the top card from the discard pile. The player will then discard one card from his or her hand.

4. Play continues until a player has one (three cards) or two (six cards) sets of three cards each with matching answers at which time he or she places a discard card face-down and shows his or her triplet matching cards to all players.

A deck of cards is made of 30 cards composed of six different sets of five possible matches. To begin, find six different "targets" for the topic on which cards will match. For example, if you are creating a multiplication game, the targets can be six different products. Once the targets are established, create four more cards that will match to the target. Figure 4.12 shows a triplets multiplication example.

For any game, you can adjust readiness simply by adjusting cards. It will still address interest because it is a game, and students recognize that everyone is playing the game and do not tend to notice whether different levels of the game are going on. For example, in the multiplication game earlier, perhaps you

FIGURE 4.12

TRIPLETS MULTIPLICATION CARDS

Target	12	24	32	64	48	16
Card	3×4	6×4	8×4	8×8	12×4	4×4
Card	6×2	12×2	16×2	4×16	16×3	8×2
Card	$4 + 4 + 4$	$6 + 6 + 6 + 6$	$8 + 8 + 8 + 8$	$32 + 32$	$8 + 8 + 8 +$ $8 + 8 + 8$	$4 + 4 + 4 + 4$
Card	• • • • • • • • •	3×8	4×8	32×2	24×2	(4×4 grid)

would want more basic products and more representations as a more basic tier of the game. On the other hand, perhaps you want to raise the readiness level and include some cards with the distributive property. These adjustments to the game do not change the interest factor, and all students continue their study of multiplication.

Build-A-Square Build-a-square is a puzzle game created from puzzles called "Crazy 'Noun'" puzzles, such as the Crazy Plane puzzle. There are nine cards with portions of the plane, or whatever is on the puzzle, on each edge. For example, there could be the front of the plane with a propeller on one edge and the tail section on the edge of a different tile. The cards are aligned in a 3×3 formation where every edge that meets between cards makes a complete plane and, thus, completes the puzzle. Build-a-square was born out of this concept. Simply put, problems and/or answers are on the edges of the cards. Cards are then matched based on the answers of the problems. Figure 4.13 shows a completed build-a-square puzzle for kindergarten subitizing.

Figure 4.14 shows a completed build-a-square for fifth-grade fraction addition and subtraction. Notice that the number of cards is increased, and there are symbols in the center of the cards. These symbols act as an answer key for the teacher instead of having to check every connecting side. Students can also record the order of the symbols to turn in as an answer key.

FIGURE 4.13

KINDERGARTEN SUBITIZING BUILD-A-SQUARE

···

1		4
6		6
3		5
	1	
7		

The full size cards can downloaded at http://resources.corwin.com/everymathlearnerK-5.

FIGURE 4.14

FRACTION ADDITION AND SUBTRACTION BUILD-A-SQUARE

···

9/10 − 1/5	5/8 − 1/3	5/8 + 1/3
2/3 − 1/5 · 2/3 − 2/9	1/3 + 1/9 × 3/4 − 2/9	1/3 + 7/36 ✦ 4/5 + 6/7
3/4 + 1/5	2/3 − 1/6	7/8 − 5/6
7/10 + 5/20	1/4 + 2/8	7/12 − 13/24
2/3 + 1/5 + 3/8 + 1/4	5/6 − 5/24 ○ 1/4 + 3/5	9/10 − 1/20 ▽ 2/3 − 4/6
1/2 − 1/5	8/8 − 19/21	5/8 − 3/10
1/10 + 1/5	3/7 − 1/8	5/8 + 1/8
3/7 + 1/8 # 3/10 + 1/2	6/15 + 2/5 ★ 3/4 + 1/8	13/13 − 1/8 ◈ 1/2 + 5/10
1/12 + 1/15	1/3 + 1/4	1/2 − 1/6

The full size cards can downloaded at http://resources.corwin.com/everymathlearnerK-5.

Neuroscience supports the advantages to students when learning with interest. They include:

1. High motivation leads to greater attention, increased willingness to learn, and persistence.

2. High motivation leads to greater interest, and high interest is intrinsically motivating.

3. The motivation a student experiences when learning something interesting is often more rewarding than when he or she is learning for "award" (Sousa & Tomlinson, 2011).

When designing for interest differentiation, and allowing students choice of task, be aware of possible snares. Even though we encourage students to choose a task based on their best learning outcomes, sometimes when you give students a choice, they can choose poorly. Students may choose a task based on the task a friend has chosen instead of the task that seems most interesting to them. One way to avoid this is to explain the options and have students write their choice on a note card or sticky note. Once students record their choices, tasks are given out or groups are formed.

Additionally, when students choose a task, whether designed by interest or learning profile, they may often choose a task because it seems easier to them. When offering choice, be careful to design tasks that remain true to the learning goals and require the same amount of work and time commitment. That way, if students choose a task because it seems easier, it will be because it appeals to how the student best learns rather than the nature of the task.

LEARNING PROFILE DIFFERENTIATION

Learning profile differentiation is often a comfortable starting place for differentiation. The learning profiles themselves suggest appropriate task design, and students can be offered the choice of task to complete based on their interest. Chapter 2 discusses the specific structures of the learning profile intelligences (Sternberg's Triarchic Theory and Gardner's Multiple Intelligences).

WATCH IT!

As you watch Video 4.3, *Planning for Learning Profile Differentiation*, consider the following questions:

1. How are the tasks the teacher chose aligned to Sternberg's learning profile?
2. What is Ms. Farless's goal in designing learning profile differentiation?
3. How do each of the three seemingly very different tasks all address the same learning objective?

Video 4.3 Planning for Learning Profile Differentiation

When designing learning profile tasks, keep in mind that the thinking and reasoning is more important than the actual task activity. In Chapter 2, the types of reasoning related to the various learning profiles are outlined.

WATCH IT!

As you watch Video 4.4, *Differentiating for Learning Profile in a Fourth-Grade Classroom*, consider the following questions:

1. How did Mrs. Garoutte design learning profile tasks incorporating tasks she already had with a need for additional new tasks?
2. How can instructions for differentiated tasks be given efficiently and succinctly?
3. In what ways does Mrs. Garoutte balance assigned and choice tasks within learning profile differentiation?

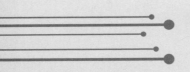

Video 4.4 Differentiating for Learning Profile in a Fourth-Grade Classroom

STRATEGIES

Sternberg Triarchic Theory Robert Sternberg (2005) suggests that students organize learning primarily in one of three ways: analytically, practically, and creatively. Most students will be a combination of two, and occasionally a student will be evenly balanced among all three. Tasks can be aligned according to these descriptions. Figure 4.14 provides task examples for each area of Sternberg's theory of intelligence.

FIGURE 4.15

STERNBERG-ALIGNED TASKS

Intelligence	Possible Tasks for Mathematical Concept or Skill
Analytical The ability to analyze and think in linear and logical-sequential ways. Analytical learners tend to be "school smart."	• Bullets • Lists • Steps • Worksheets • Tables, Charts • Venn Diagrams • Timelines • Sequencing • Flow Charts • Compare and Contrast • Puns and Subtleties • Identify Key Parts • Find the Error • Evaluating • Sorting and Classifying • Appealing to Logic • Critique and Criticize • Explaining Difficult Problems to Others • Making Inferences and Deriving Conclusions • Graphic Organizer • Timeline • Patterns • Classifying • Definitions • Cause and Effect • Codes • Graphs • Database

(Continued)

FIGURE 4.15 (Continued)

Intelligence	Possible Tasks for Mathematical Concept or Skill
	• Blueprints • Newspaper • Fact File • Worksheets
Practical The ability to put ideas into action and to apply ideas to the real world. Practical learners draw from personal experiences. Practical learners tend to be "street smart."	• Working Your Way Out of a Problem • Notes to Self (what questions to ask myself, how to make sense it for myself) • Here Is a Problem, Explain What Happened • Analogies • Draw Real-World Examples • Advising and Convincing Others (Advice columns) • Hands-on Activities • Taking Things Apart and Fixing Them • Understanding and Respecting Others / Friendships / Resolving Conflicts • Putting Things Into Practice • Adapting to New Situations • Explaining How Things Can Be Used • Developing a Plan to Address a Problem • Help Classmates Understand • Scenarios • Role Plays • WebQuest • Job Shadowing • Dialogs • Newscasts • Letters to the Editor • Flyers • Demonstrations • Experiments • Surveys

Intelligence	Possible Tasks for Mathematical Concept or Skill
	• Field trips
	• Petitions
	• "Cheat Sheets"
	• Lesson Plans
Creative The ability to imagine possibilities and think outside the box. Creative students think of their own ways to explain and demonstrate and often have unique and correct solution paths. Creative learners are "imagination smart."	• Figure Out a Way to Explain • ABC or Other Creative "Books" or Guides on a Topic • How to Represent • Make Your Own Interpretation • Pictures or News Bulletins to Describe • Designing New Things • Alternative Solutions and Methods • Thinking in Pictures and Images • Noticing Things Other People Tend to Ignore • Suppose Something Was Changed . . . What Would Happen If? • Acting and Role Playing • Inventing • Become a . . . and Use Your New Perspectives to Help Us Think About . . . • Use Humor to Show . . . • Explain or Show a New and Better Way to . . . • Figure Out a Way to Explain . . . • Pictures, Picture Books, Doodles, and Icons • Songs • Riddles • Mime or Charades (Think Vocabulary!) • Play • Bumper Stickers or Headlines to Summarize Learning

Figure 4.16 provides an example of differentiating addition tasks by Sternberg's Triarchic Theory.

The following example in Figure 4.17 gives an example of fifth-grade order of operations tasks differentiated by Sternberg's Triarchic Theory.

FIGURE 4.16

STERNBERG ADDITION TASKS

Primary Addition Tasks	
Analytical	Be the Teacher: A student has completed all of the addition problems on the worksheet incorrectly. You need to find all of the mistakes the student made and correct them. Show many different strategies to prove that your new sums are correct.
Practical	Addition in Our World: Find five different times we would need to use addition in our lives. Draw or write your stories, and show the addition equations that go with each story. Model different strategies to prove your sums are correct.
Creative	Make an addition chart with addends from 0 to 10. Find patterns within the chart that model addition facts. Find ways to help us remember the addition facts from memory or, at least, very quickly. You can use manipulatives and mental images as well.

FIGURE 4.17

STERNBERG ORDER OF OPERATIONS TASKS

Fifth-Grade Order of Operations (Smith, 2016)	
Analytical	Make a chart that shows all the ways you can think of to use order of operations to equal 24. Be sure to include all operations and symbols of inclusion. Find a minimum of 10 expressions, and prove that each is equal to 24. Explain how the nature of the operations determines the order of operations.
Practical	A friend is convinced that order of operations is not important. Convince your friend that without using them, you won't always get the correct answers! Show how the same expression could equal two different values if order of operations is not followed. Explain how the nature of the operations determines the order of operations.
Creative	A book company wants help designing pages for a mathematics book that will explain the order of operations. Your pages should include vocabulary, what the order of operations are, why the order is what it is, and examples. The publisher wants the pages to be creative—full of pictures and possibly riddles or other fun ways to engage students with order of operations problems.

Multiple Intelligences Gardner's Multiple Intelligences may be the most familiar of all the learning profile structures. Keep in mind that when you design a lesson based on Multiple Intelligences, you do not have to design tasks for all of the intelligences. Choose the most appropriate tasks for the topic—do not try to force a task to an intelligence just to have it. Figure 4.18 provides possible task ideas for the different Multiple Intelligences.

FIGURE 4.18

MULTIPLE INTELLIGENCE TASKS

Intelligence	Possible Tasks for Mathematical Concept or Skill
Linguistic "The word player"	• Use storytelling to explain . . . • Write a poem, short story, or news article about . . . • Create a mnemonic to remember a process or mathematical facts • Give a presentation • Lead a class discussion • Create a talk show radio program or PSA announcement
Logical/Mathematical "The questioner"	• Interpret or translate the concepts into a mathematical formula, or explain a formula in terms of concepts • Demonstrate, model, or justify a mathematical skill or concept • Make an instruction book on the skill or concept • Design a test with an answer key • Demonstrate how this topic can be linked to other topics we have learned
Spatial "The visualizer"	• Chart or graph . . . • Design a computer presentation, bulletin board, or mural about . . . • Create a piece of art that demonstrates . . . • Make a video finding the concept or skill in the real world
Musical "The music lover"	• Write a song, jingle, or rap that explains . . . • Explain how the music of a song relates . . . • Create a jingle or rap to memorize . . . • Use sheet music to learn fraction addition

(Continued)

FIGURE 4.18 (Continued)

Intelligence	Possible Tasks for Mathematical Concept or Skill
Bodily/ Kinesthetic "The mover"	• Create (and/or perform) a skit that explains . . . • Choreograph a dance that shows steps to a procedure or concept • Build a model • Use manipulatives to learn, practice, or demonstrate . . . • Make or play a game that includes the concepts and skills
Interpersonal "The socializer"	• Conduct a class meeting that discusses . . . • Organize or participate in a group task • Tutor another student • Peer teach
Intrapersonal "The individual"	• Create a personal analogy for . . . • Write notes to self, journal entries, and reminders about the skill or concept • Work independently
Naturalist "The nature lover"	• Describe any patterns you detect • Explain how the concept or skill can be found in the environment • Show how the concept or skill could be applied in nature

(Adapted from Sousa, 2015, p. 204)

Figure 4.19 gives an example of a second-grade lesson on time with tasks designed by Multiple Intelligences.

Modality Another common way that teachers will differentiate tasks is based on learning modalities: Visual, Auditory, and Kinesthetic. This is a learning preference (often referred to as a learning style) rather than a learning intelligence; thus, the research has not shown that using this structure directly increases student achievement. Nevertheless, designing tasks according to modalities can increase buy-in and student interest. Figure 4.20 provides different possible tasks for each area.

FIGURE 4.19

TIME MULTIPLE INTELLIGENCES

Second-Grade Time	
Logical / Mathematical	Use a Venn diagram or Top Hat organizer to compare and contrast analog and digital clocks.
Verbal / Linguistic and Visual / Spatial	Make a picture book explaining how to tell time with analog and digital clocks.
Body / Kinesthetic	Use analog clocks to model digital time. Draw a time out of the envelope, and arrange the hands on the analog clock to show the time. Check with your partners. Or play Time Charades by using your arms to show the time on a clock. Have your friends guess the time.
Naturalist	Draw or find pictures of nature at different times of the day. For each picture, show an appropriate time on an analog or digital clock.

FIGURE 4.20

MODALITY TASKS

	Possible Tasks
Visual	• Make graphs, charts, illustrations, posters, or other visual aids for learning mathematics • Write visual notes—add icons, color, and other symbols to highlight and explain notes • Color code solutions • Read or write mathematical texts, such as write a paragraph to explain . . . • Draw pictures to model or explain . . . • Design / use graphic organizers
Auditory	• Oral presentations or discussions • Present infomercials or PSAs (or other skits) • Create question lists

(Continued)

FIGURE 4.20 (Continued)

		Possible Tasks
		• Books / instructions on tape / recording answers on tape
		• Self-talk (Whispies)
		• Interviews
Kinesthetic		• Use mathematical manipulatives
		• Games
		• Skits
		• Create gestures to fit steps to a process
		• Model mathematics with concrete materials
		• Play charades to reinforce mathematical vocabulary or concepts of number

Figure 4.21 gives a sample lesson for third-grade equivalent fractions differentiated with modality in mind.

FIGURE 4.21

EQUIVALENT FRACTIONS

	Equivalent Fractions
Visual	Make a picture book to explain equivalent fractions. Show many models as to why the fractions are equivalent. Write captions to explain your pictures. Select four different fractions, and find three equivalencies for each.
Auditory	Play Shout Out (groups of three or four): One player serves as a reader and draws a fraction out of the envelope. All other players shout out an equivalent fraction. Each player scores a point if he or she can prove their fraction is equivalent. The next player becomes the reader, and play continues.
Kinesthetic	Model equivalent fractions in several ways: 1. Fold and shade paper 2. Use fraction strips 3. Use fraction circles Record your equivalencies on your paper.

For older students, specific strategies for studying may be helpful. Figure 4.22 gives study suggestions based on Visual, Auditory, and Kinesthetic strategies.

FIGURE 4.22

STUDY STRATEGIES

	Study Strategies
Visual	• Color code notes • Make and use flash cards • Make tables and bulleted notes • Keep study area clean and clutter-free • Sit toward the front of the class to make eye-contact with the teacher
Auditory	• Read notes out loud • Tape-record notes and replay them • Say the steps to solve a problem out loud as you write them • Discuss explanations and procedures with a friend or family member • Put it to music—create your own jingles and mnemonics
Kinesthetic	• Use flash cards as a match game • Make foldables • Use manipulatives to check your answers • Squeeze a stress ball or other squishy object as you study—bring it to a test with you • Take frequent stretch breaks

CLASSROOM STRUCTURES

A final consideration in planning for differentiation is how the classroom should be structured, including movement. In a differentiated classroom, multiple structures for working conditions are used flexibly. A given mathematics period might consist of a whole class, small groups or pairs, and individual work. There is no specific pattern for how or when different configurations are used, but among these, there is generally an ebb and flow. The most typical pattern in a mathematics class is starting whole, moving into guided practice in pairs or groups and ending with individual practice. This structure may be appropriate at times, but it should not be the only sequence used. In fact, this series of arrangements is in contrast to a constructivist approach to learning mathematics where students engage in an activity to explore and make connections. A constructivist approach begins with a small group or paired activity to engage with sense-making and introduction to a topic, concept, or application; then we come together to discuss findings, solidify key ideas, and get any further direction before moving into small groups or pairs for further exploration and finally ending with individual practice. These are just two classroom progressions that are possible. Depending on the day and the lesson, any combinations can be designed.

Most of the differentiated tasks described earlier in the chapter could be done in small groups, pairs, or individually. You need to make the decisions based on the complexity of the task and perhaps on students' preferences for work. The working structure for a specific task could also be a matter of choice for the student.

In designing a differentiated lesson, the classroom structure needs to be considered based on the strength of the structure and the desired outcome:

- *Whole class*—for common knowledge, creating common vocabulary, sharing work, and rich discourse
- *Small group*—for collaborative tasks that benefit from multiple perspectives, multiple tasks, problem solving, and discourse
- *Pairs*—encourages greater participation as students cannot refuse to talk with only one other person, but they can hide in a small group
- *Individual*—for individual accountability, practice, and reflection

When choosing the structure for each segment of the lesson, remember above all that students need to take ownership of their learning. As much as possible, learning should be active and students need to be doing the work, which is more difficult to achieve in whole class than with groups, pairs, or individual task assignments.

CONCLUSION

Remember that differentiation, in essence, is up to the teacher making purposeful decisions about the best ways for each of his or her students to learn and demonstrate important content. There are no ironclad "if-thens." It would be easier if there were, but unfortunately there are not. When designing differentiated tasks for a mathematics lesson, consider:

1. Determine the specific KUD for the lesson from the unit's KUD.

2. Determine what should be differentiated, and what will not be differentiated. Decide how you want to differentiate: readiness, interest, or learning profile. Remember that these can also be combined. Base your differentiation on the students' learning needs.

3. Design or find the differentiated activities or tasks.

   • Most strategies you already use can be differentiated. Look at the strategy or task, and decide which students would best benefit from it as written. Determine what would prevent other students from learning well with the task or strategy as written. Adjust the strategy or task accordingly, or determine a related strategy or task for other learners.

   • Gather a collection of ideas from colleagues, resources, the Internet, and your imagination. Instead of choosing the one task that you think will best work, decide which students may benefit from a particular approach or task and why. Then use all of the ideas for which students could best benefit.

   • No matter how you are choosing to differentiate, remember that all tasks should address the same broad learning outcome. For example, you might differentiate based on a strategy preference (base 10 blocks vs. a hundreds chart), but all students are still exploring place value and addition using strategies and models.

4. Decide which parts of the lesson will be done in which classroom arrangement: whole class, small groups, pairs, or individually.

This chapter has provided many different ways to differentiate for your students. Please remember that these are ideas from which you will choose. If you are continuing your journey in differentiation, I hope this provides you with further ideas and examples. If you are at the start of your journey, consider some advice. Do not try to do too many things at once, combine too many aspects of differentiation into single lessons, or become overwhelmed. Start with what makes most sense to you. Start with a single activity that is differentiated. Start small, but start.

FREQUENTLY ASKED QUESTIONS

Q: How do you decide whether to differentiate by readiness, interest, learning profile, or a combination?

A: The decision by what to differentiate is largely a teacher decision. The overwhelming factor is the need you see in your students for differentiation. If there are learning gaps in essential prerequisite learning, readiness needs to be the choice. Readiness can also be accomplished through learning profile or interest-differentiated tasks mixed with readiness, and either adjusting readiness within the tasks or having students with a higher readiness coaching those with a lower readiness. Learning profile provides specific structures by which to design tasks, and students can be given the choice of tasks, which will make it an interest differentiation. Keep in mind the purposes of interest (motivation) and learning profile (ease of learning) in making your choices. Sometimes you might want to choose a specific structure or aspect simply because it has not been used in quite a while and you need some novelty in class.

Q: How often should lessons or tasks be differentiated?

A: There is no correct number of times to differentiate. When a teacher is first beginning the journey of differentiation, trying to differentiate one task or lesson every week or two is probably enough. It becomes easier and more natural the more often you try, though. In fact, you will find that over time, it becomes as natural to plan a differentiated lesson as it does a whole class lesson. Often, you will find that the whole class lesson does not work any longer because you will recognize the students for whom the lesson will not work or fit, and wonder what to do about them. That's when you realize that it's happened . . . you are now fully differentiated.

Keepsakes and Plans

What are the keepsake ideas from this chapter, those thoughts or ideas that resonated with you that you do not want to forget?

Differentiation and KUD:

1.

2.

3.

Strategies: Choosing to Differentiate

1.

2.

3.

Strategies: Readiness

1.

2.

3.

Strategies: Interest

1.

2.

3.

(Continued)

(Continued)

Strategies: Learning Profile

1.

2.

3.

Classroom Structures:

1.

2.

3.

Based on my keepsake ideas, I plan to:

1.

2.

3.

CHAPTER FIVE

SET IT UP

ESTABLISHING THE RIGHT TONE
TO MAKE DIFFERENTIATION DOABLE

Where learning takes place is one of the intangible factors for learning. A safe learning environment where students collaborate and grapple with deep concepts, view mistakes as learning opportunities, and a growth mindset is promoted will enable differentiation and learning to flourish. In this chapter, you will find:

I once worked in a district where the attitude seemed to be that the students just couldn't _____. You fill in the blank. Students would look at you and say, "We don't do that here. Don't you know we are from (name of district)" or "I can't do that. I'm from (district), you know." Sitting around a conference table working on lessons and activities with a group of teachers, I quietly tallied how many times I was told that their kids couldn't do something. In frustration, I finally told the teachers that they were right. Their kids couldn't do these things. Nevertheless, it was probably more about their mindsets and attitudes about the students rather than the students themselves. They had said "these kids can't" 12 times in 20 minutes. On digesting this information, one teacher finally said, "Well, maybe they can. But they won't." Most likely you have worked with students also who "won't." Establishing a learning environment where all students are willing to try, are not afraid to fail, and value both as part of the learning process is foundational to all learning and especially to learning in a differentiated mathematics classroom.

We have now looked at most of the essential components of building a differentiated mathematics classroom: Understanding the big picture of differentiation; getting to know our students as learners; clarifying mathematical content through determining what students should Know, Understand, and be able to Do; and purposefully choosing and designing tasks and activities based on your students and content. Designing instruction to invite your students to learn is essential for differentiation; yet building the learning community is equally essential. It is possible to design a beautiful lesson and have it fail because the classroom environment was not established and maintained for successful differentiation or the learning of mathematics. The learning environment is often one of the intangibles that makes or breaks the quality of student learning.

A HEALTHY LEARNING ENVIRONMENT

Students today want to belong. They want to be accepted for who they are, strengths and weaknesses, and they want to know that they are known. They come to us with their own experiences and beliefs about their capabilities in mathematics and learning mathematics, as well as how they fit. Sometimes their background experiences can break our hearts if they have been told explicitly or experientially that they do not measure up. As teachers we quickly recognize the student with whom no one else wants to partner, or the withdrawn child who can't wait for recess, or . . . you name the type of child. Establishing a classroom community that expects that we all learn together and with each other in various pairings or groupings, that embraces and provides a safe place for mistake-making in the mathematical learning process, can go a long way to establishing a safe environment where students know one another and are known. This collaboration and belonging does not "just happen." It is taught and nurtured.

WATCH IT!

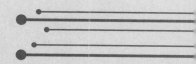

While watching Video 5.1, *Establishing and Maintaining a Healthy Classroom Environment*, consider the following questions:

1. What similarities and differences do you see among the teachers' approaches to developing a healthy mathematics classroom environment?

2. What is the role of student leadership and ownership in a healthy learning environment?

3. What are indicators of a healthy mathematics-learning community?

Video 5.1 Establishing and Maintaining a Healthy Classroom Environment

Since much of learning mathematics and designing differentiated learning tasks depends on collaboration, expectations for group functioning should be taught and maintained. For example, Figure 5.1 shows a poster from Jayne DeMeuse's classroom that promotes positive group work.

During the first weeks of school, I spend as much time—and sometimes more—establishing my environment, norms, and routines as I do with content. I hear the panic in your mind right now as you think, "But we have so much content to get through now!" I understand, but firmly know that a strong and healthy learning environment will increase effective learning and, thus, stretch your learning time over the long haul. In fact, brain research connects the physiology of the brain, learning environment, and the ability to learn (Sousa & Tomlinson, 2011; Willis, 2006).

FIGURE 5.1

GROUPS

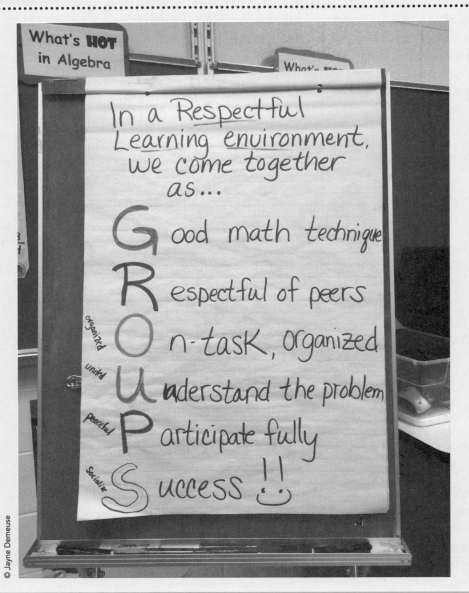

According to David Sousa and Carol Ann Tomlinson (2011), before a brain can pay attention to the learning process, students must feel physically safe and emotionally secure. If a student is feeling strong negative emotions, the limbic system of the brain kicks in and stops our cognitive processing and at the same time increases our memory of any negativity to support survival. By contrast, a positive learning environment increases endorphins in the bloodstream, which creates a positive feeling. This in turn stimulates the brain's frontal lobe to support a positive memory of the learning objective as well as the experience. Finally, a negative learning environment leads to increased cortisol in the bloodstream, which raises the learner's anxiety level, shuts down any processing of the lesson content (the brain considers it to be low priority) to prioritize the stressful situation. So you see, a healthy learning environment is much more important to establish and maintain than we might have given it credit. Our own physiology prevents us from learning when we don't feel safe and accepted!

The relationships we build among our students impact the learning of our students. One way to have students make connections yet show their own uniqueness is an activity called "Uniquely Me."

TRY IT! UNIQUELY ME

Give students an index card on which they put their name at the top and number from 1 to 5. Students will write a <u>true</u> statement about themselves on each line. Warn students that these will be read out loud, so each statement should be appropriate to be shared in class.

- Line 1—Write something that is true about yourself that is also true of **almost everyone** else in the room ("I'm a math student").

- Line 2—Write something that is true about yourself that is also true of **most** people in the room ("I like to be challenged in math").

- Line 3—Write something that is true about yourself that is also true of **some** people in the room ("I have more than one pet").

- Line 4—Write something that is true about yourself that is also true of a **few** people in the room ("I play the drums").

- Line 5—Write something that is **uniquely true about you** ("I am a twin").

- The teacher randomly draws a card from the stack and reads the first statement. If the statement is true about you as a student, stand up. If not, stay seated.

- Read the second statement. If it is also true, the student stays standing. If it is no longer true, the student sits down. Once a student is seated, he or she stays seated throughout the reading of the rest of the card.

- Continue to read through the card with students sitting down as the statements are no longer true about them.

- When the last statement is read, hopefully only the student whose card is being read will be standing. Have all students clap and welcome that student.

(Smith, 2017)

In a healthy learning environment, everyone should feel accepted and welcome, and all students make the other students feel welcome and accepted too. So how do you do it?

- Begin by modeling what it looks and sounds like to listen to each other, find out about each other, and appreciate each other.

- Use "get to know each other" activities such as People Bingo and Interest Inventories, especially at the beginning of the year.

- Continue community-building activities throughout the year as quick energizers. Be aware if the community is starting to break down to avoid the typical cliques and outcasts that are often found within a classroom.

- For more specific activities, look at the following Try It! activities.

TRY IT! ALL FRIENDS

Purpose: To get to know one another and to continue to build relationships

1. Have the class number off by twos, dividing the class into two groups. Have the "ones" form a tight circle, and then turn out so that the students' backs are toward the center of the circle and the students are facing out. Have the remaining students (the "twos") face one of the "ones," forming an outer circle. This structure is called "Inside-Outside" circles or a Wagon Wheel.

2. The teacher stands in the center of the concentric circles so that he or she can lean in any direction and hear the conversations occurring. The teacher in the center poses questions, and each pair of students tells each other their answers.

3. Questions can be anything that will help students get to know each other and make connections. It would be appropriate to share mathematics experiences as well.

4. After both partners answer the question, the teacher rotates one of the circles. For example, you might have the outside circle rotate three to the left. Now everyone has a new partner and another question is asked.

5. Continue this for the allotted amount of time, alternating which circle rotates, and ensuring that after each rotation, students are with someone new.

Note: This structure is effective for reviewing content as well! Give each student a review problem (or a current practice problem, counting card, etc.). Students work each other's problems (for more complex problems, I put the answers on back) and then check their answers. They trade cards and rotate in a circle. With every rotation, students are "experts" with a new problem and a new partner.

All Friends is a great activity to build class community and, as noted, can be used throughout the year in a wide variety of ways. The next activity emphasizes the importance of working together and listening to each other.

TRY IT! HE SAID, SHE SAID

Purpose: Developing listening and reporting skills

To encourage students to listen actively to one another, have them share something about someone that was only told to them by that person.

1. Following an introductory paired activity (questionnaire, drawing of me, or other get-to-know-you game), have students introduce each other to the class.

2. Whenever students work in pairs or groups throughout the year, challenge students to share something they heard or learned from their partner or group member instead of sharing what they have said.

It can be a challenge learning to listen, for all of us! We often are thinking of what we want to say rather than listening to what the person talking is saying. We interrupt each other. The next activity is designed to help a class listen to one another and time responses.

TRY IT! COUNT TO TEN

Purpose: Develop discourse skills

This activity is very quick and usually pretty funny. I do this to establish strong listening and responding habits.

1. Tell the class that we are going to count to ten together. Easy, right?

2. Here is the catch: I will begin by saying "one." Only one person can count the next number, so if two people talk at the same time we have to start over.

3. If there is too long of a gap before someone says the next number, we have to start over. I've had a class take three months to make it to 10!

4. As students continue to interrupt, speak at the same time, or have speaking gaps, be sure to remind students that we are learning to listen to each other and time our responses. It is important that as we talk together, we truly listen to each other and think about how and when to reply. This exercise practices that skill.

One way to establish that we all learn together and with each other is to be sure to mix groupings and pairings of students continually. We want students to wonder with whom they will be working today. We encourage the idea that we can all learn from everyone else in the classroom. Often, when I ask pairs or groups to share out, I only allow the speaker to share something that someone else said. This greatly increases the importance of listening and understanding each other as we work together. Another strategy to share what students have in common is called Get on the Bus. This is an activity that students of all ages, and adults, have fun with.

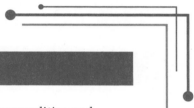

TRY IT! GET ON THE BUS

Purpose: Establish community and celebrate commonalities and differences

1. Divide the students into two groups. Have students line up side by side, facing each other with a space in between the two lines.

2. Make a statement for the students to agree or disagree with, for example, "I enjoy solving hard problems."

3. If students agree, they "get on the bus" by stepping forward into the space. This will show students whom they have connections with in different areas. Depending on the statements you make, this can be learning and personal preferences. Some statement ideas:

    • I love animals (dogs, cats, horses, etc.)

    • I have older/younger brothers or sisters

    • I love number puzzles

    • I like playing math games

    • I read for pleasure

    • If I need to concentrate, I need things to be quiet

    • I like working with others better than alone on schoolwork

- I like to watch someone do something first; then I will try it

- I would rather jump in and try something than watching or listening to someone do it

- I like using a lot of color when I take notes (or work on a project)

- I sometimes get frustrated with homework and stop doing it

In a learning community, students need to appreciate one another, especially their similarities and differences.

EMBRACING FAIR

I often hear the concern from teachers that if they differentiate, students will ask why different things are happening in the classroom, and that students will perceive that it "isn't fair that I have to do this and they get to do that." This is a legitimate concern if you differentiate without establishing an environment to support differentiation. The first step to establishing this environment is to help students understand the basics of differentiation. I explain to students that in our classroom we are all teachers and we are all learners together, but since we learn differently from each other, sometimes it is necessary for us to do different tasks in order for each of us to learn. Students understand this. An excellent third–fourth-grade teacher, Judy Rex, told me that one of her students went up to a substitute teacher who was following her lesson plans and informed her that they didn't really learn like this. When the substitute asked what he meant, he said, "You see, we all learn differently so Mrs. Rex makes sure we each get what we need to learn. We never all do the same things. That wouldn't be fair because we wouldn't all learn that way." He certainly understood the basis of differentiation, and why different learning opportunities may be needed to maximize learning. There is a quote often used that says, "Fair isn't everybody getting the same thing. Fair is everybody getting what they need." It is important for students to redefine "fair" in this way so that different tasks and assignments become natural and appreciated instead of questionable.

There are several ways to teach students about differentiation, and the amount of detail you explain to students should depend on the age of the students. It is interesting that no student is concerned whether they have a different interest than another, or a different learning preference than another. Nevertheless, readiness can carry a stigma that should not be. One way to talk to students about readiness differences is to look around the class and point out that not many students are wearing glasses. Since not everyone wears glasses, no one should be allowed to wear glasses. Have students discuss the silliness of this. This same principle should apply to learning—if there is support needed, support should be given. The goal is that everyone is able to enter the learning process where they need to enter, and learn!

TRY IT! TARGETING READINESS

Purpose: Develop understanding and acceptance of readiness differentiation

1. Put up a chart with three columns: Too Easy, Just Right, and Too Hard.

2. Ask students to tell how they feel when a task or lesson is too easy. How does it feel when it is too hard? How does it feel when it is just right?

3. List their descriptions in the columns.

4. Tell your students that it is your job as their teacher to hit each student's target and to get it "just right" for each student. The problem is that "just right" is not the same for each student. That is why we might do different tasks or someone may seem to be doing something easier or harder than I am. As your teacher, I want everyone to work equally hard! It is important that we all work hard so that we all learn. Figure 5.2 gives an example of Targeting Readiness.

FIGURE 5.2

TARGETING READINESS

Too Easy	Just Right	Too Hard
• Bored		• Bored
• Waste of time		• Waste of time
• Mind wanders		• Mind wanders
• Slow		• Dumb
• Sleepy	• Smart	• Embarrassed
• Mad	• Proud of myself	• Mad
	• Excited	
	• Energized	

Another way to build community as well as to continue to teach our students about differentiation is to extend some of the "get-to-know-each-other" activities to include talking about our learning profiles as well. In Chapter 2, Meet Up, there were several methods shared for determining students' learning profiles. For example, letting students share their favorite mathematical learning activity and asking who else enjoys that will form learning connections. When discussing learning profile with students, have students raise their hands to identify which learning profiles they most naturally align to in mathematics. As students look around the class, they see who learns in similar ways and who does not. This also creates more understanding about differentiation for students, and why you will often have different tasks for different students. It creates a learning environment where doing different things is not only acceptable but also appreciated.

EVERYBODY LEARNS

We are about learning. Sometimes that gets lost. In my classroom, I had a big banner across the back that simply said, "Everybody Learns." If students asked why they had to do something,

I pointed to the banner. We repeatedly discussed that in our class, everybody learns. In our class, it doesn't matter where you enter learning, it matters that you DO enter learning. It doesn't matter how you want to learn and practice, it matters that you do. And the bottom line of everything we do is that everybody learns. Between understanding that we all learn differently and that we all can learn, we have the foundation for understanding differentiation.

Unfortunately mathematics is one of the subjects in which students carry a belief that they are unable to learn. Parents tell their students that they were not good in mathematics. We often have an uphill battle in mathematics when it comes to learning attitudes. A teacher told me yesterday about a student in her class who constantly says that she isn't any good at mathematics and can't learn it. She then told me that the first time she met the student's mother, the mother introduced her daughter by saying that she isn't very good at mathematics . . . before she ever said her name! These attitudes cannot be allowed in our classrooms.

MINDSETS

Attitudes and belief systems shape everything in our lives, even when we are not aware of them. This is especially true with learning. What we believe, as teachers or students, about what constitutes "smart" or "good at math" effects our effort in learning and even how we talk with one another. We use the term "mindset" (Dweck, 2006) in conversations regularly regarding student attitudes. Dr. Dweck's work describes two types of mindsets: growth and fixed. Figure 5.3 provides examples of each type of mindset, and how the different mindsets affect teachers' and students' mathematics beliefs.

Dr. Jo Boaler has advanced the study of mindset, specifically for mathematics. In her latest book, *Mathematical Mindsets* (2015), Boaler explains that research shows how elastic our brains truly are. In fact, she points out that practicing a task 10 minutes a day for 15 days has been shown to change the synapses and connections within our brains. This is exciting news. Additionally, teaching students about this research has a significant impact on student performance.

> Just telling students that their intelligence is under their own control improves their effort on school work and performance. In two separate studies,

FIGURE 5.3

MINGSETS

Teacher Fixed Mindset	Teacher Growth Mindset
I can't do much about the way kids come to me. Some are just too far behind in mathematics.	With support, multiple approaches and belief in my students, I believe most students can accomplish most tasks in mathematics.
There are some people who just can't learn mathematics.	Everyone is able to learn deep concepts and strategies in mathematics, perhaps at different rates and with different experiences. There is no gene-determining ability for or against mathematical learning.
Students can't go far without memorizing mathematical facts.	Knowing mathematical facts certainly eases many mathematical processes, but knowing facts does not precede reasoning. In fact, reasoning can help make sense of mathematical facts in order to recall them more fluidly.
I stick to my mathematics textbook because I don't want my students to ask a question to which I don't know the answer	Learning and reasoning together is the most powerful learning of all—for both the teacher and the students. Most set programs do not give the depth of understanding or problem solving that current standards demand.
Student Fixed Mindset	**Student Growth Mindset**
You are born smart or you aren't, and success comes from genetics. How your parents were in math is how you will be too.	Effort in math has more to do with success than how I was born.
Challenge is scary.	Challenge is invigorating.
Mistakes are wrong and bad.	Mistakes grow my brain.
I am who I am and there isn't much anyone can do about it.	I am constantly changing and growing, and new tasks and challenges help make me who I am.
Math is hard for most people.	I can be successful at math if I give my best effort.
Math is right and wrong, and you have to be good at memorizing.	Math is connections, patterns, and problem solving. If you understand the connections and reasoning, most problems can be figured out.
I'm good at math because I know my facts and can do problems faster than most.	I'm good at math because I can problem solve, use multiple strategies and representations, and communicate.

students [were taught] how the brain works, explaining that the students possessed the ability, if they worked hard, to make themselves smarter. This erased up to half of the difference between minority and white achievement levels. (Nisbet, 2009)

Even more and more morning announcements at various schools end with the message to "make it a great day . . . or not. The choice is yours." How wonderful to enforce to students that their attitude is really in their own control. We also need to empower our students to understand that their effort makes the greatest difference for their success . . . and we probably need to educate our parents as well. No longer shall we allow "but I'm not a math person, and neither is my mom" in our classrooms!

Indicators of students' growth mindsets include their willingness to take a risk, make mistakes, combine and invent strategies, and in general, go for it!

WATCH IT!

As you watch Video 5.2, *Encouraging a Growth Mindset in Primary Classrooms*, consider the following questions:

1. How do teachers teach and create a growth mindset with their students?

2. How do the teachers continue to enforce a growth mindset?

3. How do students exhibit a growth mindset?

4. How does the classroom environment and culture add to the mindset disposition of both students and the teacher?

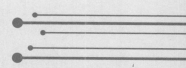

Video 5.2 Encouraging a Growth Mindset in Primary Classrooms

One way by which we can establish growth mindsets in students is simply to have phrases and expectations that express growth mindsets. Figure 5.4 shows a bulletin board from Kim Farless's classroom promoting practical changes in thought processes to promote growth mindset.

FIGURE 5.4

GROWTH MINDSET BULLETIN BOARD

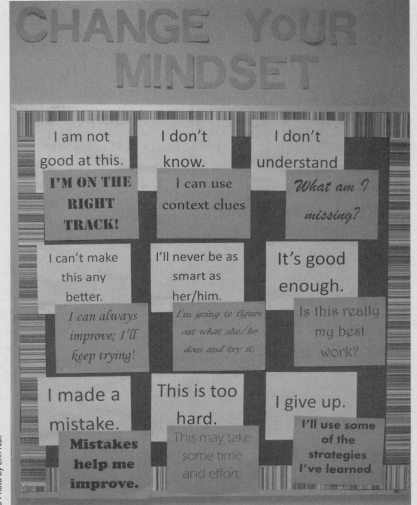

© Photo by Erin Null

WATCH IT!

As you watch Video 5.3, *Introducing a Growth Mindset in the Intermediate Classroom*, consider the following questions:

1. How does the teacher introduce a growth mindset?

2. How would you relate mindset and struggle? How do the students in the video?

3. How do students exhibit a fixed mindset?

4. How does Mrs. Potter explain the value of mistakes? How can you explain this to your students?

5. What analogies and comparisons are, or could be, used to make sense of growth mindset?

Video 5.3 Introducing a Growth Mindset in the Intermediate Classroom

Not only is it important to teach our students about having a growth mindset, but we also need them to practice adopting a growth mindset. The following activities can be done in class to help students develop a growth mindset and a learning environment to support productive struggle.

TRY IT! TRASHING FEARS

Purpose: Establish a safe place to learn mathematics

What fears do your students have about learning mathematics? Have them write their fears on quarter sheets of scratch paper—one fear per sheet. Then wad them up and throw them away! Your fears are trashed because in our classroom, that won't happen. I believe in you, and your classmates will support you until you believe in yourself.

Research indicates that teaching students that their brains grow with effort will directly impact their effort. As teachers we need to make explicit connections among effort, brain growth, and success. The next two activities are ways to have students voice their own understanding of the connections.

TRY IT! YOUR BRAIN WITH EFFORT

Purpose: To solidify the belief that effort matters most

1. After discussing the plasticity of the brain and the current research on mindset and effort, have students draw a "Before Effort and After Effort" of their brains.

2. Have students research or create their own sayings about effort and brain growth. Create bumper stickers and posters. (Adapted from YouCubed.org)

Even though these Try It! activities will reinforce what a growth mindset is, and the importance of effort for your students, it is also important to embed discussion about effort and mindset within a learning task or as part of the closure to a lesson. This will help make growth mindset and the willingness to struggle a more natural part of learning, in general, and learning mathematics, in particular.

WATCH IT!

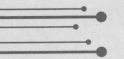

As you watch Video 5.4, *Discussing Productive Struggle*, consider the following questions:

1. What is the difference between productive struggle and frustration? How do you recognize it as a teacher? How can a student recognize it?

2. What are some ways to reinforce the positive role of struggle within a task?

3. How can discussing struggle, difficulty, and ease change students' views of what it means to be "good in math?"

Video 5.4 Discussing Productive Struggle

Praise

Perhaps one of the most powerful, yet easy, adjustments we can make to facilitate a healthy mindset is to be aware of how and for what we praise students. We should continue to praise effort and helpfulness. In addition, add praising mistakes (and willingness to share a mistake) and great questions. Do not praise results or speed, and NEVER say anything along the lines of "you're so smart. . . . " Try praising students in the following ways:

1. Praise the process, not the person or result. Eliminate words that imply it is about anything other than effort. Don't praise good scores or say a student is smart!

   - I am so proud of how long you worked on this.

   - What a great strategy to try!

   - You really caught your mistake there.

   - Thank you for trying so hard and not giving up.

   - I can see that you put a lot of time and thought into this.

2. Give real and specific praise. Keep it real and don't praise something that isn't demonstrating growth or effort. Students will know it is false. Acknowledge growth.

   - It's ok. Everyone makes mistakes and that is how we learn and grow our brains.

   - Look at the progress you made on this problem compared to the last time you tried.

3. Be positive.

   - I know you are struggling right now, but I also know you can do this.

   - I've seen how hard you tried when you ___, so I know you can do it again.

A healthy learning environment is dependent not only on the emotional climate but also on the routines that make differentiation run smoothly.

CONCLUSION

The learning environment is a make-or-break factor in successful differentiation. Creating a culture where students understand

and value struggle as the necessary process for success not only promotes the necessary growth mindset in students but also erases the potential stigma of differentiating by readiness. It is clearly understood that everyone in our class works equally hard, works together in various configurations, and is supported and challenged appropriately. In our class, we value and appreciate our differences and recognize that we learn as much if not more from others who think and work differently from us. No matter what it takes to learn in our classroom, that is what we are about. For in our class, Everybody Learns!

FREQUENTLY ASKED QUESTIONS

Q: What do we do with a student who will not work until I am standing or sitting with him or her?

A: Students who do not engage with work until a teacher is present have learned that behavior. To break their dependence, do not reinforce it. As described earlier, help students clearly understand the task at hand, and how to take the first step. Have students explain back to you the first step to be sure they understand what they are to do. Once they can tell you what the step is, walk away and have them complete the step on their own. Circle back to check on their progress, and then repeat the process with the next step or two. In this way, encourage their independence while supporting them as needed. This process will allow them to feel successful and develop a growth mindset that focuses on effort.

Q: What do I do with students who refuse to work with other students?

A: There are times when students are not permitted to work together because of a discipline plan, a 504 accommodation, or other legal document. These specifications must be followed. Other than that, do not allow put downs or refusal to work with other students. It is important that students know and understand how to work with others, whether they are friends outside of class or not. One way to encourage all students working together is to remind students that working groups are flexible, often for a specific task or designated number of minutes. With this said, learning is the most important outcome of our classrooms, and if a specific pairing of students will prevent learning, do not put the students together.

Keepsakes and Plans

What are the keepsake ideas from this chapter, those thoughts or ideas that resonated with you that you do not want to forget?

A Healthy Learning Environment:

1.

2.

3.

Embracing Fair:

1.

2.

3.

Everybody Learns:

1.

2.

3.

Mindset and Praise:

1.

2.

3.

Based on my keepsake ideas, I plan to

1.

2.

3.

CHAPTER SIX

POWER ON

MASTERING AND MODELING DAILY ROUTINES FOR ACHIEVEMENT ALL YEAR

We continue our look at the learning environment. A safe learning environment for students is based not only on the students' affect but also on the day-to-day running of the classroom. There is a sense of confidence in both the teacher and the students in a class where expectations and routines are understood and well organized. In this chapter, you will find:

Classroom Routines
    Assigning Groups
    Giving Directions
    Monitoring the Work
    Planning Flexible Time

Frequently Asked Questions
Keepsakes and Plans

Have you ever noticed how crazy classrooms can look on a teen sitcom? Kids are all over the place, throwing things, talking to each other on topics having nothing to do with learning . . . you've got the picture. Thankfully that is not how classrooms generally look, although I have seen some that come close. No matter how beautiful a lesson can be designed on paper, learning cannot occur if the learning environment is not set up for success, if routines are not established and followed consistently, or if differentiated tasks are not monitored correctly.

CLASSROOM ROUTINES

One concern that many teachers have as they consider differentiating instruction is how to manage different tasks and groups simultaneously. Truthfully, there is not too much difference between managing groups doing the same task and managing groups doing different tasks. You need to be able to

- Effectively assign groups or partners if that is the classroom structure being used
- Give directions for the various tasks
- Monitor the learning
- Have a plan for students who finish early or need more time

ASSIGNING GROUPS

The most important aspect about assigning groups is determining who will be in each group. One hallmark of a differentiated classroom is flexible grouping (Tomlinson, 2001). Flexible groups means that a group can be put together for the next 10 to 15 minutes for a specific task only, or longer standing groups that will change periodically throughout the year such as assigned seating groups. The specific group you will assign for a given task should be dependent on the task and not on student proximity.

Task Groups

If you have designed a differentiated task and want to assign students to groups for the specific task, the first step is to determine by what aspect of differentiation the task is designed: readiness, interest, learning profile, or a combination.

For assigned groups, the task will most likely be based on readiness or a previously determined interest or learning profile preference.

When grouping for readiness:

- Determine whether the group should be mixed readiness or a more homogeneous readiness grouping to address specific needs. There will be time for both. If addressing specific readiness needs, the groups will need to be more homogeneous.

  - For a more homogeneous grouping, design the tiered activity (see Chapter 4). With your roster, make a list of every student who can do the highest tier task. Next, list all of the students who can do the next level task, and so on. Continue until all of the students are assigned a specific task. Make random groups from the lists by tasks.

  - For more heterogeneous readiness groups, blend bands of readiness such as high to mid-high; mid-high to mid-low; and mid-low to low. These will be more beneficial working groups than the traditional high-low-middle-middle that usually do not function as well.

When grouping for interest:

- Determine whether you want to allow students to choose their own groups based on the task or with whom they would want to work. One possible flaw with having students choose their groups on the fly is that they will likely choose a task based on who else chose that task, rather than the task that will most likely work best for them.

- If you want to assign interest groups, survey students for their choices prior to assigning groups. One way is to explain the optional tasks, and have students list their top two choices on a sticky note or index card. From the list of their preferences, form the groups. A similar option is to have students write down their choice of task prior to forming groups. They can write their choice on a sticky note and then find a partner or small group based on their sticky notes.

WATCH IT!

As you watch Video 6.1, *Empowering Students with Choice,* consider the following questions:

1. How were students' interest used to form the working groups in this lesson?

2. How else was interest used throughout the activities?

3. How does Mrs. Francis use interest to develop student ownership and responsibility for learning?

Video 6.1 Empowering Students with Choice

When grouping for learning profile:

- One option for learning profile groups is to design the tasks according to learning profile and to allow students to choose the task they would like to do. If you would like to have groups, follow the strategies for interest grouping stated earlier.

- To assign learning profile groups, determine from the task what aspect of learning profile is being accessed. Align this with your knowledge of how your students best learn. Form groups from there.

Standing Groups

Standing groups are groups or pairings that are arranged in advanced and maintained for a period of time. Standing groups can be changed on marking periods or four to five times during the year to add variety. There are several ways to form and manage standing groups.

Clock Partners

Clock Partners is a structure to predetermine partners. To make a clock partner, a student asks another student to be his or her partner at a specific time, for example, 12:00. Each student writes the other student's name on the 12:00 line, and they now have an appointment at 12:00. A sample clock is shown in Figure 6.1.

On one clock, a variety of partners can be established:

- Allow students to choose partners at 12:00, 4:00, and 8:00.

- At 2:00, assign a partner that has a similar mathematics learning profile (see Chapter 2).

- At 6:00, assign a partner with a similar mathematics readiness level.

- At 10:00, assign a partner who will approach problems in a different manner. This can be through a different preference for representation, how to practice, or a different approach to problem solving.

On a single clock, you now have six different partners, three that are student chosen and three that are teacher chosen for differentiation. To use the clock, tell students which appointment time they will be meeting with for the task. If all students are working on the same task, use one of their choices at 12:00, 4:00, or 8:00. If the task is differentiated, use the appropriate time of 2:00 for learning profile, 6:00 for readiness, or 10:00 for an open-ended, problem-solving task.

Quadrilateral Groups

Similar to the clock partners, quadrilateral groups form groups of four instead of pairs. I have students form their own groups of four with the parallelogram and square shapes, and I assign trapezoid, rhombus, and rectangle groups. You can assign students with similar learning profile characteristics to the trapezoid group, similar readiness to the rhombus group, and a mixed readiness or learning profile group for the rectangle group. Figure 6.2 gives an example of quadrilateral groups.

The names of the group members are written inside the quadrilateral.

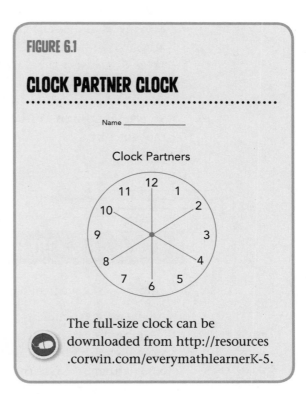

FIGURE 6.1

CLOCK PARTNER CLOCK

Name _____

Clock Partners

The full-size clock can be downloaded from http://resources.corwin.com/everymathlearnerK-5.

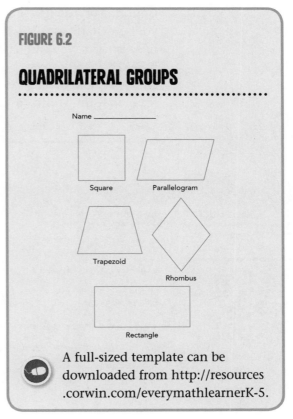

FIGURE 6.2

QUADRILATERAL GROUPS

Name _____

Square Parallelogram

Trapezoid

Rhombus

Rectangle

A full-sized template can be downloaded from http://resources.corwin.com/everymathlearnerK-5.

Moving in and out of groups should not take a long time, although in most classes, it does. Having groups preassigned saves this wasted time. Having students practice moving in and out of groups, including moving any desks if needed, should be practiced to save even more time, and it provides an element of fun as students try to beat their previous movement times.

TRY IT! STOPWATCH DRILLS

Purpose: To move in and out of groups quickly and fluidly

Challenge your students to see how quickly they can form their groups, sit together, and be ready to learn. I conduct stopwatch drills by telling students they will work with their 6:00 partners. . . . Go! Time how long it takes for the class to be seated and ready, and record the time on your whiteboard. Continue practicing at random times to see whether you can beat your previous best time. If you teach more than one section of mathematics, you can have the classes compete for the quickest time. This is a fun race, but it serves to get students moving effectively and quickly. Most classes should be able to move and be ready to learn within 75 seconds.

WATCH IT!

As you watch Video 6.2, *Clock Partners Grouping Strategy*, consider the following questions:

1. How does the teacher move students into pairs?

2. How do the students know what to do with their partners?

3. How efficiently do students move to be with their partners and begin work?

Video 6.2 Clock Partners Grouping Strategy

GIVING DIRECTIONS

Many students have difficulty following multistep directions—imagine hearing several sets of directions for various tasks all at once, of which you will only being doing one. This only serves to create confusion or to cause students to want to do something that another group is doing. Giving directions for differentiated activities can be confusing, and so they need to be given carefully. The key to giving directions with differentiated tasks is to give only the directions that are needed to the students who need them.

Depending on the age of the student, directions can be given in different ways. Young students can be directed to a specific area of the room, and specific instructions can be given once they are in place. Primary students should have familiar tasks with which to work independently, such as games that have been played as a whole class previously, or paper-and-pencil activities that have already been established. When the students get to the designated area, the activities are set up and students know how to begin. Figure 6.3 shows Lori Everson's MATH rotations that she uses daily for mathematical differentiation: M for Math Games, A for All On My Own, T for Teacher Time, and H for Hmmmm, which is usually something new. Students often have choices at each station, or they may only do one or two of the stations based on their current need. Students are told at which station they are to begin and then follow the rotation.

One way to provide directions to young children at stations is to record your directions and have students play the directions at the station. To make the recorded directions more clear, have a completed model at the station. Another strategy for giving directions with younger students is to prepare a "station leader" for each station. Prepare a student with how the station should work and what are the directions for the station. The student will begin at that station but also go back to the station at each rotation to help the next group with directions.

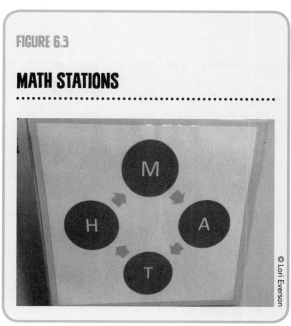

FIGURE 6.3

MATH STATIONS

© Lori Everson

Older students will be able to follow a task card for directions. Task cards can be placed in a folder with the supplies needed for a specific task or placed at the location where the task will occur. Often task cards can be put on a group of desks or a table where the group will be working on that specific task.

Of course, as students are working, the first step for monitoring the different pairs, groups, or individuals will be to circulate and make sure that everyone understands their task and is working correctly.

MONITORING THE WORK

Monitoring the work in a differentiated mathematics classroom has little difference from monitoring the work when all students are doing the same task. If students are working in pairs or groups, be sure to make your way to each grouping, beginning with the pair or group about whom you have the greatest concern. A word of caution though: It is possible to get "sucked in" to one specific group, and the rest of the class could grow restless or wander off-task while you work with only a small number of students.

It is more effective to talk with struggling groups only about the next step, and then go check other groups and bounce back to the original to see whether they have completed that first step.

TIPS FOR ELL/SPECIAL EDUCATION STUDENTS

1. Underline key words in the directions on a task card, and provide a picture of what the word means.

2. Whenever possible, reduce the number of words in the directions.

3. Provide a completed step-by-step model for students who are learning the language.

4. Have students practice saying the directions to another student and then showing what the directions mean by modeling or drawing.

After that, discuss the next step and go check other groups, bounce back to see whether step 2 is completed, and so on. In this way, you do not get caught helping a few students all the way through a task or process, and you begin to train independence in those students who tend to be dependent on a teacher's presence to begin or to try.

Another tip for monitoring groups is to set some group rules and/or roles. It is important to teach students explicitly the expectations of working together, how to be productive, and how to deal with conflict should there be a problem. Since different groups will most likely be involved in different tasks in a differentiated mathematics class, it is even more important that groups can function independently since they might be the only group on a specific task. The particular roles you choose for your groups are probably not as important as everyone having a role and feeling that they are an important member and need to contribute for the success of the group. Some group roles include

- *Director*—Reads directions out loud and makes sure that the directions are being followed as the group works.

- *Facilitator*—Helps the director to keep the group on task and moving. May assign specific jobs to the members to complete the task. Checks to see that everyone is contributing and trying.

- *Technician*—Helps check accuracy of calculations, may give suggestions for the plan to solve a problem, and makes sure that everyone is recording the group's work if required. May also be in charge of technology if part of the task.

- *Material Manager*—Gathers materials, makes sure all are using the materials appropriately, and after the group cleans up its area, returns the materials.

- *Time Keeper*—Budgets the time for each part of the task and makes sure the group continues to make progress and does not waste time.

- *Scribe or Recorder*—If only one finished product is required, the recorder would write the group's conclusions and fill in any graphic organizers or other documents to turn in.

- *Encourager*—Monitors the group member to be sure everyone is contributing and working hard to do their own jobs and prevents put-downs as much as possible.

As you set up your groups, consider which jobs will be most needed for the group's success and assign specific students to jobs. I do not recommend assigning a "spokesperson" as a group role. I want all students to be ready to share the group's work so that they will pay attention to the group's process. I recommend randomly calling students from each group to present rather than letting students know in advance who will be speaking. It is also important that a standard and expected group rule is that the group is not truly finished until everyone in the group answer a question about their work. I often check on this by asking different students in the group a question about their task. If a student is not able to answer me without help, the group is not finished.

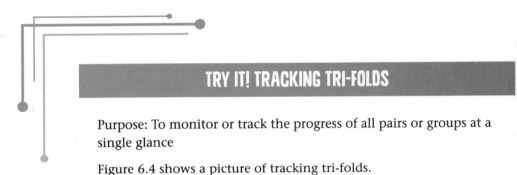

TRY IT! TRACKING TRI-FOLDS

Purpose: To monitor or track the progress of all pairs or groups at a single glance

Figure 6.4 shows a picture of tracking tri-folds.

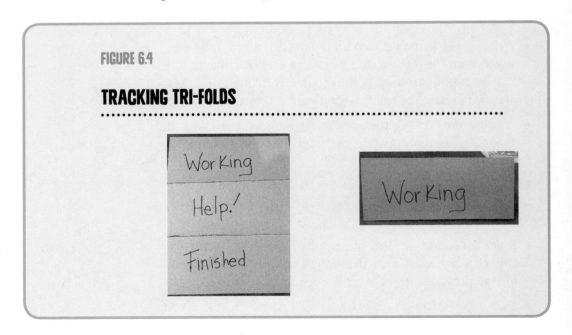

FIGURE 6.4

TRACKING TRI-FOLDS

Working

Help!

Finished

Working

Tri-fold a piece of construction paper or card stock horizontally. In the top section, write "Working." In the middle section write

"Help," and in the bottom section, write "Finished." Fold the paper into a triangular prism. Tell the students to face the side that shows how they are doing (working, need help, or finished) toward the front of the room. The teacher can go to the front of the room and at a glance see how the pairs or groups are doing—who is still working, who needs help, or who is finished.

PLANNING FOR FLEXIBLE TIME

One thing you can count on whenever your students work in groups is that they will not finish at the same time. Planning for "ragged time" will ensure that learning continues and that the classroom environment does not deteriorate. From the beginning of the year, students should have a list of accepted activities to do if they finish early. These activities are called "anchor activities."

Anchor Activities

To continue the learning in mathematics, anchor activities for mathematics class should be mathematics specific. Possible anchor activities can include

- Finish missing or incomplete assignments
- Play a mathematical game (alone or with a friend)
- Solve a logic puzzle
- Practice mathematical facts
- Solve the problem of the day (or week)
- Solve Sudoku or KenKen puzzles
- Help a friend (with permission)
- Create a mathematical puzzle (search-a-word, crossword, or coloring sheet)

The list of anchor activities should start at a more basic level with fewer options at the beginning of the year and grow throughout the year. As you compile your anchor activities, consider the following characteristics that would be considered high quality (Tomlinson & Imbeau, 2010):

- Engaging, contain an element of fun
- Focused on essential learning

- Address a broad range of student interests
- Open-ended to allow for multiple solution paths and representations
- Clear directions so that students can work independently
- A check sheet, rubric, or form of monitoring system is included for students to gauge quality work

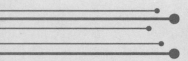

WATCH IT!

As you watch Video 6.3, *Using Anchor Activities for Classroom Management,* consider the following questions:

1. How do students know what they are to do when they finish early?

2. How independently do students work on anchor activities?

3. How does working on an anchor activity increase student engagement and collaboration?

Video 6.3 Using Anchor Activities for Classroom Management

Anchor activities give students who finish early something to extend and stretch their learning. Some students will require additional time to do their best work to complete their tasks.

Extra Time

Some students work and process more slowly than others. Time should not be a determining factor as to the amount of effort or the quality of work a student puts into a task. Unfortunately, with firmly set due dates, this can become an issue for students who work and think at a slower pace than others. I am not suggesting that every student who does not finish a task on time has worked hard and just needs more time—we all know students who waste time and do not focus until the last few minutes before something is due. Nevertheless, for students who honestly could complete a task with maximum effort if given more time, a plan should be in place.

Students who need additional time can request it using a form to explain what they have already completed, why they need more time, when they will continue their work, and their requested due date.

When allowing students to request extra time, it is important that students understand that the request is not a guarantee of extra time. Students should not think that they can put off working on a task and then request extra time. Figure 6.5 shows a sample of a request for extra time.

FIGURE 6.5

REQUEST FOR EXTRA TIME

··

Request for Extra Time

Name

_____

Project

_____

Explain what you have done so far:

For what will you use your extra time?

When will you continue your work?

Proposed due date

_____

Teacher decision:

The full template can be downloaded from http://resources.corwin .com/everymathlearnerK-5

Appropriate flexible time when students can work on tasks should be brainstormed among the students and the teacher. Possible time slots can include

- Station work
- Warm-up or transition times
- Lunch bunch
- Planned intervention times
- After-school tutoring times

Consider It!

Brainstorm a list of flexible times throughout your day that can be used to provide students with extra time.

Using flexible time for students who finish early or need additional time is one adjustment needed to make differentiation successful. The use of flexible time is needed despite whether students are engaged with different tasks because the speed at which students work is one of the learning differences inherent in a class of different students.

CONCLUSION

There is a saying that I understand and appreciate now more than any other time in my life: The devil is in the details. This is true in so many different areas but especially the classroom. We have all witnessed the demise of order, concentration, and often learning in one way or another as a result of misplaced papers, interruptions, and various lack of routines. Sometimes the mundane procedures are just what are needed to allow students to focus on learning and free a teacher's mind to give attention to what is most important.

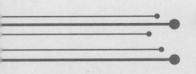

WATCH IT!

As you watch Video 6.4, *Ten Tips on Classroom Routines and Management*, consider the following questions:

1. How can classroom routines and management become a natural part of our mathematical learning?

2. How can you keep all students accountable for working and learning even when you are not present?

3. What are your favorite tips from this video that you want to be sure to implement?

Video 6.4 Ten Tips on Classroom Routines and Management

Smoothly run classrooms facilitate learning, whereas chaotic or disorganized classrooms can lead to confusion and frustration that prevent freedom to learn. In this chapter, we have seen various procedures and structures to move students in and out of groups, monitor group work, and encourage students to work together in groups as well as take responsibility for their learning. Having specific structures in place allows for maximum effort and time to be spent on the most important thing of all—learning.

FREQUENTLY ASKED QUESTIONS

Q: How can you have groups work together when your room is very small?

A: Many times space limits the desk or table arrangements; yet even the smallest rooms can facilitate groupings. For example, if desks are already in pods, those become set spaces for groups to meet. If desks are in pairs, two desks (or just the chairs) at a time can be rotated 180 degrees to make a group of four with the pair of desks behind them. Other times, desks do not need to be moved at all, but students may choose to sit together on the floor, under a table, in a corner, or wherever. Space should never be the determining factor as to whether pairs or small groups are used for differentiation.

Q: Do you accept late work?

A: I do. I know it is a challenge keeping up with the paperwork, but I always try to remember that the learning is what is important. I would rather have students do the work of learning than adhere to rules that just don't work in a particular case. I usually give my students "OOPS!" passes (about three per quarter) that they can use for late assignments without any type of penalty. Sometimes life interrupts and they can't get the work done that night. I know I didn't always get papers graded in the time frame my students wanted.

Keepsakes and Plans

What are the keepsake ideas from this chapter, those thoughts or ideas that resonated with you that you do not want to forget?

Classroom Routines—Grouping:

1.

2.

3.

Classroom Routines—Directions:

1.

2.

3.

Classroom Routines—Monitoring:

1.

2.

3.

Classroom Routines—Flexible Time:

1.

2.

3.

Based on my keepsake ideas, I plan to:

1.

2.

CHAPTER SEVEN

STEP BACK

TOOLS FOR ASSESSING AND EVALUATING IN A DIFFERENTIATED CLASSROOM

M ost of us love the process of planning lessons and of being in the classroom with the kids. Planning for differentiation is completely dependent on knowing our students well, determining the best entry points and strategies for learning for each lesson, and making sure students are progressing as planned. In this chapter, you will find:

Assessment *For, Of,* and *As* Learning

Principles to Develop Assessments

Designing Effective Assessments

Frequently Asked Questions

Keepsakes and Plans

I remember my first year of teaching mathematics. I couldn't wait to give a test or quiz so I could take them home and grade them. Yes, I'm serious. I thought all of my students would receive an A or a B on the test. After all, my lessons had gone well. My students asked questions in class, and most did their homework (it was a long time ago). Surely all my students would be able to perform with 80% mastery or above. And then I graded the tests. I couldn't understand it. There were students earning a C or a D and even some who failed. What had I done wrong? How could I have not realized this? The answer is very simple. I taught. I didn't assess. The most beautifully designed lessons, implemented well in a growth-mindset learning environment, may still not produce the desired results if we are not keeping track of exactly which students are succeeding, which are struggling and making progress, and which are completely lost.

ASSESSMENT *FOR, OF,* AND *AS* LEARNING

As a new teacher, I thought assessment and evaluations were synonymous in the life of a student. Assessments in my mind were the same as the items that I used to create points for my grade book, which were basically homework assignments, tests, and quizzes. We now have a much more robust view of assessment that benefits students. Assessment is no longer about evaluating students and assigning a grade but much more about helping students understand their own learning progress, informing next steps for learning and instruction, and determining the summary of learning at the end of the unit.

Assessment should provide a wide view of a student's learning progression through a unit. It begins with determining what students know, understand, and are able to do in regard to the upcoming unit before any instruction. This includes assessing for the essential prerequisite knowledge as well as for the upcoming learning. It continues with monitoring each student's learning throughout the unit in a moment-by-moment fashion, and it concludes with determining the summation of content knowledge and understanding at the end of the unit. Throughout the unit, students self-evaluate their progress, what strategies are working for them, and what their next steps should be. In essence, this is the meaning of assessment—from preassessment to formative assessment to summative assessment and even the students' self-assessment.

Balance is the key when considering assessment design in a differentiated classroom. Assessments should be balanced between differentiated tasks where students can best show what they truly know, understand, and are able to do and tasks that are common for all and/or more traditional in format. Furthermore, whether in your state or district mathematics is assessed with paper and pencil or on a computer, it is important to provide students the opportunities to use the same formats that will be used in high-stakes testing.

A second aspect of balancing assessment is that assessment needs to be a consistent and ongoing look at student learning throughout a unit. It should be a "picture of the entire forest" rather than a "picture of a tree." In other words, conclusions about students' learning should never be based on a single measure, a single type of measure, or sporadic measurements.

"Assessment *for* learning, assessment *of* learning, and assessment *as* learning" are now frequently used in developing a complete picture of assessment. Assessment *for* learning accentuates the use of information by the teacher to plan instruction that will benefit and move students to the desired learning outcomes for the unit. It also includes student self-assessment to enable students to reflect on their current strengths in regard to the upcoming unit, areas for growth, and to be able to set learning goals for themselves. When we assess our students for their interests and learning profiles (see Chapter 2), we are using assessments for learning as this information informs us as to the best ways to reach and hook our students. Preassessment for each unit provides readiness information prior to the start of a unit. Because these assessments are to provide information about how to design specific instruction, they are not graded.

Assessments *of* learning, on the other hand, are summative in nature. They are to measure the degree to which students have reached the learning goals of the unit.

Assessments *as* learning integrate the assessment process into instruction and learning. It has the goal of letting both the teacher and the student know the progress toward the learning goal. They show the areas in which the student is strong and is working toward mastery, areas in which more progress is needed, or areas in which there is no progress. Formative assessments are assessment *as* learning.

Make a list of the assessments you typically use throughout a unit. Next to each assessment make a note as to whether it is *for (f), of (o),* or *as (a)* learning. What conclusions can you draw from your list? What goals will you set?

PRINCIPLES TO DEVELOP ASSESSMENTS

As you plan your unit or lesson, you should also be thinking about appropriate assessments. No matter what type of assessment you are going to create, first and foremost use your unit's KUD (what students will come to *know, understand,* and be able to *do*) to guide the construction. Not all KUDs will be on every assessment—prioritizing which learning objectives will be included on the specific assessment, and how students will demonstrate their level of knowledge and understanding of the objectives, is the "big idea" of assessment design. Preassessments and summative assessments should be planned before instruction begins, and instruction follows the assessment plan. Formative assessments are embedded within the instruction plan, and they can be designed during the specific lesson planning. The details on how to use the KUD to guide the assessment design are included in the specific assessment sections later in this chapter.

Once the specific goals based on KUDs are established, the following are guiding questions to help design the specific assessment:

1. Which strategies and structures best allow my students to demonstrate what they truly know, understand, and can do? Should the specific assessment be more traditional in format (paper and pencil), be project-based or an

alternative form of assessment, or even perhaps be online? Should it be a blend?

2. Should the assessment be differentiated and, if so, how?

3. How will I organize the assessment? Should the assessment escalate in challenge? Should it be organized by skill or topic? Should it be organized with a skills (Know) section and an explanation and conceptual (Understand) section?

4. What will I do with the information? We tend to think of using only the information from preassessments and formative assessments for next-step instruction, but summative assessment data also let us know whether students are ready to move on to the next unit with confidence, which skills and understandings might need to be reinforced to move on, and which students might need to have some kind of remediation as they move on.

5. How will I keep track of the information?

6. How will students take action on their assessment information?

Before discussing the specifics for each type of assessment, consider one more form that can be used for any type of assessment: authentic performance assessment.

Authentic performance assessment creates a scenario in which students grapple with a real-world situation, come to a decision of some kind, and create an explanation or report with mathematical defense as evidence of learning. Authentic performance assessments are sometimes summative and can take the form of a project or larger task, but they can also be short formative assessments that are part of class instruction. Authentic performance assessments can even be posed as a preassessment to see how students reason about the application of the knowledge and understandings of the upcoming unit. Figure 7.1 gives an example of an authentic performance assessment for third-grade multiplication.

FIGURE 7.1

SNACK CONTROL

Standard	Solve two-step word problems using the four operations
Know	Multiplication and division facts within 100
Understand	• Multiplication and division share a unique inverse relationship that allows their facts to be used to solve each other's problems. • Multiplication and division operate on groups or areas that can be combined to find a greater total (multiplication of whole numbers) or segmented into smaller groups to find several groups or items in a group (division of whole numbers). • Addition and subtraction give a final count of things that are alike.
Do	Apply the four operations in real-world situations
Authentic Performance Task: Top Tier	You are in charge of the snacks for the third-grade field trip. Every student needs a bottle of water, a bag of chips, and a package of fruit snacks. There are 98 students going on the field trip. Bottles of water come in packages of 8. Bags of chips come in packages of 6. Fruit snacks come in packages of 5. There are already 6 bottles of water, 8 bags of chips, and 3 fruit snacks left from a classroom party. How many packages of water, chips, and fruit snacks need to be bought? Will there be any left over for the next event? Explain your answers in two different ways: Show the arithmetic steps and model in a second way.
Authentic Performance Task: Mid Tier	You are in charge of the snacks for the third-grade field trip. Every student needs a bottle of water, a bag of chips, and a package of fruit snacks. There are 98 students going on the field trip. Bottles of water come in packages of 8. Bags of chips come in packages of 6. Fruit snacks come in packages of 5. How many packages of water, chips, and fruit snacks need to be bought? Will there be any left over for the next event? Prove that your answers are correct so that we do not make a mistake in ordering.

Standard	Solve two-step word problems using the four operations
Authentic Performance Task: Lower Tier	You are in charge of the snacks for the third-grade field trip. Every student needs a bottle of water, a bag of chips, and a package of fruit snacks. There are 96 students going on the field trip.
	Bottles of water come in packages of 8.
	Bags of chips come in packages of 6.
	Fruit snacks come in packages of 4.
	How many packages of water, chips, and fruit snacks need to be bought?
	Show how you know your answers are correct.

TRY IT! WHO DOES IT?

For the topic you are currently teaching in mathematics, make a list of all possible scenarios and professionals who use the skill or concept. This list can provide the roles and situations for a performance assessment. Use this list to sketch the initial idea for an authentic performance assessment. Would your idea be a preassessment, formative assessment, or summative assessment?

No matter how you design your assessment, whether it is differentiated by readiness, interest, or learning profile, the essential learning being assessed does not change.

DESIGNING ASSESSMENTS

When designing differentiated assessments, remember that whether differentiated or not, the purpose of the assessment needs to remain the focus. Any assessment strategy you currently use can be differentiated by readiness, interest, or learning profile.

DIFFERENTIATING ASSESSMENT FOR LEARNING: PREASSESSMENT

Assessment for learning informs teachers and students of where they are as they enter a new unit of learning. Preassessing a unit is essential if we are to determine most effectively how to provide the appropriate support and challenge for our students. Preassessment does not necessarily mean a pretest. You might try to use other forms to gather information rather than a test format for finding out what your students already know or don't know, or about what they might have misconceptions. Chapter 2 gives several examples of formats for preassessment.

In designing an effective preassessment, consider:

- The Know and Understand from the unit design. Isolate the most important skills, formulations, and processes, as well as the undergirding understandings that make sense of the knowledge.

- The Do list that describes what students will be able to do as a result of both knowing and understanding the content of the unit. This will help guide the formation of the specific task or questions used in the preassessment.

- The prerequisite learning to be successful. List the essential prerequisite skills coming into the unit. Be sure that you think about what is truly essential—what do students need to know and understand in advance to be successful with the new unit?

These points will provide the content for the preassessment. The next group of considerations is the structure and possible differentiation of the preassessment. With a preassessment, the goal is to find out where students are in relation to the upcoming unit. To do this, the structure of the task should not prevent students from being able to show what they know and understand.

- What structures will best allow students to demonstrate their current knowledge and understanding?

- Should the preassessment be differentiated? If so, how?

    o Readiness—Provide a word bank to stimulate key vocabulary and ideas, allow multiple methods for explanation including pictures, modeling, or oral explanations or scaffolded examples.

    o Interest—Provide options for students to choose how to show their learning. Give several questions to assess a given learning objective, and allow students to choose which one or two they want to complete. Another interest differentiation would be to provide multiple formats, such as traditional mathematics work, models, pictures, or explanations, from which students can choose.

    o Learning Profile—Design assessment tasks according to one of the learning profile structures (see Chapter 4). Allow students to choose which format to use.

A final consideration in planning the preassessment is when to give it. Often teachers begin a new unit with the preassessment. Nevertheless, to use the information from the assessment effectively, it should be given several days in advance to allow the information to be analyzed and to plan the start of the unit accordingly. If the preassessment is given as the first step in the new unit, there is no time to analyze and plan. You are already starting. Additionally, if the preassessment is given as a whole class discussion (as is often the case when developing a K-W-L chart), the information is often what the most vocal or most advanced students know rather than giving specific information about each student. Be sure that whatever preassessment you choose to give, individual students are responsible for showing what they truly know.

Figure 7.2 shows a preassessment planning template.

Specific strategies and examples of preassessments are given in Chapter 2. These are included as a method for assessing students' readiness.

Consider It!

- How have student differences been apparent as you begin new units of study? How have you previously addressed these differences at the start of a unit?

- What are the advantages of giving a preassessment several days before the unit begins (during the previous unit)? What are the disadvantages?

FIGURE 7.2

PREASSESSMENT PLANNING TEMPLATE

Unit Title _____ Date _____

From the unit design, list the specific Know, Understand, and Do that need to be assessed.	
Know	
Understand	
Do	

Based on the content of the unit, what essential knowledge and understanding should students already have in order to be successful in this unit?	
Know	
Understand	

What structures, designs or strategies will best access students' learning?	
Possible structures, designs or strategies, for the assessment	

Does the preassessment need to be differentiated? If so how, and for whom?

How?	Differentiation	For Whom? (list names)
Readiness		
Interest		
Learning Profile		

 Templates can be downloaded at http://resources.corwin.com/ everymathlearnerK-5.

Preassessment data are used to determine the best methods for beginning a unit. These data will predominantly be about your students' readiness in relation to the upcoming unit. As such, how you begin will depend on what your information reveals.

To begin to make sense of your data, sort the student's work into piles showing significant differences in relation to demonstration of the KUDs. This may take some different tries to determine the significant differences. It might be easy to see which students have mastered the prerequisite information and which have not, or which students already know some of the strategies that are upcoming in the unit and which have no clue. This might sound straightforward, but we also know there could be students who are approaching mastery in some areas but not others, or students with the ability to solve specific types of problems, but they are not able to explain mathematically why the process is correct, the meanings of the operations or properties involved, or why their answer is reasonable. Sorting and resorting students' work along different criteria will give a full picture of the entry points of all of your students.

With the full picture of where students are in relation to the beginning of the unit, the first few days are ready to be planned. Begin with the initial concepts and overview of the unit. All students should participate in this discussion or activity to develop common vocabulary, concepts, and direction the unit will take. The next task will most likely be differentiated according to the preassessment data. Consider various stations or tasks to develop the first skill or concept in your unit. For students who have already demonstrated proficiency, design a related task, interest application, or a processing task that asks students to explain the "how and why" of the objective. This reasoning can continue to be used as the unit develops, but it will be based on more current and accurate formative assessment.

DIFFERENTIATING ASSESSMENT *AS* LEARNING: CHECKS FOR UNDERSTANDING, THE FORMATIVE ASSESSMENT PROCESS, AND STUDENT SELF-ASSESSMENT

Most often, assessment *as* learning is referred to as "ongoing assessments." These broad terms encompass many moments in daily instruction from simple checks for understanding, to engagement in a full formative assessment process that provides students with feedback, to students' self-evaluation. What these three types of assessments have in common is that they occur throughout the unit and let both the teacher and students know how they are progressing with their learning through the unit.

Checks for Understanding

Checks for understanding provide the teacher with information about where the students are in the moment. They can be formal or informal. Figure 7.3 provides several descriptions of checks for understanding.

FIGURE 7.3

CHECKS FOR UNDERSTANDING

Strategy	Example
Signals	Signals can be anything from thumbs up, down, and sideways; fist of five with 0 = no clue, 1 = just beginning, 2 = a little bit, 3 = pretty good, 4 = strong, and 5 = I can teach this; Windshield checks have students compare their understanding to a windshield covered in mud, splatted by bugs, somewhat spotty or crystal clear. Another signal can be red, yellow, and green cups or paper tents signaling whether the students are full steam ahead, getting stuck, or completely stopped. Signals can be used before, during, or after a specific problem. If before, ask who thinks they know what this problem means and how to start? If after, ask how students did, and if during, use the signal as a device for help.
Exit or Entry Cards	Exit or entry cards should have no more than three questions posed specifically related to the day's lesson (exit card) or the previous lesson or homework (entry card). Teachers can use exit cards to assess how well students understood the lesson, and then group students according to readiness groups when beginning the next day's lesson. Entry cards can be sorted into readiness groups as well. One type of exit card often used is a 3–2–1 card that asks 3 tips for solving the problems we did today are . . . 2 connections I can make between the problems and big ideas are . . . 1 question I still have is . . .

Strategy	Example
White Boards	White boards are used for students to hold up individual work or short answers to specific questions that could include vocabulary; true/false; or always, sometimes, or never.
	White boards can also be used as a means for groups to report out after discussing a problem. The "scribe" should change within the group with each problem.
	Another way to use white boards in class is to have students sit back to back, and when both partners have finished working, turn and compare their work. The partners work out any differences in their processes they might have, compare solution paths, and discuss any other points of interest. The teacher monitors and records the pairs' solutions and paths.
Any Written Work	Recording evidence of learning from any written work, whether group or individual, can serve as a check for understanding as long as the information is recorded. It can be recorded in check sheets against standards or learning objectives, on index cards in a card file or by creating a flip chart, or electronically.

Anything that happens in a classroom can and should serve as a check for understanding—even simply paying attention to the types of questions and comments students make. The trick is to keep track of the information you are observing for each student.

The Formative Assessment Process

Formative assessment is the area of assessment often discussed because of its importance in learning. It is so important that it has reached the status of initials . . . FA!

Yet the interpretation of just what is a formative assessment is sometimes dependent on the school, district, or book you are reading. The term *formative assessments* has been used to describe purchased, standardized tests administered at prescribed intervals; benchmarks created by a district team; quizzes and homework; and various other descriptors or tools. For our purposes, though, formative assessment has a broader definition. It is the process of evaluating anything that occurs in the classroom that will give the teacher insight into students' mathematical understanding, provide specific feedback to students on which they will take action, and allow teachers to make instructional choices in response to student understanding.

John Hattie (2012) suggests that the effect size of providing feedback to students is 0.75, which puts it in about the top 10 influences on achievement. Nevertheless, the effect size of engaging in a formative assessment (or formative evaluation, as Hattie calls it) process, which involves using assessment data *as* learning and provides students *with* feedback, has a walloping 0.9 effect size.

So if we want formative assessment to have the impact we desire, we need to think of it as more of a process (Popham, 2011) than a task. To be effective

- Specific and timely feedback must be provided to students
- Students must be actively involved in their own learning and take action on the provided feedback
- Teachers need to react to and make adjustments to the teaching trajectory based on their professional observation and assessment data
- Students must self-assess and take steps or set goals to improve
- Teachers must recognize the affect assessment has on motivation and the self-esteem of students (Wiliam, 2011)

Furthermore, a formative assessment is not the same as a check for understanding (Dixon, Adams, & Nolan, 2015). A check for understanding provides information to the teacher to determine where students are in relation to a learning target, as well as to make instructional adjustments. A formative assessment can be formal or informal, graded or not graded.

Consider It!

What separates a formative assessment and a check for understanding? What are the benefits of each in a lesson?

For a formative assessment to have the full effect on learning that it can have, feedback and students taking action on the feedback must be a priority. Additionally, not just any feedback will do. Several qualities determine whether the feedback being given will be effective (Tomlinson & Moon, 2013; Wiggins, 2012; Wiliam 2011). Figure 7.4 gives the criteria and descriptions of effective feedback.

FIGURE 7.4

FEEDBACK CRITERIA

Characteristic	Description
Understandable	Feedback needs to be provided in such a way that the student understands what is meant. Be sure students understand any shorthand notations or academic vocabulary that might be written. If providing verbal feedback, ask the student to echo back what he or she is hearing or to ask you a follow-up question.
Specific and Focused	Students need to know precisely what to do to improve, and feedback should enable students to persevere with the mathematical task. For example, "Be careful" or "Close!" may not be clear to the student as to what he or she needs to attend. "You have several arithmetic errors" or "Watch the labeling of your graph" are more specific and understandable without providing the correction to errors. Feedback should be focused on the learning objectives to keep a narrowed intent on improvement.
Accurate	It is possible to give students feedback that is not accurate because the mistake I assume a student is making is not the same as determining the reason for the error. Be sure to find out why an error occurred by asking, "explain what happened at this step" when giving face-to-face feedback. Be sure that the feedback provided will help students understand the mathematical task or devise a corrected solution pathway.
Frequent and Timely	Feedback needs to be provided as "in the moment" as possible. You are the best provider of feedback, but student-to-student feedback should be taught and encouraged as part of the mathematical practices and discourse. As you circulate through the room, listen for these conversations and affirm or correct the feedback being given. Try to spend no more than 19 seconds with any group of students, to keep circulating, and to offer feedback that is timely (Kanold, 2016).
Action Oriented	Feedback should enable students to take the next step in understanding and completing the mathematical task. It should be explicit enough for students to take action without doing the work for the student.
Differentiated	Feedback can be used to stretch students' learning when appropriate, or it can be used to help students get "unstuck." Some questions and prompts may be preplanned and are called "advancing questions" to help students move beyond and extend their mathematical understandings and skill, whereas others are called "assessing questions" to help students move forward when they are stuck (Kanold & Larson, 2012). Additionally, different models, manipulatives, representations, and suggestions may be offered as feedback based on how students best make sense of the mathematical content.

As described earlier, the formative assessment process has one of the largest impacts on student learning of anything we do in the classroom. James Popham (2011, p. 63) states that "recent reviews of more than four thousand research investigations highlight that when the (formative assessment) process is well-implemented in the classroom, it can essentially double the speed of student learning, producing large gains in students' achievement. At the same time, it is sufficiently robust so different teachers can use it in diverse ways and still get great results with their students."

When planning for formative assessment, consider:

- The specific K, U, and/or D on which the lesson is focused. Lessons may be about building a specific skill, so the focus will be only on specific Know targets from the unit design. Other times it may be a concept-building lesson or a combination. The formative assessment will target the lesson's learning objective.

- How will effective feedback be given to students? Who will provide it? Will you circulate among students to provide feedback, will feedback be given from peers, or will there be a combination of both?

- When will time be provided for students to take action on the feedback? Will it be simultaneous with the feedback? Given as homework?

When engaging in the formative assessment process, the best sources of uncovering student learning on which to provide feedback are tasks that are high level and multifaceted. Chapter 3 describes how to "teach up" to ensure these types of tasks. Additionally, all of the strategies and activities in Chapter 4 can be used as formative assessments.

Figure 7.5 shows student's work on a complex task.

Student work © Abigail Williams.

FIGURE 7.5

STUDENT WORK ON AREA

The Fencing Task

Ms. Brown's class will raise rabbits for its spring science fair. Students have 24 feet of fencing with which to build a rectangular rabbit pen in which to keep the rabbits.

- If Ms. Brown's students want their rabbits to have as much room as possible, how long would each of the sides of the pen be?

- How long would each of the sides of the pen be if they have only 16 feet of fencing?

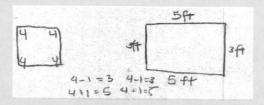

- How would you go about determining the pen with the most room for any amount of fencing? Organize your work so that someone else who reads it will understand it.

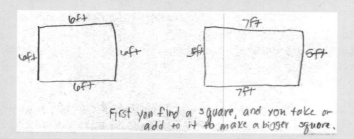

Problem Source: Stein, Smith, Henningsen & Silver, 2009, p 2.

What feedback would you give the student in Figure 7.5 on her work? List out what you would ask about and suggest for her next steps.

Using Ongoing Assessment Information

As always, ongoing assessment data are used to help teachers and students evaluate what the next learning steps should be. In a third-grade class, students were learning to find perimeters and areas of rectangles, including squares. Based on an exit card, the teacher determined that some students had mastery of calculating area and perimeter with rectangles and did not get them or their operations confused (group 1). Some students could calculate area or perimeter but not both (group 2). Some students got the two confused (group 3). Some could not calculate either (group 4). Figure 7.6 shows the tasks given to groups of students based on their exit cards.

FIGURE 7.6

NEXT STEPS WITH AREA AND PERIMETER

Group	Task
Group 1	Students were asked to draw their own figures for a given perimeter or area.
Group 2	Students were paired with mixed strengths: one student who is strong in perimeter with a student strong in area. They teach each other and practice together finding perimeters and areas of rectangles. Students alternate which measure (area or perimeter) they are finding.
Group 3	Students were given square tiles and graph paper. They were given a worksheet giving dimensions of rectangles and asked to either build the rectangles with tiles or trace them on graph paper. They had scaffolded directions. The first rectangles told students to trace the outside of the rectangle and count each segment forming the sides to find perimeter. Write the equation of the sides to show the perimeter. Next count the number of squares that make up the rectangle to determine area. Show how the side dimensions lead to the total number of squares. These directions gradually reduced to calculate simply the perimeter and area for the rectangle.
Group 4	These students began with the teacher for a reteach on area and perimeter. They were then asked to work in pairs on the group 3 assignment.

The third-grade teacher who was working with area and perimeter noticed that two students in group 1 finished the task very quickly and had drawn several correct rectangles for each given perimeter and area. The teacher decided to see how far these students could extend their understanding by giving them the task shown in Figure 7.5. All students were able to reach the required standard as well as describe the difference between area and perimeter and why perimeter required addition and area required multiplication. Many students were able to move beyond standard through their tasks.

Student Self-Assessment

One area of assessment that is often overlooked is having students assess their own learning. From the earliest grades, students should be aware of how they are doing in their learning. Student self-reflections can be just about anything such as rating their effort and success on a specific skill from 0 to 5 or circling a smiley face, straight face, or frowney face to describe how well they understand the lesson. As students get older, journal prompts and other writing opportunities (exit cards, reflection questions on homework, tasks, quizzes, or tests) are appropriate. Figure 7.7 gives examples of possible self-reflection tools for primary and intermediate students.

Assessments *for* and *as* learning are largely differentiated. Throughout the unit, we are primarily concerned that students learn the mathematical content fully in whatever manner will work the best for them. Sprinkled throughout the unit should be standardized assessments that model any high-stakes test the students may encounter, as well as measure student progress strictly against the standard. But these should be the exception throughout the unit rather than the norm.

DIFFERENTIATING ASSESSMENT *OF* LEARNING: SUMMATIVE ASSESSMENT

Summative assessments usually occur at the end of a unit, but any cumulative assessment can be regarded as a summative assessment. These may be mid-unit quizzes or other assessments, district or quarterly benchmark exams, or any other assessment that evaluates students' progress at a particular point in time. Summative assessments can be in the form of a paper-and-pencil assessment, a presentation, or an authentic performance assessment. The key to designing a valuable summative assessment is that it remains true to the learning goals of the unit as determined by the unit's KUD. When designing a summative assessment, be sure to

FIGURE 7.7

STUDENT SELF-REFLECTION TOOLS

Primary Example

Name _____

My Math Today

Today I worked hard on _____.

I am really good at _____.

I need more practice on _____.

I am proud of myself because _____.

I used my time well

I helped my classmates

I gave my best effort

Intermediate Example

Math Self-Assessment

Read each sentence and mark on the number line the number that best describes your math work today.

1. I stayed on task and gave my best effort today.

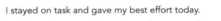

| 0 | 1 | 2 | 3 | 4 | 5 |

I did not   Most of   All the
      the time   way

2. I participated during class discussions

| 0 | 1 | 2 | 3 | 4 | 5 |

I did not   Most of   All the
      the time   way

3. I participated during class work

| 0 | 1 | 2 | 3 | 4 | 5 |

I did not   Most of   All the
      the time   way

4. I persevered and did not give up on independent work

| 0 | 1 | 2 | 3 | 4 | 5 |

I did not   Most of   All the
      the time   way

On the back, please tell me what you learned today in math. What are you confident you know well? With what do you need more practice? Do you have any questions for me, or anything else you want me to know?

 The full tools can be downloaded at http://resources.corwin.com/ everymathlearnerK-5.

- Reflect the same importance of the learning goals on the assessment as in the unit. On the summative assessment, the number of items relating to a particular standard or K, U, or D should be in the same proportion as the instruction and tasks throughout the unit.

- The depth of the questions or tasks should be at the same level of cognitive demand as throughout the unit and as specified by the standard. I know a few teachers who believe that being rigorous means giving exceedingly difficult assessments. On the other hand, I know teachers who give relatively easy summative assessments so that students do not struggle too much. Neither of these is the correct stance. The rigor and depth (not difficulty) of the assessment is determined by the standard.

- If differentiated applications, strategies, or methods were used throughout the unit, they should also be reflected in the assessment.

Consider It!

What are the pros and cons of differentiating a summative assessment? What are the possible concerns or constraints?

Summative assessments may be differentiated by readiness, interest, and learning profile as well, but carefully.

Readiness differentiation should allow students to show what they know, understand, and are able to do. Readiness differentiation strategies could include:

- Formatting a test with larger print and more writing space

- Including multiple representations and solution paths

- Providing manipulatives, multiplication charts, word banks, and so on

- Providing oral or pictorial mathematical explanations

Figure 7.8 gives an example of a tiered first-grade assessment. The knowledge being assessed is as follows: place value, adding one more, one less, ten more, and ten less. The understanding being assessed is that only like things can be added (tens + tens, ones + ones). Notice that the readiness differentiation is in providing models and hints while the questions remain the same.

Interest and learning profile differentiation on a summative assessment may include:

- Having a section on a test that is required for all students, but also providing a bank of questions and point values and allowing students to choose problems to acquire a certain number of points.

FIGURE 7.8

READINESS SUMMATIVE ASSESSMENT DIFFERENTIATION

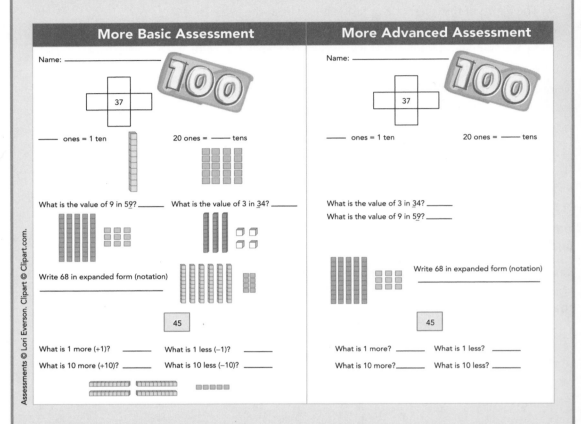

The full assessments can be found at http://resources.corwin.com/ everymathlearnerK-5.

- Giving a choice of the applications for a topic on which to be assessed.

- Providing choices in format for the assessment: paper and pencil, presentation, creating a test and answer key, or "designing" a text book chapter on the topic.

- Designing authentic performance assessments that allow for multiple roles or products.

TIP FOR ELL/SPECIAL EDUCATION STUDENTS

Be sure that any Individualized Education Plan (IEP) or 504 accommodations are strictly followed when designing assessments. For English-language learners (ELLs), consider providing a word bank to help with explanations or allow other methods for explanations such as pictures or demonstrations. Record instructions and questions in the student's native language if possible, or use models, pictures, and/or gestures to help students understand the tasks and expectations.

To guarantee the validity of the summative assessment, no matter the design or differentiation, ensure that the same learning targets are being assessed in the same proportion and to the same depth of knowledge.

CONCLUSION

Assessments are to be a way of determining students' progress toward the learning goals as established by the unit's standards and corresponding KUD. Assessment allows us to make "next-step" decisions about instruction. Differentiated assessments allow us to determine what students truly know, understand, and are able to do. These same assessments should serve as a method of reflection for our students as they also self-assess and determine their own next steps in learning.

The structure or design of an assessment is not as critical as the content that it assesses. Almost any strategy can be used for preassessments, checks for understanding, and formative assessments. Mathematical summative assessments tend to most often be paper-and-pencil, presentation, or authentic performance assessment.

Finally, do not confuse grading and assessing. Assessments inform instruction for both the teacher and the student. Grades merely record some form of percentage or other measure of proficiency.

FREQUENTLY ASKED QUESTIONS

Q: Is it fair if tests are differentiated?

A: Assessments, including tests, are to measure what students know, understand, and are able to do in regard to specific learning targets at a specific point in time. The structure of the test or assessment should not restrict the student's ability to show his or her learning. In some ways, differentiated assessments are more fair than nondifferentiated ones. With that understanding, it is also important to realize that part of mathematics is the ability to write and solve problems. There are times when paper-and-pencil assessments are the appropriate measure and other options should not be used. In the same way, not all assessments need to be differentiated, but neither should all assessments be the same for all students.

Q: What about grading?

A: The first principle of grading in a differentiated classroom (in fact, in all classrooms) is that not everything should be graded. Students should not rely on a grade as motivation to complete tasks. Grades tend to shut down intrinsic motivation and end learning. There is ample research evidence on the importance of feedback over grades for learning. With that established, for most of us, grades are a necessary evil in our educational system. To grade consistently and fairly with differentiated tasks is to grade against the learning targets regardless of the specific task or differentiation. The most consistent strategy for this is to design a rubric based on the mathematical expectations. If desired, a nominal number of points could be assigned to the quality and neatness of the work in the task.

Keepsakes and Plans

What are the keepsake ideas from this chapter, those thoughts or ideas that resonated with you that you do not want to forget?

Assessment *For, Of,* and *As* Learning:

1.

2.

3.

Principles to Develop Assessments:

1.

2.

3.

Designing and Using Preassessments (*For* Learning):

1.

2.

3.

Designing and Using Ongoing Assessments (*As* Learning):

1.

2.

3.

Designing and Using Summative Assessments (*Of* Learning):

1.

2.

3.

Based on my keepsake ideas, I plan to

1.

2.

3.

CHAPTER EIGHT

CLOSE UP

A WEEK IN THE LIFE OF A DIFFERENTIATED MATHEMATICS CLASS

The goal of this book has been to bring the various pieces and processes of differentiating mathematics instruction together for you, step-by-step, into a cohesive and doable endeavor.

But what does it look and sound like when all the pieces are in place? What does a week in the life of a differentiated classroom look like? In this chapter, you will find:

A Look Into a Week in a Primary Classroom

A Look Into a Week in an Intermediate Classroom

Advice From the Field

Conclusion

A LOOK INTO A WEEK IN A PRIMARY CLASSROOM

Laurie Salazar, a first-grade teacher, is planning her unit on adding a two-digit number to another number with sums within 100. Ms. Salazar builds her unit by focusing on the group of standards addressed throughout the unit, and she develops lessons by using resources and activities she has as well as finding new resources online.

Her standard specifies that the addition could be a two-digit number and a one-digit number or a two-digit number and a multiple of ten. The related standards for the unit discuss the role of place value and using multiple strategies to find sums. This example models how to construct differentiated lessons within a unit, beginning with the unit plan as described in Chapter 3—Teach Up, developing a general sequence of lessons on a planning calendar, and finally making the day-to-day decisions for differentiation.

FROM UNIT TO LESSON PLAN

As Ms. Salazar begins the unit, she knows that some of her students do not have a solid understanding of place value, much less its role in addition. Some students demonstrate place value fluently with base 10 blocks that can be touched but struggle with paper-and-pencil strategies. She has some students that are fluent with single-digit addition and close to fluent finding a sum of double-digit and single-digit numbers. Still others can add two two-digit numbers. As she makes initial plans for the unit, she begins with the standards, KUDs (what students will come to *know*, *understand*, and be able to *do*), and possible assessments on the unit-planning document. Figure 8.1 shows the unit plan for Ms. Salazar's unit.

Ms. Salazar uses her lesson plan book, to sketch out her daily lessons for the unit, which will last approximately four weeks. She begins her lesson planning with the daily big ideas and skills for the unit, as well as with the activities that already has that will fit with each day's goal. She will differentiate each day's lesson from the day's goal and/or topic, and any information from prior lessons that inform decisions about what her students need to best move forward in learning. Her initial planning calendar is shown in Figure 8.2.

Throughout the unit, Ms. Salazar will reinforce various strategies that have been introduced earlier in the year when students added single-digit numbers. The strategies Ms. Salazar will use in this unit are base 10 blocks, tally marks in a chart of tens

FIGURE 8.1

"ADDING THINGS THAT ARE ALIKE" UNIT PLAN

· ·

Unit Title: *1st Grade "Adding Things That are Alike": Addition of 2-Digit Numbers*

Standards Addressed:

1.NBT.B.2 *Understand that the two digits of a two-digit number represent amounts of tens and ones. Understand the following as special cases:*

    A.   *10 can be thought of as a bundle of ten ones—called a "ten"*

    B.   *The numbers from 11 to 19 are composed of a ten and one-nine ones*

    C.   *The numbers 10, 20, 30-90 refer to 1-9 tens*

1.NBT.C.4 *Add within 100, including adding a two-digit number and a one-digit number, and adding a two-digit number and a multiple of 10, using concrete models of drawings and strategies based on place value, properties of operations, and/or the relationship between addition and subtraction; relate the strategy to a written method and explain the reasoning used. Understand that in adding two-digit numbers, one adds tens and tens, ones and ones; and sometimes it is necessary to compose a ten*

1.NBT.C.5 *Given a two-digit number, mentally find 10 more or 10 less than the number, without having to count; explain the reasoning used.*

By the end of the unit, what will students come to . . .

Know	Understand	Be Able to Do
Place value Value. vs. digits	Students will understand that only like things can be added (tens + tens, ones + ones)	The students will be able to verbally explain how they solved a 2-digit addition problem
Tens & ones		
Expanded form	Students will understand that numbers can be broken apart to make addition more clear:	
Strategies—Base 10		The students will be able to model strategies to solve a 2-digit addition problem
100 chart	28 + 12 = 28 + 10 + 2	
Jump method (open number lines)	Students will understand that different strategies can be used to solve the same problem	The students will be able to show the role of place value in 2-digit addition (tens + tens, ones + ones)
Tally method		

Preassessment Ideas: Have students show various 2-digit numbers using base 10 blocks, discussion of putting things together (looking for place value understanding)

Summative Assessment Ideas: Verbal explanation of 2-digit addition and teacher-made test based on KUD.

Formative Assessment Ideas: Within the small group stations, accountability sheets will be checked daily and verbal/written explanation on white boards in Teacher Time station will demonstrate students' understanding. Mission Possible using 2-digit addition problems will be checked daily as well.

Resources: White boards, 100 Charts, Base 10 manipulatives, cards, 2-digit addition games (Three-in-a-Row, Addition War, etc . . .)

© Lori Everson

 Download the full unit plan from http://resources.corwin.com/everymathlearnerK-5

FIGURE 8.2

TENTATIVE UNIT PLANNING CALENDAR

Math Planning Calendar

Unit: Adding things that are alike: two-digit addition

Duration: 4 weeks

Monday	Tuesday	Wednesday	Thursday	Friday
2/1 What can be added? Place values with tens Hundreds chart patterns	2/2 Strategy review with single digit addition—tie into Hundreds Chart for larger numbers	2/3 Mystery Clues: Hundreds charts & manipulatives (10 more, 20 less, has 5 tens and 2 ones, etc)	2/4 Picture addition problems and riddles	2/5 Mystery Clues Advanced
2/8 Concept check: place value of 2-digit numbers, adding multiples of tens to numbers	2/9 Adding with Hundreds board	2/10 Adding with Hundreds board and open number line; 2-digit plus 1-digit (Hundred chart where we "do" it, Number line is where we record it)	2/11 Adding with Hundreds board and number line; 2-digit plus 2-digit	2/12 Adding with Hundreds board and number line; 2-digit plus 2-digit
2/15 Base 10 Block Addition with Number Line and/or Hundreds Chart	2/16 Base 10 Block Addition	2/17 Base 10 Block Addition Tally method	2/18 Tally method	2/19 Tally method; choose a method and record answers on paper
2/22 Choose a method and record answers on paper; Bonding to 100 and tie to money	2/23 Friendly numbers getting to 100	2/24 Choose your favorite methods Explain role of place value (only same things can be added)	2/25 Choose your favorite methods Explain role of place value (only same things can be added)	2/26 Concept Check

 A blank planning calendar and the completed calendar for this unit can be found on http://resources.corwin.com/everymathlearnerK-5

and ones, a hundreds chart, jumps on a number line (an open number line method), and paper-and-pencil algorithms including number bonds and the standard algorithm. She plans to review each strategy and extend it with the more advanced numbers for several days, but along with using the strategy to add, she will also continue to reinforce the essential understandings for the unit through modeling, questioning, and discourse. The understanding that only things that are alike can be added together was the primary emphasis to reinforce the role of place value in addition. This understanding has been built into conversations, including adding different pieces of fruit; story problems that involve different nouns, such as trees and birds that ask for a total number of birds alone; and asking students to talk about things they can add in their lives. She knows that this foundational understanding about addition will be important throughout her students' mathematics career.

DAILY PLANNING—DAY 1

As Ms. Salazar prepares for the third week of the unit, she draws on formative assessments given throughout the previous weeks, especially the observations and formative assessments from the last three days. From her observations and anecdotal records, she has the following concerns:

The entire week's lesson plans and blank lesson planning templates can be downloaded from http://resources.corwin.com/everymathlearnerK-5.

- Four students understand addition of a two-digit number and a multiple of ten (the required standard) and can model and explain it with all strategies, and two students have their own invented (and correct) strategies. They will need to be extended and challenged beyond the standard's requirement.

- Eight students still confuse movement within the hundreds chart for adding ten (down) or one (right). Two students still count each square, one-by-one, instead of adding tens. Figure 8.3 shows examples of student work adding on the chart.

- Most students can model addition moves on the open number lines, describing the addition of 10 as a jump, and the addition of 1 as a hop; yet, four students still draw miscellaneous "loops" without understanding the addition of a ten or a one. Figure 8.4 provides the open number line

FIGURE 8.3

ADDITION ON A CHART

Example A (correct)

26 + 30 = 56

1	2	3	4	5	6	7	8	9	10
11	12	13	14	15	16	17	18	19	20
21	22	23	24	25	26	27	28	29	30
31	32	33	34	35	36	37	38	39	40
41	42	43	44	45	46	47	48	49	50
51	52	53	54	55	56	57	58	59	60
61	62	63	64	65	66	67	68	69	70
71	72	73	74	75	76	77	78	79	80
81	82	83	84	85	86	87	88	89	90
91	92	93	94	95	96	97	98	99	100

Example B (Movement of ones and tens confused)

26 + 30 = 29

1	2	3	4	5	6	7	8	9	10
11	12	13	14	15	16	17	18	19	20
21	22	23	24	25	26	27	28	29	30
31	32	33	34	35	36	37	38	39	40
41	42	43	44	45	46	47	48	49	50
51	52	53	54	55	56	57	58	59	60
61	62	63	64	65	66	67	68	69	70
71	72	73	74	75	76	77	78	79	80
81	82	83	84	85	86	87	88	89	90
91	92	93	94	95	96	97	98	99	100

Example C (counting by ones)

26 + 30 = 56

Example D (counting by ones, weaving movement)

26 + 30 = 56

1	2	3	4	5	6	7	8	9	10
11	12	13	14	15	16	17	18	19	20
21	22	23	24	25	26	27	28	29	30
31	32	33	34	35	36	37	38	39	40
41	42	43	44	45	46	47	48	49	50
51	52	53	54	55	56	57	58	59	60
61	62	63	64	65	66	67	68	69	70
71	72	73	74	75	76	77	78	79	80
81	82	83	84	85	86	87	88	89	90
91	92	93	94	95	96	97	98	99	100

record of an addition problem that students first solved using a chart an then recorded their thinking with the open number line.

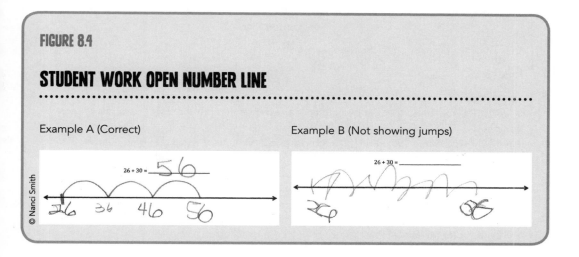

FIGURE 8.4

STUDENT WORK OPEN NUMBER LINE

Example A (Correct)   Example B (Not showing jumps)

© Nanci Smith

- When building numbers with base 10 blocks, seven students do not recognize the difference between a ten-rod and a unit cube. For example, when building the number 24, students will try to count out 24 ten-rods. Still others do not recognize the value of the tens digit and count out single-unit cubes.

With these concerns in mind, Laurie Salazar begins to plan Monday's lesson (Week 3) by consulting the unit's plan and determining the specific standards and KUD that will be addressed for this lesson. These are cut and pasted into the lesson-planning sheet. Figure 8.5 shows the beginning of the lesson-planning sheet with the standards and KUD from the unit plan inserted.

Miss Salazar wants to connect the work from the prior two weeks with adding two-digit numbers and either a single digit or a multiple of ten through the hundreds chart and open number line strategies with the new lesson's strategy of base 10 blocks. She wants her students to discover that the new tool (10 blocks) are showing the same thing as the other strategies for addition, which

FIGURE 8.5

STANDARDS AND KUD IN LESSON-PLANNING SHEET

Daily Lesson Plan
Day 1

Date: 2/15

Standards:

1.NBT.B.2 *Understand that the two digits of a two-digit number represent amounts of tens and ones.*

1.NBT.C.4 *Add within 100, including adding a two-digit number and a one-digit number, and adding a two-digit number and a multiple of 10, using concrete models of drawings and strategies based on place value, properties of operations; relate the strategy to a written method and explain the reasoning used. Understand that in adding two-digit numbers, one adds tens and tens, ones and ones; and sometimes it is necessary to compose a ten.*

Standard for Mathematical Practice:

SMP5: Use appropriate tools strategically.
SMP6: Attend to precision.
SMP7: Look for and make use of structure (place value).

K: Place value
Value vs. digits
Tens & ones
Expanded form

U: Students will understand that only like things can be added (tens+tens, ones+ones)

Students will understand that numbers can be broken apart to make addition more clear:
$28 + 12 = 28 + 10 + 2$

D: The students will be able to verbally explain how they solved a 2-digit addition problem

The students will be able to model strategies to solve a 2-digit addition problem

The students will be able to show the role of place value in 2-digit addition (tens+tens, ones+ones)

is that you are still adding tens with tens and ones with ones. To correlate the strategies and reinforce the understandings for the lesson, she decides to begin with whole class modeling is and discourse.

To remind students of how base 10 blocks model place value, which they have used from the beginning of the year but not very recently, she will have students build numbers with the blocks. She will pay special attention to students who did not previously show mastery with using ten-rods and unit cubes for place value. She plans to give students 11 ten-rods and 17 unit cubes so that students who try to count one-by-one without place value will not have enough cubes or rods to show the whole number. She will begin by asking students to model the number 28 and check with a partner. For students who count out cubes, rods, or a combination of the two to total 28, Ms. Salazar plans to ask about making exchanges or comparing the size of the rods and cubes. She also plans to have students explain their various models and how they thought about making the number. For students who did not originally model the number correctly, she will ask them to explain what they originally did and how they would now change it. This process will be repeated with the number 54 and, finally, 13. If the modeling of 54 is not consistently correct, she will insert another number to model prior to 13.

When students have modeled the number 13, she will ask her students to slide the 13 blocks to the top of their work mat and then model the number 40. She will then ask the students whether there is some way to add these two numbers together, and if so, what would be the sum. Ms. Salazar plans to allow her students (a) to make sense of addition as combining, (b) move the ten-rods together and keep the unit cubes separate, and (c) explain the total as 53. She will ask students to discuss why the sum wasn't eight (counting the blocks without place value) or 17 (keeping one ten and counting the "4" from the number 40 and the "3" from the number 13 together) to have students explain the role of place value, and how tens are added to tens and ones to ones. She will also show how the number 13 could be broken apart to 10 + 3, and then she will add the 10 to the 40 for 50 and finally 50 + 3 for the sum of 53.

She will repeat this process with another problem, but she will ask one student also to model the same problem using the hundreds chart. Students will explain how the two processes are alike, as well as how they are different. For the next problem, this entire process will be repeated, but as one student explains the movement on the chart and another with the base 10 blocks,

Ms. Salazar will draw an open number line on the board. She will ask students to interpret the number line and how it can show either the base 10 blocks or the chart. She will repeat this combination two or three more times depending on how quickly the students make connections, with all students building with the blocks and two student volunteers showing the chart and open number line.

Ms. Salazar will next place her students for this particular lesson in groups of three based on same readiness. Each group will have a set of base 10 blocks, a chart, and a set of number lines with which they will model several problems at their appropriate readiness level (two-digit plus ten, two-digit plus a multiple of ten, and two-digit plus any other two-digit). Each student will use one of the strategies, base 10 blocks, hundreds chart, or open number line to find the sum and compare and explain their thinking and answers. They will rotate strategies for each problem ensuring that each group member models with and explains each of the three strategies.

Finally, students will be asked to solve one (or two if time) problem using base 10 blocks that they will draw on their paper and one other strategy of their choice as a formative assessment. Figure 8.6 shows the remaining lesson plan.

Ms. Salazar will carefully review her anecdotal records and her students' individual problems to refine her plans for Tuesday.

DAILY PLANNING—DAY 2

After observing students' work and reviewing the individual addition problems from Day 1, Ms. Salazar recognizes that

- Now ten students understand addition of a two-digit number and a multiple of ten (the required standard) and can model and explain it with all representations. They will need to be extended and challenged beyond the standard's requirement.

- Four students continue to confuse movement within the hundreds chart for adding ten (down) or one (right). The two students who counted each square instead of recognizing groups of ten are still counting by ones.

WHOLE CLASS, SMALL GROUP, AND INDIVIDUAL FORMATIVE ASSESSMENT

Whole Class:

1. Review modeling numbers with Base 10 (28, 54, 13 . . . leave 13 move to top of work mat)
2. Now show me 40. If we added these, what would you do and how did you figure it out? (Repeat)
3. As students build numbers, have one student show it on the Hundreds chart to connect the two methods.
4. Model the open number line in conjunction the first time; then have students take turns modeling the three strategies.

Small Group:
Groups of 3: base 10 blocks, Hundreds chart and Open number line. Rotate roles explaining what they did to compare final answers.

Readiness groups to change problem challenge. Some two-digit plus 10, some two-digit plus multiple of 10, some any two-digits plus any two-digit.

Individual:
Given a single problem, show addition with Base 10 blocks plus one other method of their choice

Formative Assessment/Check for Understanding: Individual task

- When adding two-digit numbers with base 10 blocks, five students do not recognize the values of the ten-rods and unit cubes. Although they can now model numbers with the blocks more accurately (although three are still having trouble even with that), they can combine tens and ones separately but still either count the total number of blocks as a final answer or count all the blocks by tens.

Day 2 is a continuation from the previous day, so the mathematical standards and KUD remain the same from Day 1. Nevertheless, Ms. Salazar realizes that the activities for this day's lesson will use different mathematical practices, so she adds Standards for Mathematical Practice (SMP) 1, 2, 4, 5, 7, and 8 to the lesson plan template.

Day 2's lesson will put more focus on adding with the base 10 blocks than on the previous strategies of using the hundreds chart and open number line. Ms. Salazar decides to use her MATH stations today to connect the addition understandings for the unit with the strategies being used, as well as to serve as a bridge to Day 3 when she will introduce the tally method for addition, which will be introduced originally as a way to record the base 10 block addition.

Ms. Salazar will allow her students to pick a partner with whom they would like to work at each station. She will provide differentiated options within the stations based on choice (interest). She will be able to address some of the readiness concerns as students come to her in the T—Teacher Time— station even though the students will more than likely be in mixed-readiness pairs based on their choices of partners.

The lesson will begin with a whole class review from Day 1. Ms. Salazar will have the students sitting in their chosen pairs, one with a white board and the other with base 10 blocks. She will present an addition problem of a two-digit plus a multiple of ten, and one partner will write the problem and record the final answer on the white board while the other partner finds the sum with the base 10 blocks. Partners will change roles with each problem. After several problems and answers are recorded on the class white board in a list, the students will be asked whether they see any pattern in adding a two-digit number and a multiple of ten. Ms. Salazar will let students present their patterns and demonstrate why their pattern is true with the hundreds chart. She will question students and guide them into describing place value of tens and ones, connecting the pattern to the tens-rods and moving down on the hundreds chart. She will conclude the whole class time by having students explain to their partners why only the tens digit changes when you are adding these two types of numbers, listening for the key understanding that you can only add tens and tens and ones and ones.

After the whole class time, Ms. Salazar will assign groups of pairs to each station to begin the rotation. She is looking to mix readiness pairs at each station, so that if any pair of students experiences difficulty, they can ask another pair of students for help. The stations will be set up as follows:

M—Math Games—Popsicle Stick Addition—Using two cans of popsicle sticks: one can with random two-digit numbers and the other can with numbers of multiples of 10—10, 20, 30, 40. Students draw a stick from each can, show them with base 10 blocks, and add them together. Each partner will be able to choose the challenge level of their addition problem by either choosing two sticks from the can with random two-digit numbers, one from each can, or two sticks from the multiples of tens can; yet both partners will work together on the problem drawn. Students will record their problems, sketch the base 10 blocks, and write the sums on a recording sheet. Ms. Salazar will also be able to monitor the problem choices for various pairs by glancing at the recording sheets and making challenge recommendations if needed. Figure 8.7 shows this activity.

FIGURE 8.7

POPSICLE STICK ADDITION

© Lori Everson

A—All By Myself—By using a mathematical problem given to them (14 + 20), students draw a picture and write a story problem to go with it. For some students who have language difficulties, a template for a story will be given or the picture illustrating the problem concept will be sufficient. This will be collected to serve as a formative assessment to plan for the next day along with the Teacher Time records. Figure 8.8 shows a more challenging example of this activity.

FIGURE 8.8

ALL BY MYSELF MATH PROBLEM

Math Problem

35+42

Draw a picture:

_____

Write a story problem to match the math sentence above:

_____
_____
_____
_____
_____
_____
_____
_____

© Lori Everson

T—Teacher Time—Work in small groups with the teacher modeling addition with base 10 blocks. At this time, Ms. Salazar will differentiate by the challenge level of the problem, and she will have students teach each other accessing the mixed-readiness pairs. Through this peer teaching, she will be able to listen for conceptual development as well as monitor the skill progress. On her check sheet, she will keep a record of each student's progress.

H—Hmmmm . . .—100 Board Scrabble—Use blank 100 board and tiles 1 to 100, play like Scrabble (Hasbro, Pawtucket, RI), where players choose seven pieces, place one random number on the board to begin, and may play only one piece at a time (which must touch another piece already on game board). Figure 8.9 shows the 100 Board Scrabble game.

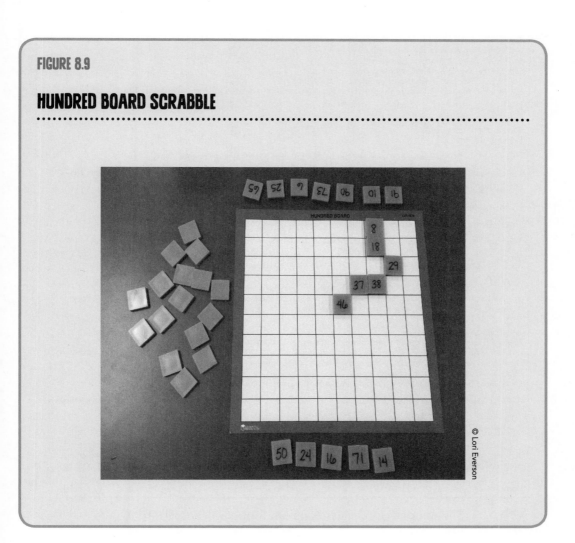

FIGURE 8.9

HUNDRED BOARD SCRABBLE

© Lori Everson

Figure 8.10 shows the lesson plan for Day 2.

FIGURE 8.10

DAY 2 LESSON PLAN

Daily Lesson Plan
Day 2

Date: 2/16
Standards:

1.NBT.B.2 *Understand that the two digits of a two-digit number represent amounts of tens and ones.*
1.NBT.C.4 *Add within 100, including adding a two-digit number and a one-digit number, and adding a two-digit number and a multiple of 10, using concrete models of drawings and strategies based on place value, properties of operations; relate the strategy to a written method and explain the reasoning used. Understand that in adding two-digit numbers, one adds tens and tens, ones and ones; and sometimes it is necessary to compose a ten.*

Standard for Mathematical Practice:

SMP1: Make sense of problems and persevere in solving them
SMP2: Reason abstractly and quantitatively
SMP4: Model with Mathematics
SMP5: Use appropriate tools strategically
SMP7: Look for and make use of structure (place value)
SMP8: Look for and express regularity in repeated reasoning (pattern in adding multiples of 10)

K: Place value
Value vs. digits
Tens & ones
Expanded form

U: Students will understand that only like things can be added (tens + tens, ones + ones)

Students will understand that numbers can be broken apart to make addition more clear: 28 + 12 = 28 + 10 + 2

Students will understand that different strategies can be used to solve the same problem

D: The students will be able to verbally explain how they solved a two-digit addition problem

The students will be able to model strategies to solve a two-digit addition problem

The students will be able to show the role of place value in two-digit addition (tens + tens, ones + ones)

Whole Class:

1. Work on adding numbers with Base 10 (36 + 20, 75 + 10, 35 + 30, etc . . .).
2. Talk about: when you add, do you see a pattern? (only tens are added, ones remain the same)
3. As students add numbers, have one student show it on the Hundreds chart and one student model the open number line to continue to connect and review the strategies.

Small Group MATH Rotations:
M – Math Games – Popsicle Stick Addition (using two cans of popsicle sticks – one can with random two-digit numbers and the other can with numbers of multiples of 10—10, 20, 30, 40). Students draw a stick from each can, show them with base 10 blocks, and add them together. Differentiate with different levels of sticks—higher groups choose two sticks from the can with random two-digit numbers, while students that are struggling may only have sticks with 10 and 20 on them. Recording sheets for problems to be handed in.

A – All By Myself – Using a math problem given to them (14 + 20), students draw a picture and write a story problem to go with it.

T – Teacher Time – Differentiated instruction (based on readiness) with Base 10 blocks

H – Hmmmm – 100 Board Scrabble (Use blank 100 board and tiles 1 to 100, play like Scrabble where players choose seven pieces and place one random number on the board to begin; players may play only one piece at a time (which must touch another piece already on game board).

Formative Assessment/Check for Understanding: Recording sheet from Popsicle Stick activity and story problem.

 The entire week's daily plans can found on the website at
http://resources.corwin.com/everymathlearnerK-5.

DAILY PLANNING—DAY 3

When planning for Wednesday of Week 3, Laurie Salazar reviewed her students' individual written work and her check sheet and anecdotal records from the previous days. She found

- Several of her students are now proficient with adding any two-digit numbers, and almost all of her students can add a two-digit number and a multiple of ten using base 10 blocks.

- Half of the students can explain the role of place value, or adding things that are alike, in their own words. Some of her favorite explanations include

    o "23 + 45 you could add it as 25 + 43; it doesn't matter because those are the ones (pointed to ones units) and because those are the tens (pointed to ten-rods) I add the tens first 20 + 40 = 60, then the ones 3 + 5 = 8 so the answer is 68."

    o "These together are all the tens and these are all the ones so you just put them together . . . tens and tens and ones and ones are easier for me."

    o "When I add these (the ones units), I get my ones number and when I add these (the ten-rods) I get my tens, then it's easier because I can just count the tens and ones."

- Approximately five students do not fully grasp the difference between what the ten-rod and unit cube represent. They tend to either count all the blocks as tens, simply counting by tens as a pattern, or count each block that is present. Ms. Salazar hopes that today's work of adding a tally chart to record the base 10 blocks and addition will help clarify this misconception for these students.

For this lesson, Ms. Salazar will be introducing the tally method of adding two-digit numbers. This method will be originally introduced as an easy way to record the work with base 10 blocks so students will not have to continue drawing blocks to show their thinking. Instead, they can use tallies to record the number of tens and ones, and then they can use the tallies to find the sum. Today's lesson will continue the same two standards that have been used and will continue to be used this week. The Standards for Mathematical Practice will concentrate on SMP4 (models), SMP 5 (tools), SMP 7 (structure of place value), and SMP 8 (patterns of adding multiples of tens).

To begin the lesson, Ms. Salazar will call her students to the rug for whole class time. She will model with magnetic base 10 blocks on the white board throughout the whole class time, but students will have a white board for working. To begin the whole class time, she will post the problem 37 + 20 and will ask her students how to model it with the base 10 blocks. She will have a student come and complete the problem to review the base 10 block process. While a student is modeling the problem, she will ask the rest of the students to draw it on their white boards.

To transition to the tally method, she will ask her students how they like drawing all the blocks. She is hoping that several students will explain that it is hard or tedious (in their own words, of course). This will give an access to explaining that there is an easier way to record the blocks, just as the open number line was another way to show how they added on the hundreds chart.

Going back to the original problem, 37 + 20, Ms. Salazar will show the blocks of 37, and by picking up one ten-rod at a time followed by one unit block at a time, she will create tallies next to 37. She will repeat the process with 20. Finally, Ms. Salazar will show how the tallies can be counted using place value to find the sum. Figure 8.11 demonstrates Ms. Salazar's white board.

Ms. Salazar will repeat the process having students write the tally chart on their white boards, first with two-digit numbers and progressing to addition problems. Once she sees that most students

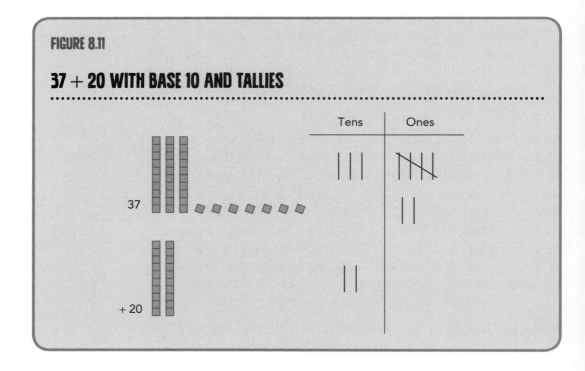

FIGURE 8.11

37 + 20 WITH BASE 10 AND TALLIES

37

+ 20

can transfer base 10 blocks to the tally chart, and vice versa, she will have them move to a paired activity.

For this activity, students will choose their partners, as well as their challenge levels. Ms. Salazar will prepare two sets of cards with problems on them. The green set of cards will have two-digit numbers plus a multiple of ten, and the yellow set of cards will have any two-digit numbers to add. Each partner team will have base 10 blocks, tally sheets, and white boards. One partner will choose a problem card and build the addition problem with base 10 blocks. The other partner will make a tally chart for the problem. They will use their models to find the sum, and they will see whether they agree. If not, they will show each other what they did to determine the answer, correcting any mistakes they see with their partner. If they do not agree, they will ask another team or see whether Ms. Salazar is available. Once the problem is complete, they will record it on the SUMS sheet and switch roles for another problem. Figure 8.12 shows the tally chart and SUMS sheet for the partners.

FIGURE 8.12

TALLY CHART AND SUMS SHEET

· ·

Tally Method

_____ + _____ = _____

Tens	Ones

Name _____

My SUMS Sheet

1. _____ + _____ = _____

2. _____ + _____ = _____

3. _____ + _____ = _____

4. _____ + _____ = _____

5. _____ + _____ = _____

© Lori Everson

FIGURE 8.13

DAY 3 LESSON PLAN

Daily Lesson Plan
Day 3

Date: 2/17
Standards:

1.NBT.B.2 *Understand that the two digits of a two-digit number represent amounts of tens and ones.*
1.NBT.C.4 *Add within 100, including adding a two-digit number and a one-digit number, and adding a two-digit number and a multiple of 10, using concrete models of drawings and strategies based on place value, properties of operations; relate the strategy to a written method and explain the reasoning used. Understand that in adding two-digit numbers, one adds tens and tens, ones and ones; and sometimes it is necessary to compose a ten.*

Standard for Mathematical Practice:

SMP4: Model with Mathematics.
SMP5: Use appropriate tools strategically.
SMP7: Look for and make use of structure (place value).
SMP8: Look for and express regularity in repeated reasoning (pattern in adding multiples of 10).

K: Place value
Value vs. digits
Tens & ones
Expanded form

U: Students will understand that only like things can be added (tens + tens, ones + ones)

Students will understand that numbers can be broken apart to make addition more clear: 28 + 12 = 28 +10 + 2

Students will understand that different strategies can be used to solve the same problem

D: The students will be able to verbally explain how they solved a two-digit addition problem

The students will be able to model strategies to solve a two-digit addition problem

The students will be able to show the role of place value in two-digit addition (tens + tens, ones + ones)

Whole Class:

1. Review addition of two-digit numbers with base 10 blocks.
2. Using magnetic base 10 blocks on the board, model two-digit addition problem.
3. Explain that base 10 blocks can be recorded on paper by use of tallies:

Show tallies

4. Lift each magnetic base 10 block and record tally under.
5. Count tallies to solve.
6. Repeat with a few problems to check for understanding prior to partner work.

Partner Work:

Use base 10 blocks to show a math problem, then record it with tallies on white boards or paper. Switch with partner to solve (students can reverse process with base 10 blocks if needed).

Formative Assessment/Check for Understanding: Observation on white boards or paper

The entire week's daily plans can be found on the website at
http://resources.corwin.com/everymathlearnerK-5

Ms. Salazar plans to observe her students closely as they work and make anecdotal records on her clipboard regarding which students are having difficulty transferring the base 10 blocks to the tally method, which students have made the place value connections and are being successful with the task, which students are working with challenge problems, and which students do not need the base 10 blocks at all but can go straight to the tally method for addition. She will use the SUMS sheet and her observations as formative assessment to inform specific groupings for tomorrow's lesson. Figure 8.13 shows the lesson plan for Day 3.

DAILY PLANNING—DAY 4

Thursday's lesson will be a continuation of using the tally method. This is a powerful strategy in that not only does it reinforce the role of place value in numbers and addition, but it also leads very naturally to the standard addition algorithm, which will be taught and required in later years. As Ms. Salazar plans for the next day's lesson, she reviews her records and the students' SUMS sheet. She sees that

- Four students still do not recognize place value and count all blocks and all tallies as either a 10 or a 1.

- Another three students whose fine motor skills are not developed enough to record the tallies neatly can correctly identify numbers and sums when given a completed tally chart.

- The majority (with the exception of the seven mentioned) of her students can correctly depict two-digit numbers with base 10 blocks and tallies.

- Fifteen students can use either model to add any two-digit numbers together correctly, not just a two-digit number and a multiple of ten.

To address the readiness needs of the students, Ms. Salazar will group the four students who do not appear to have a solid understanding of place value together, and the six most advanced students together, and she will mix the remaining students in groups of four. She plans to use her stations again to address the readiness differences most easily by changing the level of addition problem or puzzle at the stations for the different groups.

Ms. Salazar will begin with a brief whole class introduction, reviewing tens and ones and how they are seen in the hundreds chart, base 10 blocks, and the tally chart. She will next have students model two-digit addition, letting students choose their favorite method from all the methods they have done so far. This is to try to solidify the role of place value within each strategy, as well as the All By Myself Station, which will allow students to add, choosing from various methods. With each example, she will ensure that the tally method is shown clearly because it is the most recent strategy and still a focus of the day's learning.

With groups assigned, the students will begin their rotations:

M—Math Games—Dice Roll Addition—Use two 10-sided dice (0–9) and 1 place value dice (with numbers 10, 20, 30 etc.; these can also be made with different numbers to accommodate different levels). Roll two dice to make a two-digit number, and then roll the place value die to make the second number to add. Choose a strategy to solve the problem (100 board, open number line, base 10 blocks) along with the tally method. Record your problem and answer on paper. Figure 8.14 shows the dice used for this activity.

Students who demonstrate proficiency can choose to use digit cards to play two-digit addition war for added challenge.

A—All By Myself—Four Square Strategies for Addition Page—This activity is differentiated by readiness by changing the center problem and by interest by offering students a choice in their method of solution. Figure 8.15 provides an example of this activity.

FIGURE 8.14

DICE ROLL ADDITION

© Lori Everson

FIGURE 8.15

FOUR SQUARE ADDITION STRATEGIES

Strategies for Addition

100 Chart:

1	2	3	4	5	6	7	8	9	10
11	12	13	14	15	16	17	18	19	20
21	22	23	24	25	26	27	28	29	30
31	32	33	34	35	36	37	38	39	40
41	42	43	44	45	46	47	48	49	50
51	52	53	54	55	56	57	58	59	60
61	62	63	64	65	66	67	68	69	70
71	72	73	74	75	76	77	78	79	80
81	82	83	84	85	86	87	88	89	90
91	92	93	94	95	96	97	98	99	100

Open Number Line:

Math Problem:

Place Value:

Tally:

T—Teacher Time—Ms. Salazar differentiated instruction (based on learning profiles) with base 10 blocks or another manipulative—KP ten frames, paper, etc.—to help students who may struggle using the base 10 blocks.

H—Hmmmm . . . —Build-A-Square Puzzle with two-digit numbers and multiples of 10s. Different versions (levels) allow for differing levels of ability. This puzzle is put together by forming a 3 × 3 arrangement of cards where each side of a card touching a side of another card (vertically or horizontally) completes a problem. Figure 8.16 shows a completed example.

As part of her formative assessment, Ms. Salazar is going to ask students to explain how to add two two-digit numbers. She will give them the choice of explaining in words, either

FIGURE 8.16

BUILD-A-SQUARE ADDITION PUZZLE

	28 + 10			29 + 40			87 + 10	
35 + 20		42 + 10	52		35 + 20	55		71 + 20
	66 + 30			64			82	
	96			44 + 20			52 + 30	
42 + 20		54	34 + 20		29	19 + 10		43
	20 + 45			36			78	
	65			6 + 30			58 + 20	
72		34	4 + 30		41	21 + 20		87
	49 + 20			55			34	

© Lori Everson

oral or written, drawing a picture, or using a model. She will remind students to be sure to use "tens and ones" as part of their explanation. Because this is an essential understanding assessment, she wants to work with each student individually. She will do this over the course of this lesson as well as several additional days by asking students to meet individually with her during work times, station rotation with the teacher as appropriate, and other "loose" time during the day. She will also take note of explanations during the stations. For example, when she conducted the lesson, she noticed one student who was playing two-digit addition war: taking the two tens-cards and adding them and then taking the two ones-cards and adding them to find the sum of the numbers. When Ms. Salazar asked the student why she was doing that, she explained, "You have to add the tens with the tens and the ones with the ones. Otherwise you mix up the numbers for the answer." This response was logged as a correct understanding of the role of place value in addition.

Not all students could add the two-digit numbers or explain place value. For example, in working with Ms. Salazar during teacher time, one student tried to model 35 + 23. Although his thinking was somewhat on track (physically showing tens plus tens and ones plus ones), he could not get the answer. Matthew put them together, but instead of showing 35, he showed 53. He also reversed the tens and ones (put the tens on the right and ones on the left). When he counted, he counted 10, 20, 30, 40, 50, 60, 70 and told the teacher the answer was 70. When asked about the ones, he just smiled that cute smile and then continued 80, 90, . . . When he was asked to recount, he started with the ones and became confused.

Figure 8.17 shows the lesson plan for Day 4.

FIGURE 8.17

DAY 4 LESSON PLAN

Daily Lesson Plan
Day 4

Date: 2/18
Standards:

1.NBT.B.2 *Understand that the two digits of a two-digit number represent amounts of tens and ones.*
1.NBT.C.4 *Add within 100, including adding a two-digit number and a one-digit number, and adding a two-digit number and a multiple of 10, using concrete models of drawings and strategies based on place value, properties of operations; relate the strategy to a written method and explain the reasoning used. Understand that in adding two-digit numbers, one adds tens and tens, ones and ones; and sometimes it is necessary to compose a ten.*
1.NBT.C.5 *Given a two-digit number, mentally find 10 more or 10 less than the number, without having to count; explain the reasoning used*

Standard for Mathematical Practice:

SMP4: Model with Mathematics.
SMP5: Use appropriate tools strategically.
SMP7: Look for and make use of structure (place value).
SMP8: Look for and express regularity in repeated reasoning (pattern in adding multiples of 10).

K: Place value
Value vs. digits
Tens & ones
Expanded form

U: Students will understand that only like things can be added (tens + tens, ones + ones)

Students will understand that numbers can be broken apart to make addition more clear: 28 + 12 = 28 + 10 + 2

Students will understand that different strategies can be used to solve the same problem

D: The students will be able to verbally explain how they solved a two-digit addition problem

The students will be able to model strategies to solve a two-digit addition problem

The students will be able to show the role of place value in two-digit addition (tens + tens, ones + ones)

Whole Class:

1. Review tally method of addition of 2 digit numbers with Base 10 blocks.
2. Have students take turns modeling both magnetic base 10 and tally marks.

Small Group MATH Rotations:

M – Math Games – Dice Roll Addition – Use 2-10 sided dice (0-9) and 1 place value dice (with numbers 10, 20, 30 etc.. – these can also be made with different numbers to accommodate different levels). Roll 2 dice to make a 2 digit number, then roll the place value dice to make the second number to add. Choose strategy to solve (100 board, Jump Method, Base 10 or Tally). Record on paper.

A – All By Myself – Four Square Strategies for Addition page – Differentiation by readiness and interest.

T – Teacher Time – Differentiated instruction (based on learning profiles) with Base 10 blocks or offer use of other manipulative – KP tenframes, paper, etc . . . to help those who may struggle with base 10.

H – Hmmmm..- Magic 9 squares – 2 digit numbers and multiples of 10s. Different versions (levels) allow for differing levels of ability.

Formative Assessment/Check for Understanding: Four Square Strategies for Addition page

Closure and beginning summative assessment: Students explain how to add 2 two-digit numbers being sure to include the words "tens" and "ones" in their explanation. They will have the choice of:

*   Verbal or written (one or two sentences) explanation
*   Drawing a picture
*   Using a model

 The entire week's daily plans can be downloaded at http://resources
.corwin.com/everymathlearnerK-5

DAILY PLANNING—DAY 5

The final lesson of the week will be a combination of all strategies used in the unit to add two-digit numbers. Students will practice addition through a game called "Three-in-a-Row." The lesson is designed to address all areas of differentiation by having different readiness game boards and having students choose their addition strategy, which will address learning profile and interest.

Ms. Salazar will begin the lesson with a whole class activity. She will post two different addition problems on her white board, one that is a two-digit plus a multiple of ten and the other that is the sum of any two-digit numbers. She will then ask students to choose the problem that will challenge them and to choose any method to solve the problem. For the first round of problems, she will select students to present their solution methods having observed which problem and method students chose. She will choose a student to present a specific method for the first problem and then another student with the same method for the second problem. This will progress until all four addition strategies from the unit (hundreds chart, open number line, base 10 blocks, and tallies) have been presented for both problems. She will then post another pair of problems and ask students to move to a side of the rug based on their chosen problem. Once grouped by problem choice, she will ask the students to compare their methods and answers. By observing the two groups, she will determine who is ready to start playing the game and who needs more reinforcement. She will ask students to find partners in the groups they are currently in (based on problem choice and readiness) but knows she might have to move some students from one group to the other to address the challenge level of problems better.

Once students have chosen their partners, Ms. Salazar will give the pairs the appropriate game board and will review how to play:

- There are two paperclips on your addend strip. You may move only one paperclip on your turn.
- Add the two addends together, and place your marker on your sum on the gameboard.
- Paperclips can be in the same square, for example, 20 + 20.
- Use any strategy you want to find your sum.
- Record your addition sentences (equations) on the record sheet.

Figure 8.18 shows the most challenging level game.

FIGURE 8.18

THREE-IN-A-ROW HIGH CHALLENGE

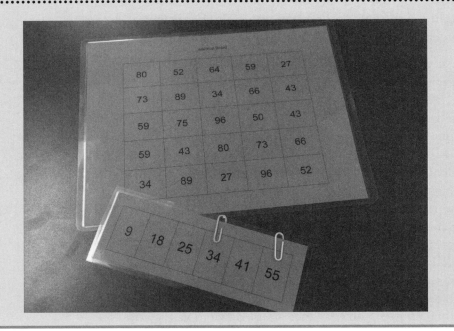

Ms. Salazar will ask a few pairs of students to come play the game with her at the Teacher Table, where she will continue to review place value and addition with these students through the game. She understands that it is important that these students also play the same game and do not feel ostracized or remediated with menial work even though they are still struggling to master the content. With these students, Ms. Salazar will have a very basic game with multiples of ten, one two-digit number other than a multiple of ten, and single-digit numbers. She will watch the strategies used, and she will reinforce with the students the place value with each number on the addend strip, as well as how tens are added to tens and ones are added to ones. She has been careful to choose numbers that will not need regrouping regardless of the addends chosen.

As students show better mastery with the game and with addition, she will give them the choice to continue playing at her table or to find another spot in the room to play. She will then be able to check in with different students, ask for the verbal explanations from students (see Day 4 closure), and give immediate feedback as students are playing the game.

Ms. Salazar plans to gather her students for a formal closure by asking students to share their most challenging problem they made while playing the game, how they solved it, what they found for the answer, and how they knew their answer was correct. After this discussion, she will give students the same Four Square addition sheet she used yesterday, but this time, the sheet will be blank. She asks students to write their most challenging problem in the center and to choose at least two different strategies to show their answer. Figure 8.19 shows the day's lesson plan.

FIGURE 8.19

DAY 5 LESSON PLAN

Daily Lesson Plan
Day 5

Standards:

1.NBT.B.2 *Understand that the two digits of a two-digit number represent amounts of tens and ones.*
1.NBT.C.4 *Add within 100, including adding a two-digit number and a one-digit number, and adding a two-digit number and a multiple of 10, using concrete models of drawings and strategies based on place value, properties of operations; relate the strategy to a written method and explain the reasoning used. Understand that in adding two-digit numbers, one adds tens and tens, ones and ones; and sometimes it is necessary to compose a ten.*

Standard for Mathematical Practice:

SMP4: Model with Mathematics.
SMP5: Use appropriate tools strategically.
SMP7: Look for and make use of structure (place value).
SMP8: Look for and express regularity in repeated reasoning (pattern in adding multiples of 10).

K: Place value
Value vs. digits
Tens & ones
Expanded form

U: Students will understand that only like things can be added (tens + tens, ones + ones)

Students will understand that numbers can be broken apart to make addition more clear: 28 + 12 = 28 + 10 + 2

Students will understand that different strategies can be used to solve the same problem

D: The students will be able to verbally explain how they solved a two-digit addition problem

The students will be able to model strategies to solve a two-digit addition problem

The students will be able to show the role of place value in two-digit addition (tens + tens, ones + ones)

Whole Class:

1. Review tally method of addition of two-digit numbers with Base 10 blocks.
2. Have students take turns modeling both magnetic base 10 and tally marks.
3. Snowball fight – use paper to write a math problem. Crumple up paper and throw – each student grabs a "snowball" and solves the problem using base 10 and tally method.

Partner Activity:

With partners, play 4 in a Row – different versions allow for differentiation based on readiness. Recording sheet to check for understanding

Re-Teach: Select students not able to show understanding of addition to the teacher table to play the basic version of the game with the teacher present. Reinforce with KP Ten frames, base-10 blocks and Hundreds chart the role of place value. Joke with students about "fair trades" to reinforce the difference of one ten and one unit.

Formative Assessment/Check for Understanding: Four Square Strategies for Addition page

Closure: What was the most challenging problem you made while playing the game? How did you solve it? What was your answer? How did you know your answer was reasonable and correct?

 The entire week's daily lesson plans can be downloaded from http://resources.corwin.com/everymathlearnerK-5

A LOOK INTO A WEEK IN
AN INTERMEDIATE CLASSROOM

Tom Mayfield is a fifth-grade teacher planning a geometry unit. The unit combines classifying polygons and volumes of right rectangular prisms. He will use the essential understandings regarding the importance of knowing and using the characteristics of shapes as a connection between the classification of shapes and determining the volume of prisms. He assigns homework practice sheets following Days 2, 3, and 4; yet the homework is not discussed in this section.

Mr. Mayfield understands that for many students, this geometry unit will be very easy as it is a concrete hands-on unit. Nevertheless, for some students, confusing aspects of measurement, formulas, and units can prove to be problematic. Additionally, Mr. Mayfield is planning to use volume as a way to review multiplication with decimals and fractions by providing fractional side lengths on the prisms, even though the standard specifies whole number measurements.

FROM UNIT TO LESSON PLAN

Mr. Mayfield begins to plan his unit by creating a unit plan and calendar. The unit plan lists the standards on which the unit is built. He unpacks these standards into the Know, Understand, and Do (KUD) and lists these in the unit plan. The KUD guides his daily instructional decisions. Finally, Mr. Mayfield lists possible assessment ideas including a preassessment for the unit to be given several days in advance, daily formative assessments and checks for understanding, and items he will want to include in a summative assessment. Figure 8.20 shows Mr. Mayfield's unit plan, which he titled "Measuring Shapes."

Once the unit plan is completed, Mr. Mayfield sketches out on a calendar the number of days and preliminary activities for the unit. He checks to be sure that all of the standards are addressed and the KUD is established and connected in his initial plans. The unit planning calendar is shown in Figure 8.21.

Throughout the unit, Mr. Mayfield plans on emphasizing the importance of the number of dimensions in a shape. This should help students as they classify two- and three-dimensional (2-D and 3-D) shapes, but more importantly, dimensions determine what can be measured about a shape and the correct units in describing the measurement. The following lessons focus on the first full week of the unit, Days 4 through 8, beginning with the concept check activity on classifying polygons.

FIGURE 8.20

MEASURING SHAPES UNIT PLAN

Unit Design Template

<u>Unit Title</u>: *Measuring Shapes (5th Grade): Classifying 2-D and 3-D Shapes and Volume*

<u>Standards Addressed</u>:

5.G.3 *Understand that attributes belonging to a category of two-dimensional figures also belong to all subcategories of that category. For example, all rectangles have four right angles and squares are rectangles, so all squares have four right angles.*

5.G.4 *Classify two-dimensional figures in a hierarchy based on properties.*

5.MD.3 *Recognize volume as an attribute of solid figures and understand concepts of volume measurement.*

   a. *A cube with side length 1 unit, called a "unit cube," is said to have "one cubic unit" of volume and can be used to measure volume.*

   b. *A solid figure that can be packed without gaps or overlaps using n unit cubes is said to have a volume of n cubic units.*

5.MD.4 *Measure volumes by counting unit cubes, using cubic cm, cubic in, cubic ft, and improvised units.*

5.MD.5 *Relate volume to the operations of multiplication and addition and solve real world and mathematical problems involving volume.*

   a. *Find the volume of a right rectangular prism with whole-number side lengths by packing it with unit cubes, and show that the volume is the same as would be found by multiplying the edge lengths, equivalently by multiplying the height by the area of the base. Represent threefold whole-number products as volumes, e.g., to represent the associative property of multiplication.*

   b. *Apply the formulas $V = l \times w \times h$ and $V = b \times h$ for rectangular prisms to find volumes of right rectangular prisms with whole-number edge lengths in the context of solving real-world and mathematical problems.*

   c. *Recognize volume as additive. Find volumes of solid figures composed of two non-overlapping right rectangular prisms by adding the volumes of the non-overlapping parts, applying this technique to solve real-world problems.*

By the end of the unit, what will students . . .

Know	Understand	Be Able to Do
Vocabulary: area, attribute, base, categorize, congruent, edge, face, hierarchy, lateral face, parallel, perimeter, polygon, polyhedron (polyhedra), prism, property, regular, right angle, unit cube, vertex, volume Names of specific polygons based on numbers of sides $V = (l)(w)(h)$ $V = bh$	Students will understand that we organize and classify shapes based on the characteristics (attributes) of the shape. Students will understand that often irregular shapes or solids can be separated into familiar shapes or solids. Then composite areas or volumes can be found. Students will understand that volume is found from measurements of area similarly to how areas are found from measurements of lengths. Students will understand that the types of units used describe what is being measured, and what is being measured has a specific type of unit.	The students will be able to classify polygons and explain the hierarchy of quadrilaterals. The students will be able to compare and contrast 1-D, 2-D and 3-D measurements (lengths vs. area vs. volume). The students will be able to explain the role of units in geometric measurement. The students will be able to correctly calculate volumes of right rectangular prisms and composite shapes made of right rectangular prisms. The students will be able to apply geometric measurement to real-world problems.

(Continued)

FIGURE 8.20 (Continued)

Preassessment Ideas: Graphic organizer on polygons to name, measure and calculate areas and perimeters (prior information). Given a rectangular right prism, ask students to describe it and find a volume with a provided word bank (upcoming learning).

Summative Assessment Ideas: Complete quadrilateral hierarchy organizer. Calculate volumes of simple right rectangular prisms and composite rectangular prisms. Apply volume to real world problems. Essay: Explain the role of units in measurements.

Formative Assessment Ideas: Exit cards, station and activity work, homework, class discourse, questioning.

 The full unit plan can be found online at http://resources.corwin.com/everymathlearnerK-5.

FIGURE 8.21

MEASURING SHAPES PLANNING CALENDAR

Math Planning Calendar

Unit: Measuring Shapes: Classifying 2-D and 3-D shapes; volume

Duration: 2½ weeks

Monday	Tuesday	Wednesday	Thursday	Friday
		4/13 Identify and classify polygons	4/14 Focus on triangles	4/15 Focus on quadrilaterals –
4/18 Concept Check: Classifying Polygons – modality activities	4/19 Review of area and perimeter; Introduction to Volume – master builder	4/20 Finding the volume of rectangular prisms	4/21 Finding the volume of rectangular prisms – exploring a formula	4/22 Finding volumes of composite rectangular prisms
4/25 Continued practice with composite rectangular prisms	4/26 Comparing volumes	4/27 More application problems	4/28 Looking at other polyhedra	4/29 Unit assessment

 A blank planning calendar and the completed calendar for this unit can be found on http://resources.corwin.com/everymathlearnerK-5

DAILY PLANNING—DAY 1

Today's lesson is a continuation from the previous Friday, and it serves as a concluding activity to classifying polygons. Mr. Mayfield plans to use the activities today as an assessment to check for mastery on the standard. From observations on Friday, he anticipates that

- Twelve students will confuse descriptive terms such as scalene, isosceles, and regular.

- Four students will not know the names of the specific quadrilaterals, confusing trapezoid, parallelogram, rhombus, and square.

Mr. Mayfield is not sure whether these students have misconceptions or whether they simply need more time and practice. He believes that today's activity will provide additional practice as well as serve as a formative assessment to verify that his students understand the attributes of polygons and how they can be grouped and classified prior to beginning the study on volume in right rectangular prisms.

To give his students the opportunity to demonstrate most fully what they know and understand about classifying polygons, he will offer three different activities, differentiated by interest. He will also allow his students a choice to work with a partner or to work alone on two tasks. The third task, however, will be an interactive task requiring a partner. He chose and designed the tasks based loosely on the modality learning profile of visual, auditory, and kinesthetic tasks. The tasks also have elements of analytical, creative, and practical tasks. No matter what the task, the essential understanding that we organize and classify shapes based on the characteristics (attributes) of the shape is addressed.

To begin the class, Mr. Mayfield will conduct a whole class discussion. He will review key polynomial vocabulary with his class, and specifically, he will review the terms *scalene*, *isosceles*, and *regular* as he knows that students often develop misconceptions related to them. For example, we do not think about applying the terms *scalene* and *isosceles* to anything other than triangles; yet, those terms also apply to quadrilaterals. This will be important in possible groupings and classification of polynomials.

After the key vocabulary and terms are reviewed, he will lead an activity he calls "Make Three Statements." This is an activity the students are familiar with as he uses this strategy often.

Mr. Mayfield will present a polygon to the class and say, "Make three statements." The students will write on their white boards three statements about the polygon and hold them up. He will then call different students to read specific statements.

The last activity he will lead in a whole class setting is a compare-and-contrast activity that the students will do in pairs. Mr. Mayfield will show two polygons, and the pairs of students will discuss how they are alike and how they are different. Responses will be logged on the white board as students give their observations. He will repeat this with several different pairings of polygons, paying attention to subtleties such as an isosceles triangle and an isosceles trapezoid or a right triangle and a square.

On the Friday prior to the lesson, Mr. Mayfield described the three choices of activities that would be offered in today's lesson. He asked his students to write their top two choices, in order, on a slip of paper. He used their choices to assign a task to them. He chose to do this because he wanted his students choosing a task they felt they could do well. At the time of the choice, they did not know they would be able to work with a partner, and he was concerned that many of his students would choose to work with a friend regardless of whether the task would be their best choice. By having them choose the task in advance, and then choose a partner from the specific list of students with the same task, he knows the partners are working together on a task on which they best feel they will be able to show their learning. To move students into their chosen activities, he uses his document camera to show the tasks and the student's names listed below the task based on their prior choices. He then allows them to find a partner with the same task choice or to work alone.

The three choices that Mr. Mayfield designed to classify shapes were a Venn diagram, a sorting activity, and a game to guess the shape. The Venn diagram compares quadrilaterals, and he knows that he will also want to challenge students to compare triangle classifications and quadrilateral classifications. He will accomplish this by asking for students to fill in an "Alike But Different" table on specific shapes on the back of the Venn diagram. He knows students who are more visual and analytical should like this task. Figure 8.22 shows the Venn diagram.

The second choice is a sorting activity. The students will be given a baggie with terms and diagrams with which they are to form groups. This is a very open task, and there are multiple ways the terms and diagrams can be correctly grouped. This task is a kinesthetic

FIGURE 8.22

VENN DIAGRAM FOR QUADRILATERALS

FIGURE 8.23

GROUPING POLYNOMIALS

and more practical task. The students will record their groupings and why they believe they went together. In addition, they will be able to draw arrows from one group to another to show another connection if needed (e.g., right triangles, squares, and rectangles all have right angles). Figure 8.23 shows the sorting activity.

The third activity is a partner game based on the child's game "Guess Who." Partner A will choose a polynomial. Partner B will ask yes-and-no questions about the attributes of the shape to guess the shape. Partners will log both the questions and answers and the final guess to turn in for accountability. Mr. Mayfield will provide a list of attributes for this game to be sure that the partner answering the questions gives correct information. Figure 8.24 shows the guessing game.

FIGURE 8.24

GUESS WHO

To close the lesson, Mr. Mayfield will ask students to gather back together and say one thing they knew really well about classifying polygons after their activity. He will "whip" around the room with each student sharing one idea. He will then ask the students to complete an exit card classifying a trapezoid and a square in as many ways as they can.

The lesson plan for the first day of this week is found in Figure 8.25.

FIGURE 8.25

DAY 1 LESSON PLAN

Daily Lesson Plan
Day 1

Date: 4/18
Standards:

5.G.3 *Understand that attributes belonging to a category of two-dimensional figures also belong to all subcategories of that category. For example, all rectangles have four right angles and squares are rectangles, so all squares have four right angles*

5.G.4 *Classify two-dimensional figures in a hierarchy based on properties.*

Standard for Mathematical Practice:
SMP3: Construct viable arguments and critique the reasoning of others.
SMP6: Attend to precision.
SMP7: Look for and make use of structure.

K: Vocabulary: attribute, classify, hierarchy, parallel sides, polygon, property, regular polygon, right angles
Names of polygons
Hierarchy of quadrilaterals

U: Students will understand that we organize and classify shapes based on the characteristics (attributes) of the shape.

D: The students will be able to classify polygons and explain the hierarchy of quadrilaterals.

Whole Class:

1. Review attributes and names of polygons, with emphasis on the vocabulary terms: scalene, isosceles, regular.
2. "Make three statements . . . "
3. Compare and contrast any two polygons
4. Review tasks and have students find partners within their chosen tasks

Paired activity based on interest:

- Venn Diagram
- Sorting Activity
- Guess Who game

Individual/formative assessment:
Exit card: Given a trapezoid and a square, give all of the categories in which they can be described.

 The entire week's daily lesson plans can be accessed at http://resources .corwin.com/everymathlearnerK-5

DAILY PLANNING—DAY 2

Today's lesson is a beginning introduction to 3-D shapes and volume. This is a shift of topic within the unit, and from yesterday's lesson, Mr. Mayfield knows that he still has eight students who do not recognize that shapes can be classified in multiple ways or that shapes can be classified within a hierarchy and "nested" within other shapes, such as a square is also a rectangle, which is also a parallelogram. He will address some issues he identified from yesterday in small readiness groups during the station time in class today.

Mr. Mayfield is planning to introduce initial 3-D (polyhedra) vocabulary at the beginning of the lesson, which will continue to be used throughout the unit; yet he is not concerned about spending a lot of time on this vocabulary or on the specific types of polyhedra today. He is planning a day toward the end of the unit on various polyhedra (see calendar 4/28), but at this time, he wants to move into the concept of volume. Since his standards only address volume of right rectangular prisms, he will spend more time with that specific polyhedron than with others.

Mr. Mayfield will begin the lesson by asking students to explain what a dimension means when it comes to shapes. He will ask them to give examples around the room of a 2-D shape and a 3-D shape, being sure to clarify that the "D" stands for dimension. He will then challenge his students to think about 1-D shapes and what that means.

He will begin to build a chart of students' responses for shapes, listing the identified shape, then types of measurements that are possible, and finally the units that could be used for each type of measurement. Figure 8.26 shows the chart and types of responses Mr. Mayfield received from his students during the opening discussion.

Mr. Mayfield's students described measuring only the sides of the desk at first, instead of the desktop, when asked what could be measured with the tops of their desks. He helped his students realize that if they measure the side lengths, they are measuring only a 1-D shape, not the entire top of the desk. They were describing perimeter, which is about lengths and only one dimension. This led the students to describe measuring area, which is measurement of a 2-D shape. From this conversation, Mr. Mayfield was able to reinforce why area always has square units (two dimensions that have been multiplied together), and length

FIGURE 8.26

SHAPE, MEASUREMENT, AND UNIT

Dimension	Shape	Measurement	Unit
1-D	Side of desk	Length	Inches or feet
1-D	Where the wall meets the floor	Length	Feet or yards
1-D	Door frame	Length	Feet or yards
2-D	Top of desk	Area	Square inches or square feet
2-D	Book cover	Area	Square inches
3-D	Our mailboxes (cubbies)		
3-D	Inside the cabinets		

is not measured with a square unit. When describing a 3-D shape, students were not sure what to measure. They kept describing measuring side lengths, which they could now correct each other as being about one dimension instead of about three. Mr. Mayfield then asked them what could be done with a 3-D shape that could not be done with a 2-D shape. To help, he brought out a box and a rectangle. Students immediately saw that they could fill up the box. This set up the introduction to volume.

Mr. Mayfield had students suggest how to measure the idea of "filling up." He explained that to begin to measure volume, they would be working with cubes that are one inch on all sides. He asked them to describe the shape (cubes), and told them that these are inch cubes, and to determine volume for today, they would be counting how many cubes it would take to fill the shape.

He introduced the stations for the day and assigned groups of students to different stations to begin. He arranged to have students together based on the results of yesterday's formative assessment and exit card on classifying polynomials because he could reengage students with that content as needed, clarify individual student's understanding, or extend learning as appropriate during the "Meet the Teacher" Station. There were three stations for class today. He had his students grouped in six groups of four or five and repeated the three stations twice as blue and red stations. The three stations were as follows:

- Master Builder: This is a partner activity where one partner builds a shape behind a file folder using the cubes. The student describes the building to his or her partner including the dimensions, how it is shaped, and the total volume. The partner tries to build exactly the same shape behind another file folder. When the partners are ready, they lift their file folders to see whether the two shapes are the same. Figure 8.27 shows one of the shapes built during Master Builder.

- Practice Sheet: Mr. Mayfield has several practice sheets for students to count cubes as a way of determining the volumes of shapes. These sheets ask for volume in terms of numbers of cubes, which will lead to the notation of cubic units (units^3) for volume tomorrow. Blocks to build the shapes are available for students who have difficulty imagining the 3-D shape from the image on paper. This will be used for Mr. Mayfield's check for understanding and provide information as he plans for the next day's lesson.

FIGURE 8.27

MASTER BUILDER

© Nanci Smith

- Meet with Me: Mr. Mayfield will call groups of students to meet with him for reengagement, explanations, and/or extensions as appropriate regarding classification of polynomials. Some students need to review perimeter and area versus volume. For students who have mastered classification, Mr. Mayfield plans to extend their thinking in comparing and classifying polyhedra, including prisms, cylinders, cones, and pyramids.

FIGURE 8.28

DAY 2 LESSON PLAN

Daily Lesson Plan
Day 2

Date: 4/19
Standards:

5.MD.3 *Recognize volume as an attribute of solid figures and understand concepts of volume measurement.*

    a. *A cube with side length 1 unit, called a "unit cube," is said to have "one cubic unit" of volume, and can be used to measure volume.*

    b. *A solid figure that can be packed without gaps or overlaps using n unit cubes is said to have a volume of n cubic units.*

5.MD.4 *Measure volumes by counting unit cubes, using cubic cm, cubic in, cubic ft, and improvised units.*

Standard for Mathematical Practice:

SMP1: Make sense of problems and persevere in solving them
SMP2: Reason abstractly and quantitatively
SMP4: Model with Mathematics
SMP5: Use appropriate tools strategically

K: Vocabulary: area, base, edge, face, lateral face, parallel, perimeter, polyhedron (polyhedra), prism, unit cube, vertex, volume

U: Students will understand that the types of units used describe what is being measured, and what is being measured has a specific type of unit.

D: The students will be able to compare and contrast 1-D, 2-D, and 3-D measurements (lengths vs. area vs. volume).

The students will be able to explain the role of units in geometric measurement.

Whole Class:

1. Discuss 1-D, 2-D and 3-D shapes. Begin with 2- and 3-D shapes, then ask students to describe a 1-D shape.
2. Ask what types of measurement we could get with a line, a rectangle, and a right rectangular prism (box). Ask if we could fill up a line or rectangle . . . discuss volume.
3. Fill up boxes with unit cubes – inch cubes and cm cubes. Describe volume as the total number of cubes that can fill a space without any gaps or holes.

Stations:

Master Builder

Meet with Teacher when called (differentiated instruction review measurement and area of rectangles. Explore the role of units. Compare area with volume using cubes – faces of cubes for area and number of cubes for volume)

Practice sheet of counting volume cubes

Closure: Think-Pair-Share-Squared "Top 2 statements about 3-D shapes."

Individual/formative assessment: Practice sheets

 The entire week's daily lesson plans can be accessed at http://resources .corwin.com/everymathlearnerK-5

For his lesson closure, Mr. Mayfield planned a Think-Pair-Share-Squared in figure 8.28. He asked students to think of two statements about 3-D shapes that they learned today and to write them down. He then asked his students to find a partner, share their statements, and record their partner's statements on their own paper. Out of the four statements they now had, they were to choose their favorite two statements. Finally, the partners paired up into groups of four and repeated the process with the other pairs' chosen two statements. Out of the four statements, they chose their favorite two and were ready to share one of the two as part of the whole class sharing. Figure 8.28 provides the lesson plan for this day's lesson.

DAILY PLANNING—DAY 3

This lesson continues to build on volume as a measurement to fill space. The students did not have any misconceptions or difficulties from the introduction to volume yesterday, so Mr. Mayfield has prepared a Math Menu for students to guide their work time today. He is hoping that by focusing activities on filling right rectangular prisms, and determining the number of cubes needed to fill the shapes without gaps, that his students will be able to generalize the volume formulae on their own. This will be formalized and applied in the next day's lesson.

To begin the lesson, Mr. Mayfield will show a picture of a square watermelon (see http://news.bbc.co.uk/2/hi/asia-pacific/1390088.stm) and will ask his students whether they have any questions. He will post the questions they ask without giving too much information. He also will assure the students that these are real and that Japanese farmers grow them.
Mr. Mayfield will not answer many questions, but he will prompt his students to keep the watermelon in mind because he would like to know how much watermelon is in one of these by the end of class.

Mr. Mayfield will ask his students why these might be called "cubic" watermelons. This will lead to a discussion of a cube, and he will ask his students to give him other examples of cubes, as well as then to list attributes of cubes. He will tie this back to earlier lessons by categorizing cubes as a specific type of right rectangular prism. He will let his students know that this year they will only work with volumes of right rectangular prisms. Before giving the menu assignment, he will ask students to describe the meaning of volume, and how cubes can help determine the exact volume, listening carefully for a description that includes filling the space without gaps.

The menu planner (see Chapter 4 for description) is designed to provide students with choice while they refine their understanding of volume. The menu for this lesson is designed for one class session, and Mr. Mayfield wants his students to become familiar with the format as he plans to use a menu (see Figure 4.10) as a differentiated summative assessment on the volume portion of the unit. The menu is designed with a main course, which includes three tasks that students must complete: building right rectangular prisms given a volume, a practice sheet determining volumes of right rectangular prisms formed from cubes, and a choice of a real-world packing problem that includes different readiness levels. Figure 8.29 shows the packing problems. Cubes will be available for any students who want to build the prisms on the sheet as it can be difficult for some students to interpret perspective drawings of 3-D shapes.

Mr. Mayfield expects that most of his students will have an intuition about a formula for volume by the end of this class period. The design of the Building Volume activity is to foster that intuition, which will be formalized in the next day's lesson.

Students will choose one game to play for their side dish. The game choices are

- Fill-a-Box: Choose a box and predict how many cubes it will take to fill. Then, fill the box and record your dimensions and volume on the menu sheet. There are a variety of boxes, large and small, and some that perfectly fit the cubes and others that do not. By using large boxes, Mr. Mayfield hopes that his students will begin naturally to connect multiplication with the total number of cubes. By using boxes that do not fit

FIGURE 8.29

PACKING PROBLEM CHOICE CARDS

Volume Fill-It Problem Cards

Michelle's jewelry box has a volume of 36 cubic inches. Build a possible jewelry box. Record the number of cubes needed:

_____ X _____ X _____

length   width   height

You have been using inch cubes to find volume. Now I need to pack them up. My box is 12" long, 4 inches wide and 3 inches high. How many cubes will it hold?

Bianca wants to pack her Duplo blocks into a box. She lines up four rows of eight blocks across on the bottom of the box. She can fill the box with five layers. How many Duplo blocks can she fit in the box?

How much space (volume) is there in your cubby? If time, find something else in our class that has volume, and determine its volume.

My granddaughter loves crayons, but she keeps breaking them (she's 2). I bought a case of big fat crayons for her. The case came with smaller boxes of crayons inside it. Each crayon box is 4" long, 6" wide and ½ " tall. There were a total of 10 boxes of crayons. What is the volume of the case?

Landon is getting an aquarium. His goldfish will need as much room as possible. He wants to buy either the aquarium that is 10" long, 8" wide, and 9" high, or 12" long, 5" wide, and 12" high. Which tank will hold more water?

_____ X _____ X _____

length   width   height

the cubes perfectly, he hopes his students will begin to think about fractional side dimensions, even though this is beyond the standard requirement. Figure 8.30 shows the start of a Fill-A-Box activity.

- Volume Memory: This is a memory game with pictures of prisms built by cubes and volume cards. The memory game will also be an option for tomorrow's class as well, but using dimensions and volumes. Figure 8.31 displays a memory game in progress.

FIGURE 8.30

FILL-A-BOX

© Nanci Smith

FIGURE 8.31

VOLUME MEMORY

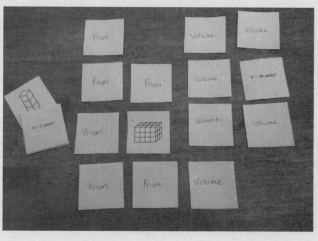

© Nanci Smith

- Online Volume Game: Several choices of online games and activities, all with filling shapes with cubes to determine volumes. One example is from NCTM's Illuminations (http://illuminations.nctm.org/Activity.aspx?id=4095).

The final section of the menu is called *dessert*, and it is there to take care of any ragged time for students who finish earlier than others. One of the two dessert options is to complete an "Exploring Volume" activity, which asks students to predict and compare volumes of two different prisms and then fill one prism with pinto beans and pour the beans into the other to see whether their comparison is correct. The second dessert choice is to play another volume game from the side dish options. Figure 8.32 provides the students' menu.

As students complete their menu tasks, they will record the prisms with which they work in the table at the bottom of the menu. They will also check in with Mr. Mayfield as they complete their side dish and each main course task.

Mr. Mayfield will then gather the students together to close the lesson. He will ask students to share any ideas, patterns, or connections they have discovered with determining volumes. Several students will have already seen the multiplication process for determining the total number of cubes. He will then revisit the cubic watermelon and tell the students that if he had one, he would cut the watermelon inside into cubes instead of balls. He learned that the boxes in which the watermelon are grown are 8" × 8" × 8". Mr. Mayfield will ask students to tell him how many watermelon cubes he could get out of the cubic watermelon if each of his melon pieces were a 1-inch cube? They will write their answers and an explanation of how they know on an index card as an exit card. The menu and exit card will be the data that Mr. Mayfield use to determine the next day's lesson adjustments. Figure 8.33 shows the day's lesson plan.

DAILY PLANNING—DAY 4

By using his students' completed Menu work, exit cards, and his anecdotal records from conversations with students, Mr. Mayfield sees that:

FIGURE 8.32

VOLUME MENU

Measuring Shapes Menu Planner
Please attach all of your work to this menu planner. Turn everything in by the end of class.

Check In

Main Course: Complete both of these activities.

- Practice sheets of counting cubes for volume
- Choose a "Fill-It" card to solve.

Side Dish: Choose one math game to play.

- Fill-A-Box
- Volume Memory
- Online Volume activity from Illuminations:
  http://illuminations.nctm.org/Activity.aspx?id=4095

Don't forget to record your volumes from your game on a piece of paper.

Dessert: If time, you may

- Complete the Exploring Volume activity
- Play another game, or repeat the game you have played

The prisms I built or worked with today:

# cubes in length	# cubes in width	# cubes in height	# cubes in total (volume)

 The full menu can be found at http://resources.corwin.com/
everymathlearnerK-5

FIGURE 8.33

DAY 3 LESSON PLAN

Daily Lesson Plan
Day 3

Date: 4/20
Standards:

5.MD.4 *Measure volumes by counting unit cubes, using cubic cm, cubic in, cubic ft, and improvised units.*

5.MD.5 *Relate volume to the operations of multiplication and addition and solve real world and mathematical problems involving volume.*

   a. *Find the volume of a right rectangular prism with whole-number side lengths by packing it with unit cubes, and show that the volume is the same as would be found by multiplying the edge lengths, equivalently by multiplying the height by the area of the base. Represent threefold whole-number products as volumes, e.g., to represent the associative property of multiplication.*

Standard for Mathematical Practice:

SMP4: Model with Mathematics
SMP5: Use appropriate tools strategically.
SMP8: Look for and express regularity in repeated reasoning (pattern in adding multiples of 10).

K: Vocabulary: area, base, edge, face, lateral face, parallel, perimeter, polyhedron (polyhedra), prism, unit cube, vertex, volume

U: Students will understand that the types of units used describe what is being measured, and what is being measured has a specific type of unit.

Students will understand that volume is found from measurements of area similarly to how areas are found from measurements of lengths.

D: The students will be able to explain the role of units in geometric measurement.

The students will be able to apply geometric measurement to real-world problems.

Whole Class:

1. Launch discussion using square watermelon: http://news.bbc.co.uk/2/hi/asia-pacific/1390088.stm

Wikimedia commons/ laughlin at http://www.flickr.com/photos/wurzle/52461952/

2. Why do this? Should we get rid of circles and spheres?

3. I can't fill up the watermelon with cubes. How could I determine how much watermelon is in there?

Menu Planner (Work alone or with one partner)

Main Course: Please complete:

- Practice sheet with volume by counting cubes progressing to seeing cube outlines of a prism and predicting volume. Differentiate by providing cubes for those who still want to build.
- Choose a "Fill-It" card to solve.

Side Dish: Math Game. Choose one to play:

- Fill-A-Box
- Volume Memory
- Online Volume game or Illuminations activity http://illuminations.nctm.org/Activity.aspx?id=4095

Dessert: If time, you may

- Complete the Exploring Volume activity – fill boxes, compare volumes, hypothesize how to find volume if you don't have cubes
- Play another game

Closure: The watermelons were grown in hard plastic boxes (polyurethane) that were 8" × 8" × 8". How much watermelon is in a square watermelon? By the way, they sell in Japan for about $83 a watermelon so most people don't buy them.

Formative Assessment/Check for Understanding: Practice sheets and record sheet from game that is chosen.

The entire week's daily lesson plans can be accessed on the website at
http://resources.corwin.com/everymathlearnerK-5

- Twelve of his students have explained that they do not need to build the shapes; they can multiply the numbers.

- Eight students have a shorter counting method for the blocks by multiplying for the base area and using repeated addition based on the height for the total volume.

- Seven students still count the blocks.

- All students can correctly describe what they are finding when they fill shapes or when asked what volume is.

- Only three students chose the most challenging (The Crayon Problem) Fill-It cards, but they got a correct answer through modeling the problem with blocks. Many students chose to find the volume of their cubby, but they tried to find it by filling it with cubes, which did not work well.

Mr. Mayfield will begin today's class by asking students to build prisms based on a given volume. They will be challenged to find every possible prism with the same volume. Figure 8.34 shows two students' work from the Building Volume activity, having selected a volume card of 24 cubic inches.

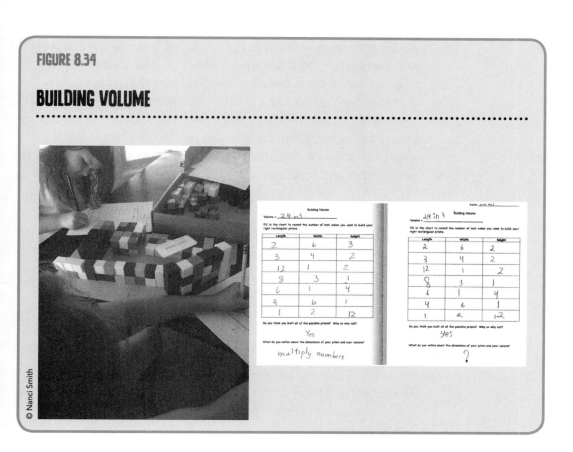

FIGURE 8.34

BULDING VOLUME

This activity will be used to springboard the whole class discussion leading to the formalization of the two-volume formulas. He will take careful note of which students are seeing the relationship between the dimensions of a prism and the total volume. Mr. Mayfield will then bring the students together after the Building Volume activity to discuss findings. Several students will be asked to explain how they built their prisms based on the given volume and whether they had any difficulties.

During the activity several students shared that they had leftover cubes when building their prisms, so they had to start over with their base dimensions to get the prism dimensions to be exact. All students agreed that a one-level prism (height of one) was easy to build. When challenged to think why this would be easy, it dawned on most students that they just had to think of two factors whose product was the volume. Mr. Mayfield had his students discuss in pairs why it was harder to build a prism with multiple layers.

After taking several answers, Mr. Mayfield asked his students to consider their Building Volume sheets. How did the dimensions of the prism relate to the total volume? Why would the dimensions work? At this point, almost all students were seeing the multiplication process, but once a student shared that you multiply the three dimensions to get the total number of cubes, the remaining students saw it as well. Mr. Mayfield then took the time to have two students model two different prisms made from the cubes and how the multiplication related to the total numbers of cubes. This was formalized into the formula $V = l \times w \times h$. He used this time to discuss why the units being used to describe volume would always be cubic. He had students talk about how the inch cubes are 1" × 1" × 1" but could be 1 ft × 1 ft ×1 ft or any other unit of measure.

After practicing two prisms with given dimensions using the formula, he asked his students whether anyone recognized $l \times w$. All students responded that it was the area of a rectangle. This led to the second volume formula, $V = B \times h$. Special care was taken to discuss why it is a capital B (because it stands for the area of the base, not a single dimension). This was followed by modeling with cubes the repeated layering of "areas of base" to form a prism. He ended the whole class discussion with teaching students how to draw a right rectangular prism two different ways.

Mr. Mayfield gave pairs of students an 11" × 17" sheet of paper and challenged them to build a box with the greatest volume by folding up all four edges equally and taping the corners. They had to measure all three dimensions of their open boxes and find their volume. Once the box was built, Mr. Mayfield filled it with popcorn for the pair to share as a treat. Of course students wanted the biggest box! A class challenge was on to find the dimensions of a box with greatest volume.

For closure, Mr. Mayfield planned a differentiated task that asked his students to summarize their learning about volume. He wanted to be sure that they understood the volume of a prism, the units used, and the use of formulas prior to beginning compound volumes tomorrow. He designed the task options using Sternberg's Triarchic Theory as a framework, but he allowed his students to choose the task they would like to complete. Figure 8.35 shows the Volume Wisdom task and one student's work.

FIGURE 8.35

VOLUME WISDOM

Name_____

Volume Wisdom!

Your task is to let me know EVERYTHING you now know about volume. To share your wisdom with me, you may

- Create a step-by-step information sheet
- Write a letter to a 4th-grade student who only knows about area
- Make a 2-page book
- Construct a 5-question quiz with answers

No matter which option you choose, your All About Volume must include the following information:

- Define the following terms: volume, right rectangular prism, dimension(s), units used for volume (2 points each – 8 points)
- Formulas related to volume and how you could use them (3 points each – 6 points)
- At least one example worked out with explanations (2 points problem, 2 points correct volume, 2 points explanation – 6 points)

Total Points: 20 points

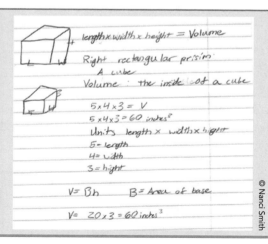

Figure 8.36 shows today's lesson plan.

FIGURE 8.36

DAY 4 LESSON PLAN

Daily Lesson Plan
Day 4

Date: 4/21
Standards:

5.MD.4 *Measure volumes by counting unit cubes, using cubic cm, cubic in, cubic ft, and improvised units.*

5.MD.5 *Relate volume to the operations of multiplication and addition and solve real-world and mathematical problems involving volume.*

   a. *Find the volume of a right rectangular prism with whole-number side lengths by packing it with unit cubes, and show that the volume is the same as would be found by multiplying the edge lengths, equivalently by multiplying the height by the area of the base. Represent threefold whole-number products as volumes, e.g., to represent the associative property of multiplication.*

   b. *Apply the formulas V = l × w × h and V = b × h for rectangular prisms to find volumes of right rectangular prisms with whole-number edge lengths in the context of solving real-world and mathematical problems.*

Standard for Mathematical Practice:

SMP 3: Construct viable arguments and critique the reasoning of others.
SMP4: Model with Mathematics
SMP7: Look for and make use of structure (dimensions to determine volume related to formulae).
SMP8: Look for and express regularity in repeated reasoning (recognize multiplication).

K:
V = (l)(w)(h)
V = Bh

U: Students will understand that volume is found from measurements of area similarly to how areas are found from measurements of lengths.

Students will understand that the types of units used describe what is being measured, and what is being measured has a specific type of unit.

D: The students will be able to explain the role of units in geometric measurement.

The students will be able to correctly calculate volumes of right rectangular prisms and composite shapes made of right rectangular prisms.

The students will be able to apply geometric measurement to real-world problems.

Build-the-volume activity

Whole Class:
Discussion around volume: from using cubes to count, to using cubes to build a specific volume, to predicting volume given dimensions, to hypothesizing a short-cut method without cubes
Practice drawing right rectangular prisms

Fold boxes and fill with popcorn to compare. Calculate your volume (If time)
Another Fill-It problem

Formative Assessment/Check for Understanding: All About Volume

Your task is to let me know EVERYTHING you now know about volume. To share your wisdom with me, you may

- Create a step-by-step information sheet
- Write a letter to a 4th-grade student who only knows about area
- Make a 2-page book
- Construct a 5-question quiz with answers

No matter which option you choose, your All About Volume must include the following information:

- Define the following terms: volume, right rectangular prism, dimension(s), units used for volume
- Formulas related to volume and how you could use them
- At least one example worked out with explanations

Closure: What is your favorite thing you just wrote or drew about volume?

The entire week's daily lesson plans can be accessed at http://resources
.corwin.com/everymathlearnerK-5

DAILY PLANNING—DAY 5

By reviewing the Volume Wisdom tasks from the prior day,
Mr. Mayfield recognizes that

- All students can correctly describe the concept of volume.

- Students have not connected why units are cubic units. Many
  students remembered to mention that the units are called
  cubic but not why they are.

- All students could now correctly use $V = l \times w \times h$ and 20
  could explain that $V = B \times h$ because $l \times w$ is the area of a
  rectangle, but only six could explain B as the area of the
  base of the prism that is layered the number of times that
  comprises the height. Mr. Mayfield is not sure whether
  students did not think to include this in their work or
  whether students do not understand the concept.
  He plans to follow up with students during Meet the
  Teacher.

- Five students added the dimensions rather than multiplied.

To begin the final lesson of the week, Mr. Mayfield will ask his
students to build any right rectangular prism that has a volume
of 24 cubic inches or less. He will tell his students to write the
volume of their prism, including units, in the corner of their
white boards in very small print to keep it secret. Next, students
will find a partner that has a prism with different dimensions
and put their two prisms next to each other. Mr. Mayfield will
call this their new shape. Because it will be made up of more
than one 3-D shape, it is called a compound shape. He will then
ask students to figure out the total volume of the compound
shape. After students figure out a way to find the compound
volume, Mr. Mayfield will ask how the total volume compares to
each of their individual volumes. Students will tell each other
how they think the volume of a compound shape is found. Mr.
Mayfield trusts that the students' discovery and explanation will
bring out the additive nature of volumes. He also anticipates
that at least one student will compare the process to finding
compound area with which they are all familiar. To summarize
this portion of the lesson, he will show his students a compound
2-D figure and a compound 3-D figure. He will ask his students
to compare finding the area of the 2-D shape with the volume of
the 3-D shape.

There are three activities for students to complete in class:

- Building Compound Volumes: This task is similar to the previous day's introductory activity. Students will draw a card stating a compound volume, and they will build a compound shape of right rectangular prisms to prove that the total volume is correct. Figure 8.37 shows an example.

© Nanci Smith

FIGURE 8.37

BUILDING COMPOUND VOLUMES

- Compound Volume Practice Sheets: It is often challenging for students to apply their knowledge to a drawing of compound shapes rather than having the physical model with which to work. The practice sheet (as well as the closing activity) will help students understand how 3-D shapes are represented on paper as well as practice using formulas and calculating compound volumes.

- Meet the Teacher: Mr. Mayfield plans to differentiate his small group instruction from reinforcing why the formulas work (multiply, not add) with students who were not correctly using or explaining the formulas, reinforcing the "layering of the base area" for the second formula, connecting volume units to the multiplication of three dimensions, and reinforcing and observing students as they calculate volumes and compound volumes.

For the final activity of the lesson Mr. Mayfield has designed an Inside-Outside circle. All students will receive a figure of either a right rectangular prism with dimensions provided or a compound figure with dimensions provided. Some figures will have an area of the base and height provided, whereas others will give all three dimensions. On the back of each figure is the correct total volume. Students will begin the activity by calculating the volume of their figures on their white boards. Mr. Mayfield will divide the class in half and have the first group form a tight circle around him with their problems and white boards. These students then turn to face out so that their backs are to Mr. Mayfield who will be in the center of the circle. The remaining students will bring their problems and white boards and face one of the students in the circle. The partners will work each other's problems and will check with each other to see whether the answer and work is correct. They will then trade questions, and Mr. Mayfield will rotate one of the circles (for example, inside circle move three to the right). Now each student will have a new partner with a new problem and repeat the process. Mr. Mayfield, who will be in the center of the concentric circles, will monitor all conversations as he moves within the center of the circle.

As a final check for the lesson, he will present a compound 3-D shape with all dimensions labeled. The students' exit cards will explain step-by-step how to find the compound volume, including units. Figure 8.38 provides the lesson plan for this day's lesson.

FIGURE 8.38

DAY 5 LESSON PLAN

Daily Lesson Plan
Day 5

Date: 4/22
Standards:

5.MD.5 *Relate volume to the operations of multiplication and addition and solve real-world and mathematical problems involving volume.*

  a. *Recognize volume as additive. Find volumes of solid figures composed of two non-overlapping right rectangular prisms by adding the volumes of the non-overlapping parts,* and apply *this technique to solve real-world problems.*

Standard for Mathematical Practice:
SMP 3: Construct viable arguments and critique the reasoning of others
SMP4: Model with mathematics
SMP7: Look for and make use of structure (adding volumes).

K: Compound volume; how to add volumes together

U Students will understand that often irregular shapes or solids can be separated into familiar shapes or solids. Then composite areas or volumes can be found.

D: The students will be able to explain the role of units in geometric measurement.

The students will be able to correctly calculate volumes of right rectangular prisms and composite shapes made of right rectangular prisms.

Whole Class:

1.   Have each student build a right rectangular prism with 24 cubes or fewer. Find the volume of their shape and write it very small in the corner of their whiteboard to keep it secret.
2.   Students find a partner and put their two prisms next to each other to form a compound shape.
3.   Students find the volume of their compound shape and compare it to their individual volumes.
4.   Discuss compound volumes and compare to compound area.

Partner Activity:
Building Compound Volumes
Practice Sheets
Meet with Teacher: Readiness differentiation

Closure: Inside/Outside Circles with compound volume cards

Formative Assessment/Check for Understanding: Exit card. Given a drawing of a compound shape (two or more prisms), explain step-by-step how to find the total volume.

 The entire week's daily lesson plans can be accessed at http://resources .corwin.com/everymathlearnerK-5

ADVICE FROM THE FIELD

The goal of sharing these two different weeks of differentiation is not to overwhelm you but to give you ideas on how to make adjustments for each day based on what you see in your students' learning from a previous day. Although this gives you the most intense picture of differentiation, bear in mind that not everything must be differentiated. Many times only one segment or one activity in a lesson will be differentiated, and often that will be a minor adjustment rather than separate activities.

Your practice in differentiating your classroom will build and grow over time, and anything you do *right now* to identify, acknowledge, and address your students' various learning needs will help them grow, succeed, and feel successful. The teachers you have heard from throughout this book have been asked to share with you their best advice for getting started or for continuing to grow in differentiation. Each teacher who differentiates begins in ways that make sense to him or her. What are your next steps?

WATCH IT!

As you watch Video 8.1, *Advice for Getting Started With Differentiation*, consider the following questions:

1. Which piece of advice motivates you to try or continue differentiation?
2. What will you do to take your next step in differentiation?

Video 8.1 Advice for Getting Started With Differentiation

CONCLUSION

A friend of mine shared a story with me that highlighted how important differentiation is. While waiting for her daughter's dance class to let out, she noticed a girl nearby who was working on some mathematics homework and was in tears, looking utterly miserable. My friend, who is a mathematics coach, asked whether there was something she could do to help. This seven-year-old girl,

FIGURE 8.39

REGINA'S NUMBER BONDS

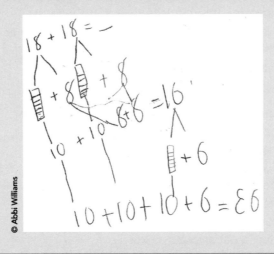

© Abbi Williams

Regina—a first grader—was working on a sheet of eight problems where she was asked to add double-digit numbers using the number-bond method. Figure 8.39 shows Regina's model of 18 + 18.

She was on the final problem, and her mother was trying to convey to her that she had to use this method and follow the steps in this exact way, just as she had for the previous seven problems, because those were the instructions. The girl seemed utterly perplexed, frustrated, and exhausted—so did her mother. My friend asked Regina to walk her through her work and explain her thinking, all of which looked correct on paper and appeared to make sense. What she realized as she probed deeper, though, was that Regina could follow the steps for this particular strategy, but she still wasn't connecting that particular strategy with any conceptual understanding of deconstructing and reconstructing numbers, the role of place value, or even the meaning or properties of addition. But because her teacher and her worksheet instructions told her she had to do all the problems that way, she did so. It took her a very long time, and her mathematical understanding was definitely cloudy. In this particular scenario, the way my friend saw it, this strategy was simply a different version of the traditional vertical addition where you add the ones and carry the tens. In other words, it was simply a different *procedure*, but it was neither borne of any conceptual understanding nor helping to build any.

My friend talked with the mother some more, who seemed equally frustrated and desperate to help her daughter really learn. She said that her daughter is bright and understands the concepts when she applies a different strategy, like an open number line, or when she uses manipulatives as she's a very kinesthetic person. She also enjoys putting things into stories, especially if they involve *Star Wars*. But Regina wasn't given those options. She was told to add 18 + 18 using number bonds, and then she was given seven more problems of the same nature with the same instructions. And so, although a student for whom this particular strategy makes sense might spend a mere 15 minutes in completing the assignment, it took Regina an hour. And there were seven other pages of mathematics homework to go. It's no wonder Regina and her mother felt so burdened! Her mother also shared that the teacher was now really picking up the pace to cover all the content she needed to cover by the end of the year, Regina was getting left further and further behind, despite all the additional work her parents were doing with her at home. They had plans for Regina to be privately tutored all the coming summer, and they felt lucky they could afford that option. But sadly, Regina had already learned to loathe mathematics . . . at seven years old.

Of course, we don't know all the details of all that was going on in Regina's classroom, and this is just one anecdotal story, but the evidence doesn't suggest that the teacher was tuned in to Regina's needs as a learner. What might have happened if the teacher had given Regina some options about how to solve these problems? What if she suggested that Regina try a different method; that she make sense of these problems by putting them into stories, drawing pictures, or pulling out some base 10 blocks or linking cubes? Perhaps the teacher could have had Regina model two problems with number bonds to show that she knows how to do that particular strategy and the other problems using a strategy of choice. Might Regina have had a more positive and enlightening experience?

Our goal in differentiation is to lift students up to their greatest potential in learning. By recognizing what is truly important in our content, where our students are as learners, how they can best take their next steps in learning, we will reach that goal. It's not easy, but it is worth it. Think of all that is at stake with the best possible education of our children. Thank you for all you do for our children.

APPENDIX A

FURTHER READING ON THE TOPIC OF ENGLISH LANGUAGE LEARNERS

Throughout the text, there are suggestions for addressing English-language learners (ELLs) that are specific to the topic of the text at the time. This does not begin to address the depth of research and knowledge in the area. We know that those struggling with language need specific vocabulary instruction, both Tier 1 and Tier 2. Warning students in advance that they will be called on, and allowing them to practice what they will say with a partner prior to having to speak, will ease some of the stress for students. Asking students to teach the class to count in their own language will help others understand the struggle to learn a new language, put the student in the role of the teacher, and help the students feel more a part of the classroom community. Pictures and motions help as well. These are just the beginnings of addressing our students who struggle with the language. The following list serves to begin the process of further reading:

Calderon, M. E., & Soto, I. (2016). *Academic language mastery: Vocabulary in context.* Thousand Oaks, CA: Corwin.

Coggins, D. S. (2014). *English learners in the mathematics classroom* (2nd ed.). Thousand Oaks, CA: Corwin

Freeman, D., Freeman, Y. S., & Soto, I. (2016). *Academic language mastery: Grammar and syntax in context.* Thousand Oaks, CA: Corwin.

Gottlieb, M. (2016). *Assessing English language learners* (2nd ed.). Thousand Oaks, CA: Corwin.

Gottlieb, M., & Ernst-Slavit, G. (2013). *Academic language in diverse classroom: Promoting content and language learning, Mathematics grades 3–5.* Thousand Oaks, CA: Corwin.

Gottlieb, M., & Ernst-Slavit, G. (2014). *Academic language, definitions and contexts.* Thousand Oaks, CA: Corwin.

LeMoyne, N., & Soto, I. (2016). *Academic language mastery: Culture in context.* Thousand Oaks, CA: Corwin

Moschkovich, J. N. (2013) Principles and guidelines for equitable mathematics teaching practices and materials for English language learners. *Journal of Urban Mathematics Education, 6*(1), 45–57.

Moschkovich, J. N. (2014). Building on student language resources during classroom discussions. In M. Civil & E. Turner (Eds.), *The Common Core state standards in mathematics for English language learners: Grades K–8.* Alexandria, VA: TESOL International Association.

Ramirez, N. (2012). *Beyond good teaching: Advancing mathematics education for ELLs.* Reston, VA: NCTM.

Rodriguez, E. R., Bellanca, J., & Esparza, D. R. (2016). *What is it about me you can't teach? Culturally responsive instruction in deeper learning classrooms* (3rd ed.). Thousand Oaks, CA: Corwin.

Tellez, K., Moschkovich, J. N., & Civil, M. (Eds.), *Latinos/as and mathematics education: Research on learning and teaching in classrooms and communities* [Research in Educational Diversity & Excellence Series]. Charlotte, NC: Information Age Publishing.

White, D. Y., & Spitzer, J. S. (2009). *Mathematics for every student: Responding to diversity, grades Pre-K–5.* Reston, VA: NCTM.

Zwiers, J., & Soto, I. (2016). *Academic language mastery: Conversational discourse in context.* Thousand Oaks, CA: Corwin.

APPENDIX B

FURTHER READING ON THE TOPIC OF SPECIAL EDUCATION

Students with diagnosed learning disabilities will benefit from the attention of differentiated tasks and lessons. This is not to imply that differentiation could, or should, replace special services. Certainly a student's Individualized Education Plan (IEP) must be strictly followed. In addition, by differentiating appropriately for all students, mainstreamed students will often feel more a part of the learning community because they are not the only students doing something slightly different or with different pacing. In a differentiated math classroom, this is true of all students at various points of time. The following list provides a starting point for reading in the field of special education:

Allsopp, D. H., Kyger, M. M., & Lovin, L. H. (2007). *Teaching mathematics meaningfully: Solutions for reaching struggling learners.* Baltimore, MD: Brookes.

Berch, D. B. *Why is math so hard for some children? The nature and origins of mathematical learning difficulties and disabilities.* Baltimore, MD: Brookes.

Fattig, M. L., & Taylor, K. T. (2007). *Co-teaching in the differentiated classroom: Successful collaboration, lesson design and classroom management.* San Francisco, CA: Jossey-Bass.

Fennell, F. (Ed.). (2011). *Achieving fluency: Special education and mathematics.* Reston, VA: NCTM.

Kurth, J. A., & Gross, M. (2015). *The inclusion toolbox: Strategies and techniques for all teachers.* Thousand Oaks, CA: Corwin.

Murawski, W. W., & Spencer, S. (2011). *Collaborate, communicate & differentiate! How to increase student learning in today's diverse schools.* Thousand Oaks, CA: Corwin.

Sousa, D. A. (2016). *How the special needs brain learns* (3rd ed.). Thousand Oaks, CA: Corwin.

Storeygard, J. (2012). *Count me in, K–5.* Thousand Oaks, CA: Corwin.

Witzel, B. S., Riccomini, P. J., & Herlog, M. L. (2016). *Building number sense through the common core.* Thousand Oaks, CA: Corwin.

APPENDIX C

FURTHER READING ON THE TOPIC OF RICH PROBLEMS AND MATHEMATICAL DISCOURSE

This book has focused on the details of differentiating a mathematics classroom. I wish I had been able to include more information on choosing rich tasks and orchestrating productive mathematical discourse. Certainly the types of tasks that are chosen are of the utmost importance for learning. Mathematical discourse is the primary manner in which students make sense of learning and communicate thinking to both their peers and their teachers. The following list is for further reading in these areas:

Chapin, S. H., O'Connor, C., & Anderson, N. C. (2009). *Classroom discussions in math: Using math to help students learn grades K–6.* Sausalito, CA: MathSolutions.

Hull, T. H., Balka, D. S., & Miles, R. H. (2011). *Visible thinking in the K–8 mathematics classroom.* Thousand Oaks, CA: Corwin.

Kazemi, E., & d Hintz, A. (2014). *Intentional talk: How to structure and lead productive mathematical discussions.* Portland, ME: Stenhouse.

Schrock, C., Norris, K., Pugalee, D. K., Seitz, R., & Hollingshead, F. (2013). *NCSM Great tasks for mathematics: Engaging activities for effective instruction and assessment that integrate the content and practices of the common core state standards for mathematics.* Reston, VA: NCSM.

Sherin, M., Jacobs, V., & Philipp, R. (2011). *Mathematics teacher noticing: Seeing through teachers' eyes.* New York, NY: Routledge.

Small, M. (2009). *Good questions: Great ways to differentiate mathematics instruction.* New York, NY: Teachers College Press.

Smith, M. S., & Stein, M. K. (2011). *5 Practices for orchestrating productive mathematics discussions.* Reston, VA: NCTM.

REFERENCES

Boaler, J. (2015). *Mathematical mindsets: Unleashing students' potential through creative math, inspiring messages and innovative teaching.* San Francisco: Jossey-Bass.

Cummings, C. B. (2000). *Winning strategies for classroom management.* Alexandria, VA: ASCD.

Dixon, J. K., Adams, T. L. and Nolan, E. C. (2015). *Beyond the common core: A handbook for mathematics in a PLC at work.* Bloomington, IN: Solution Tree.

Dweck, C. S. (n.d.). AZQuotes.com. Retrieved January 01, 2016, from AZQuotes.com Web site: http://www.azquotes.com/quote/937595

Dweck, C. S. (2006). *Mindset: The new psychology of success.* New York: Random House

Hattie, J. (2012). *Visible learning for teachers: Maximizing impact on learning.* New York: Routledge.

Hattie, J. (2013). Understanding learning: Lessons for learning, teaching and research. Accessed at http://research.acer.edu.au/cgi/viewcontent.cgi?article=1207&context=research_conference.

Jensen, E. (1998). *Teaching with the brain in mind.* Alexandria, VA: Kanold (2016), personal communication. ASCD.

Kanold, T. D. and Larson, M.R. (2012). *Common core mathematics in a PLC at work: Leader's guide.* Bloomington, IN and Washington DC: Solution Tree and NCTM.

Kilpatrick, J., Swafford, J., Findell, B. (Eds). (2001). *Adding it up: Helping children learn mathematics.* Washington DC: National Academies Press.

NCTM (2014). *Principles to actions: Ensuring mathematical success for all.* Reston: VA, NCTM.

Nisbet, R. E. (2009). Education is all in your mind. New York Times Opinion, February 8, 2009.

Popham, W. J. (2011). *Transformative assessment in action.* Alexandria, VA: ASCD.

Smith, M. S. and Stein, M. K. (1998). Selecting and creating mathematical tasks: From research to practice. *Mathematics Teaching in the Middle School, 3*(5), 344–350.

Smith, N. N. (2017) *A mind for mathematics: Meaningful teaching and learning in elementary classrooms.* Bloomington, IN: Solution Tree.

Sousa, D. A. (2015). *How the brain learns mathematics* (2nd ed.). Thousand Oaks, CA: Corwin.

Sousa, D. A. and Tomlinson, C. A. (2011). *Differentiation and the brain: How neuroscience supports the learner-friendly classroom.* Bloomington, IN: Solution Tree.

Stein, M. K., Smith, M. S., Henningsen, M. A., & Silver, E. A. (2009). *Implementing standards-based mathematics instruction: A casebook for professional development* (2nd ed.). New York, NY: Teachers College Press.

Sternberg, R. J. (2005). The theory of successful intelligence. *Interamerican Journal of Psychology, 39*(2), 189–202.

Styles, V. (2015). A primer for on personalized learning for Mark Zuckerberg – by Harvard's Howard Gardner. The *Washington Post.* Downloaded from https://www.washingtonpost.com/news/answer-sheet/wp/2015/12/02/a-primer-for-mark-zuckerberg-on-personalized-learning-by-harvards-howard-gardner/

Tomlinson, C. A. (2014). *The differentiated classroom: Responding to the needs of all learners* (2nd ed.). Alexandria, VA: ASCD.

Tomlinson, C. A. (2001). *How to differentiate instruction in mixed-ability classrooms.* (2nd ed.). Alexandria, VA: ASCD.

Tomlinson, C. A. and Imeau, M. B. (2010). *Leading and managing a differentiated classroom.* Alexandria, VA: ASCD.

Tomlinson, C., & Imbeau, M., (2014). *A differentiated approach to the Common Core: How do I help a broad range of learners succeed with challenging curriculum?* Alexandria, VA: ASCD.

Tomlinson, C., & Moon, T. (2013). *Assessment and student success in a differentiated classroom.* Alexandria, VA: ASCD.

Walkington, C, Milan, S., & Howell, E. (2014). Personalized learning in algebra. *The Mathematics Teacher, 108, (4), 272–279.*

Wiliam, D. (2011). *Embedded formative assessment.* Bloomington, IN: Solution Tree.

Willis, J. (2006). *Research-based strategies to ignite student learning.* Alexandria: VA, ASCD.

INDEX

CORWIN MATHEMATICS

Supporting Teachers, Empowering Learners

Why Corwin Mathematics?

We've all heard this—"either you are a math person, or you are not." At Corwin Mathematics, we believe ALL students should have the opportunity to be successful in math! Trusted experts in math education such as Linda Gojak, Ruth Harbin Miles, John SanGiovanni, Skip Fennell, Gary Martin, and many more offer clear and practical guidance to help all students move from surface to deep mathematical understanding, from favoring procedural knowledge over conceptual learning, and from rote memorization to true comprehension. **We deliver research-based, high-quality content that is classroom-tested and ready to be used in your lessons**—today!

Through books, videos, consulting, and online tools, we offer a truly **blended learning experience that helps teachers demystify math for students.** The user-friendly design and format of our resources provides not only the best classroom-based professional guidance, but many activities, lesson plans, rubrics, and templates to help you implement changes at your own pace in order to sustain learning improvement over time. We are **committed to empowering every learner.** With our forward-thinking and practical offerings, Corwin Mathematics helps you enable all students to realize the power and beauty of math and its connection to everything they do.

Warm Regards,
The Corwin Mathematics Team

New titles from Corwin Mathematics!

The *what*, *when*, and *how* of teaching practices that evidence shows work best for student learning in mathematics.

Grades: K–12

Everything you need to promote mathematical thinking and learning!

Grades: K–12

Move the needle on math instruction with these 5 assessment techniques!

Grades: K–8

See what's going on in your students' minds, plus get access to 340 rich tasks to use in instruction or assessment!

Grades: K–2 and 3–5

Students pursue problems they're curious about, not problems they're told to solve.

Grades: K–12

When it comes to math, standards-aligned is achievement-aligned...

Check out our free Corwin Mathematics resources at
www.corwin.com/free-corwin-mathematics-resources

A SAGE Publishing Company

CORWIN HAS ONE MISSION: to enhance education through intentional professional learning.

We build long-term relationships with our authors, educators, clients, and associations who partner with us to develop and continuously improve the best evidence-based practices that establish and support lifelong learning.